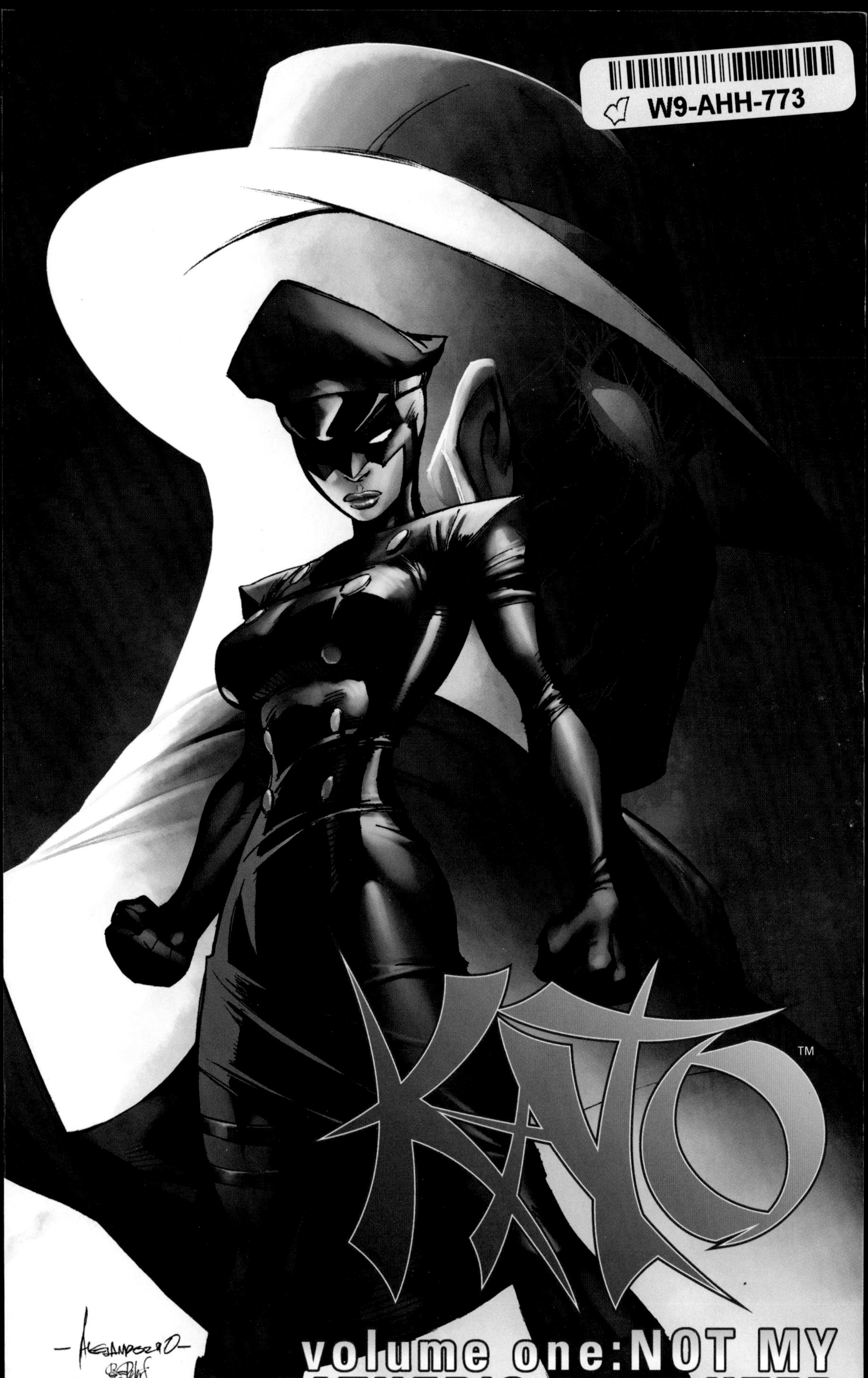
KATO™

volume one: NOT MY FATHER'S DAUGHTER

Written by
ANDE PARKS

Art by
ALE GARZA & DIEGO BERNARD

Colors by
LEONARDO-MLK/PC SIQUEIRA, ALE STARLING & ALAN FARIA

Letters by
BILL TORTOLINI

Collection cover by
ALE GARZA

Special thanks to David Grace at Green Hornet Inc.

Collection design by JASON ULLMEYER

This volume collects issues one through five of Kato, originally published by Dynamite Entertainment.

ISBN-10: 1-60690-154-0   ISBN-13: 978-1-60690-154-0. First Printing 10 9 8 7 6 5 4 3 2 1

KATO™ VOLUME ONE: NOT MY FATHER'S DAUGHTER. First printing. Contains materials originally published in Kato #1-5. Published by Dynamite Entertainment. 155 Ninth Ave. Suite B. Runnemede, NJ 08078. Copyright © 2010 The Green Hornet, Inc. All rights reserved. The Green Hornet, Inc. www.thegreenhornet.com Black Beauty, Kato, and the Hornet logo are trademarks of The Green Hornet, Inc. colophon ® 2010 DFI. All Rights Reserved. All names, characters, events and locales in this publication are entirely fictional. Any resemblance to actual persons (living or dead) events or places, without satiric intent, is coincidental. No portion of this book may be reproduced by any means (digital or print) without the written permission of Dynamite Entertainment except for review purposes. The scanning, uploading and distribution of this book via the Internet or via any other means without the permission of the publisher is illegal and punishable by law. Please purchase only authorized electronic editions, and do not participate in or encourage electronic piracy of copyrighted materials. Printed in Canada.

For media rights, foreign rights, promotions, licensing, and advertising:
marketing@dynamiteentertainment.com

DYNAMITE
ENTERTAINMENT®

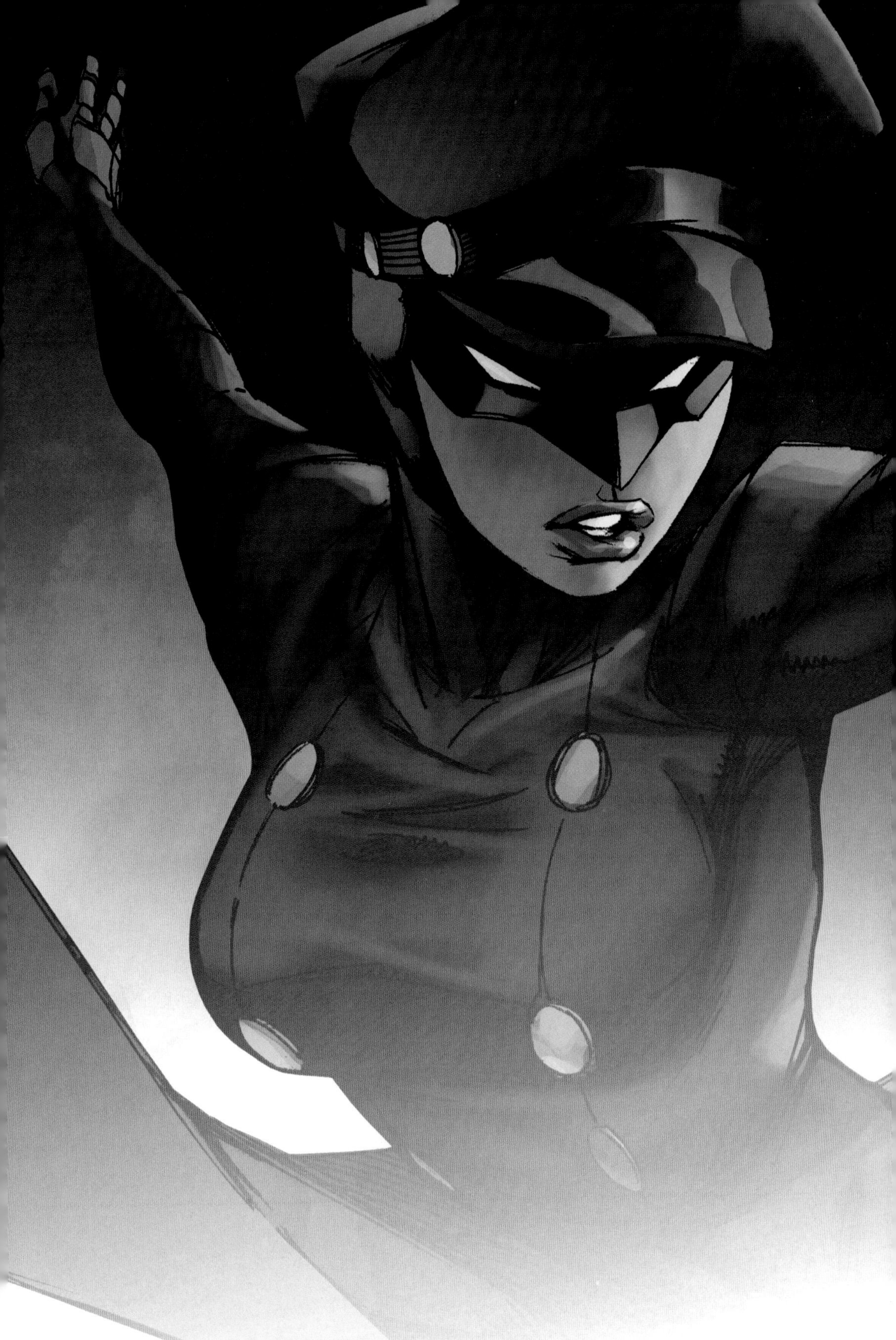

Issue ONE

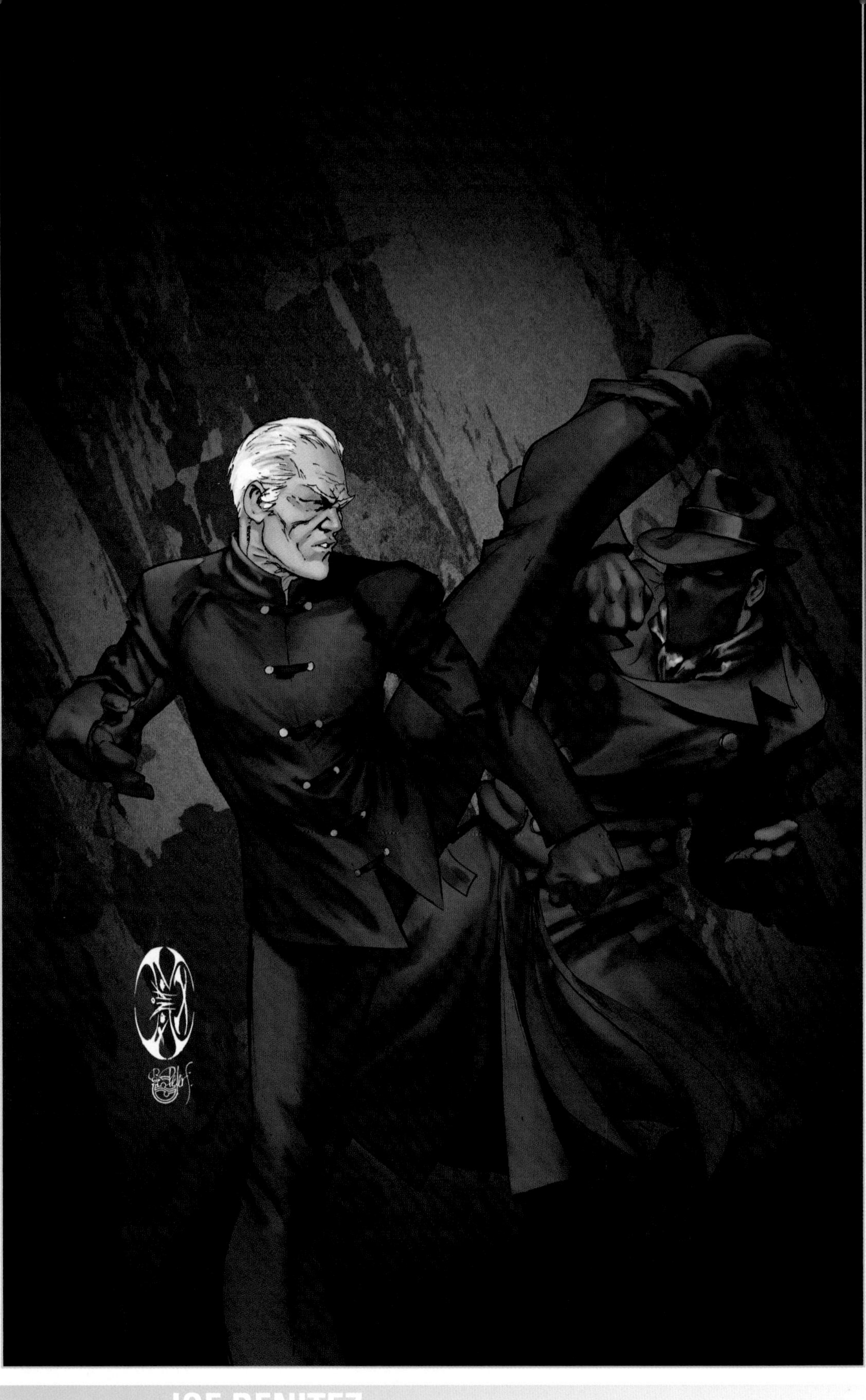

Issue one cover by **JOE BENITEZ**

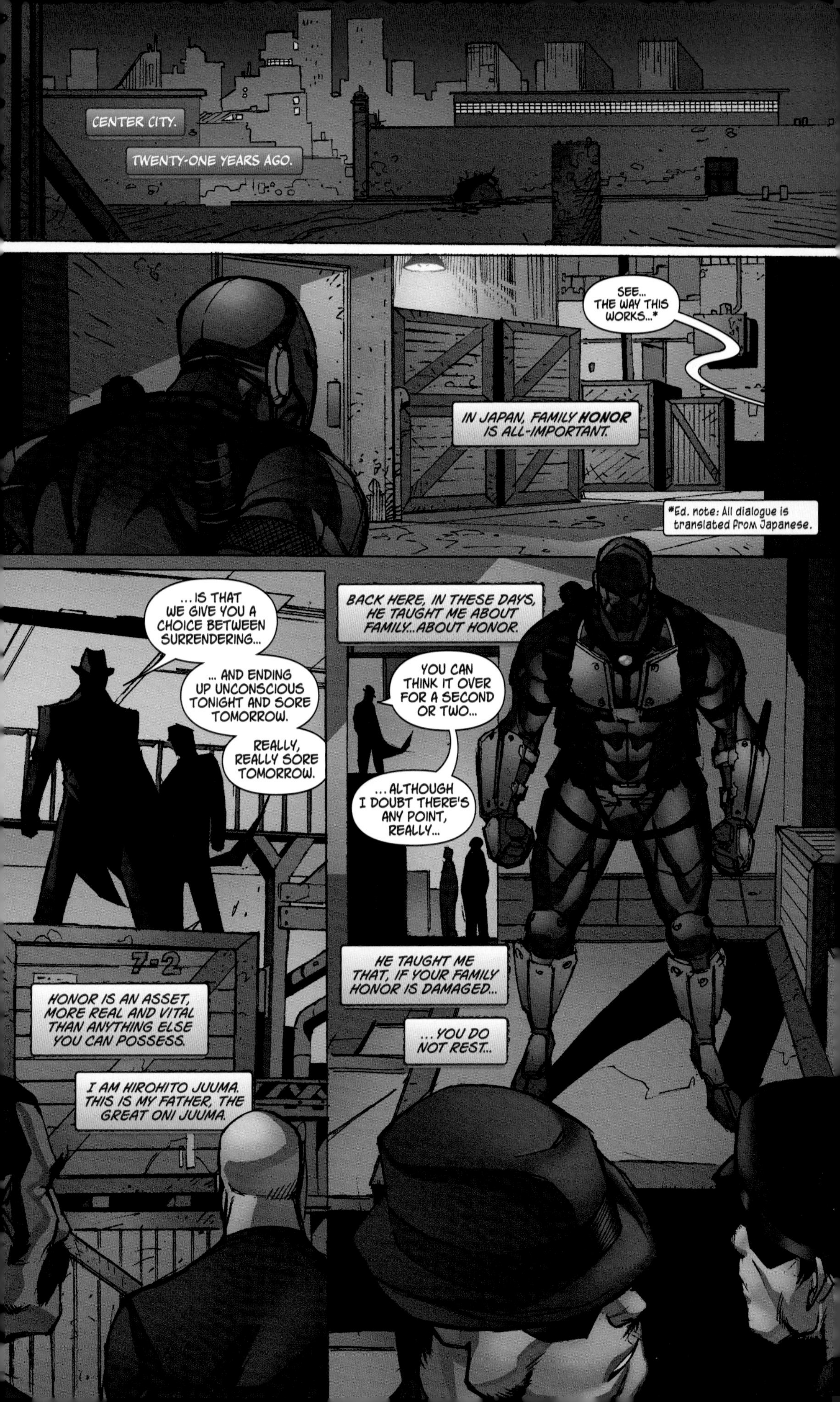
CENTER CITY.
TWENTY-ONE YEARS AGO.
SEE... THE WAY THIS WORKS...*
IN JAPAN, FAMILY HONOR IS ALL-IMPORTANT.
*Ed. note: All dialogue is translated from Japanese.
...IS THAT WE GIVE YOU A CHOICE BETWEEN SURRENDERING...
... AND ENDING UP UNCONSCIOUS TONIGHT AND SORE TOMORROW.
REALLY, REALLY SORE TOMORROW.
BACK HERE, IN THESE DAYS, HE TAUGHT ME ABOUT FAMILY...ABOUT HONOR.
YOU CAN THINK IT OVER FOR A SECOND OR TWO...
...ALTHOUGH I DOUBT THERE'S ANY POINT, REALLY...
7-2
HONOR IS AN ASSET, MORE REAL AND VITAL THAN ANYTHING ELSE YOU CAN POSSESS.
I AM HIROHITO JUUMA. THIS IS MY FATHER, THE GREAT ONI JUUMA.
HE TAUGHT ME THAT, IF YOUR FAMILY HONOR IS DAMAGED...
...YOU DO NOT REST...

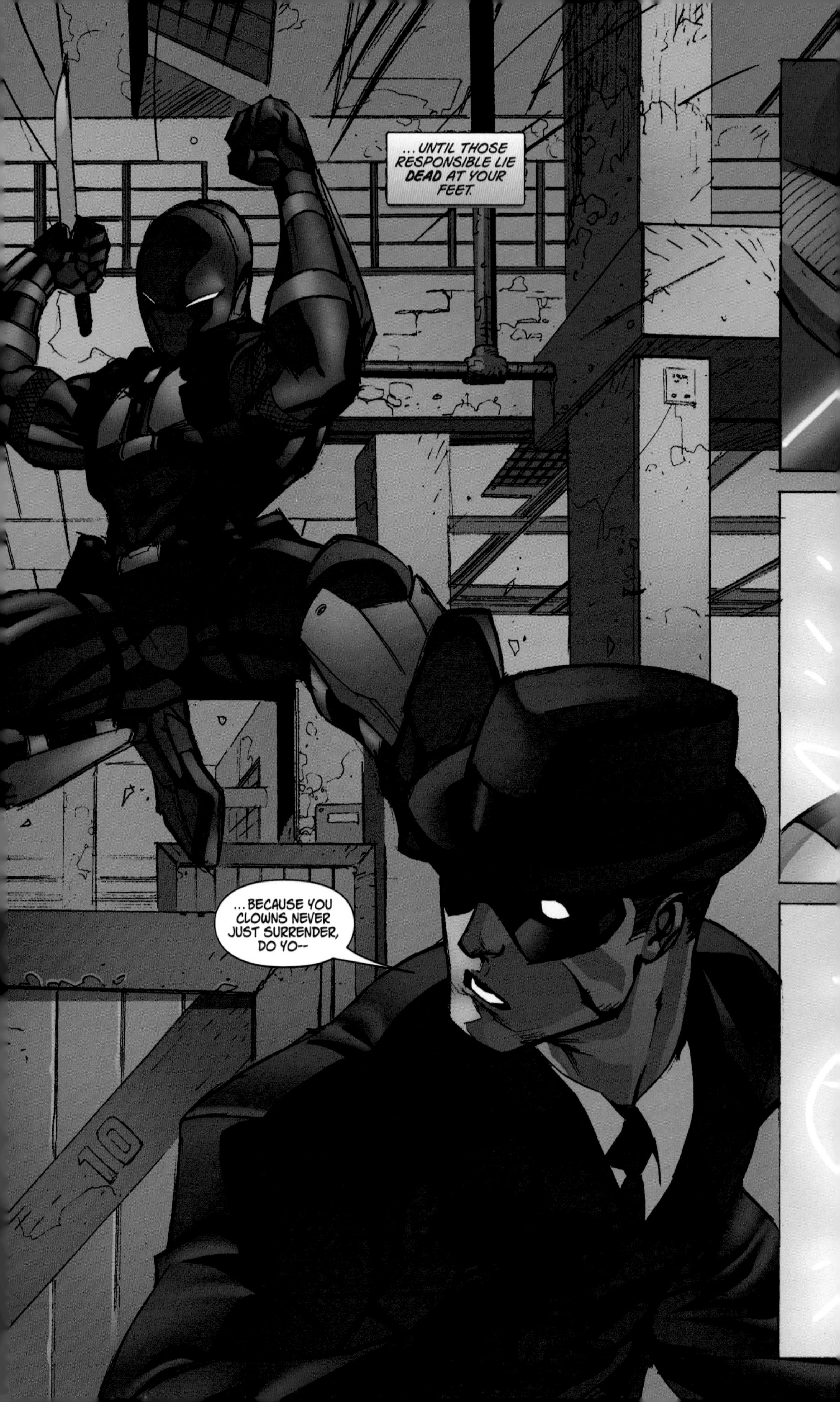
...UNTIL THOSE RESPONSIBLE LIE DEAD AT YOUR FEET.
...BECAUSE YOU CLOWNS NEVER JUST SURRENDER, DO YO--
10

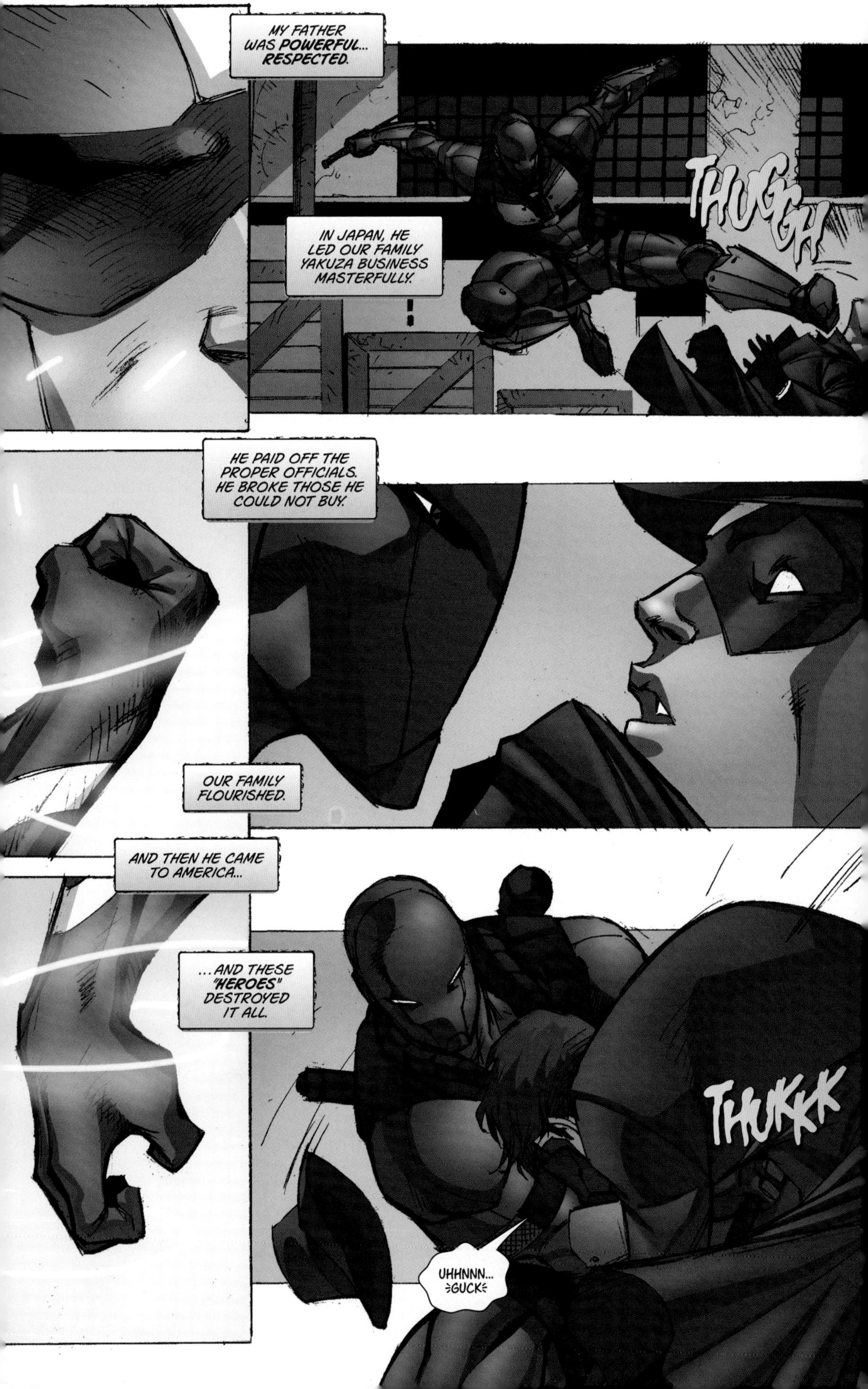

MY FATHER WAS POWERFUL... RESPECTED.
THUGGH
IN JAPAN, HE LED OUR FAMILY YAKUZA BUSINESS MASTERFULLY.
HE PAID OFF THE PROPER OFFICIALS. HE BROKE THOSE HE COULD NOT BUY.
OUR FAMILY FLOURISHED.
AND THEN HE CAME TO AMERICA...
...AND THESE "HEROES" DESTROYED IT ALL.
THUKKK
UHHNNN... GUCK

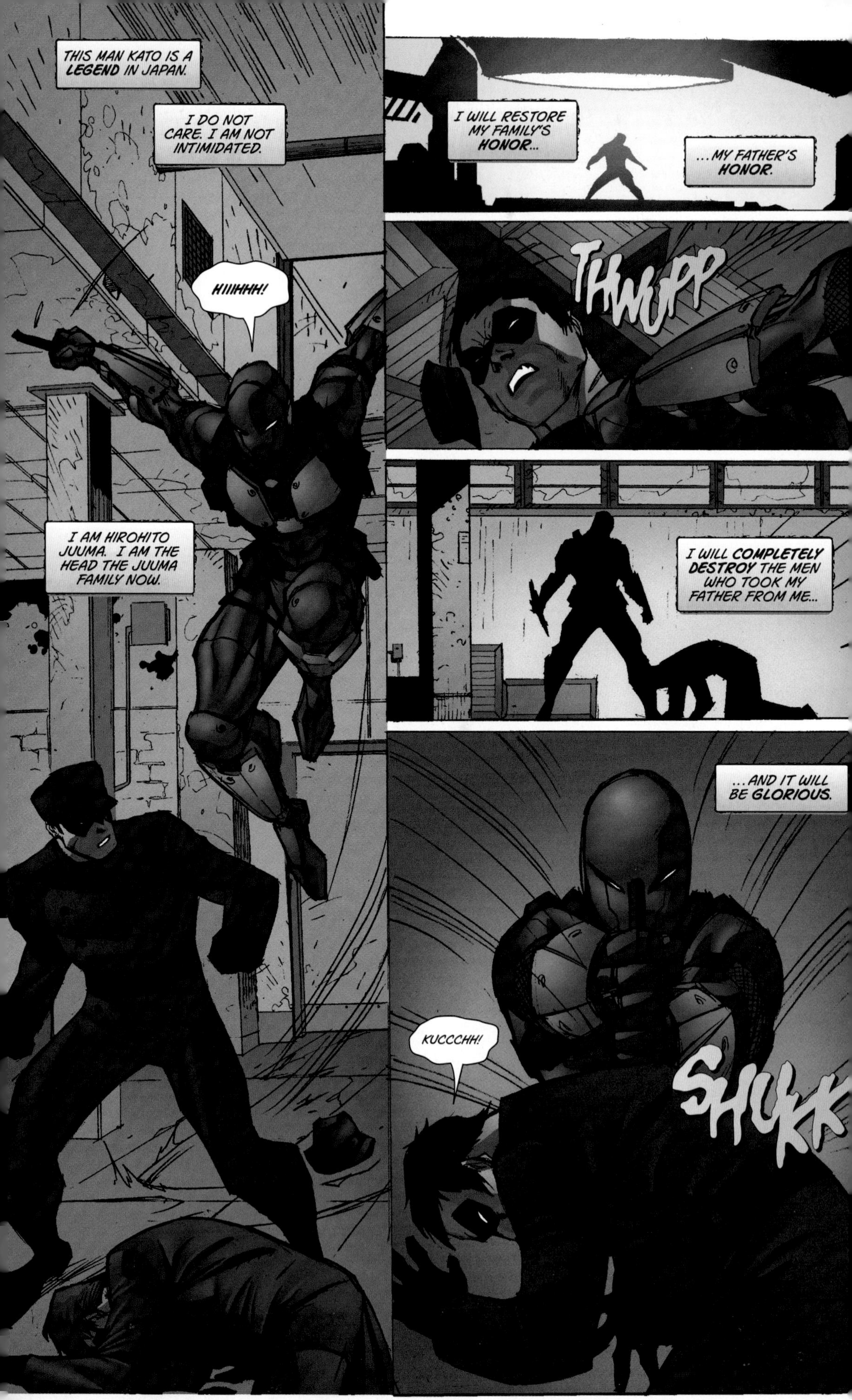

THIS MAN KATO IS A LEGEND IN JAPAN.
I DO NOT CARE. I AM NOT INTIMIDATED.
HIIIHHH!
I AM HIROHITO JUUMA. I AM THE HEAD THE JUUMA FAMILY NOW.
I WILL RESTORE MY FAMILY'S HONOR...
...MY FATHER'S HONOR.
THWUPP
I WILL COMPLETELY DESTROY THE MEN WHO TOOK MY FATHER FROM ME...
...AND IT WILL BE GLORIOUS.
KUCCCHH!
SHUKK

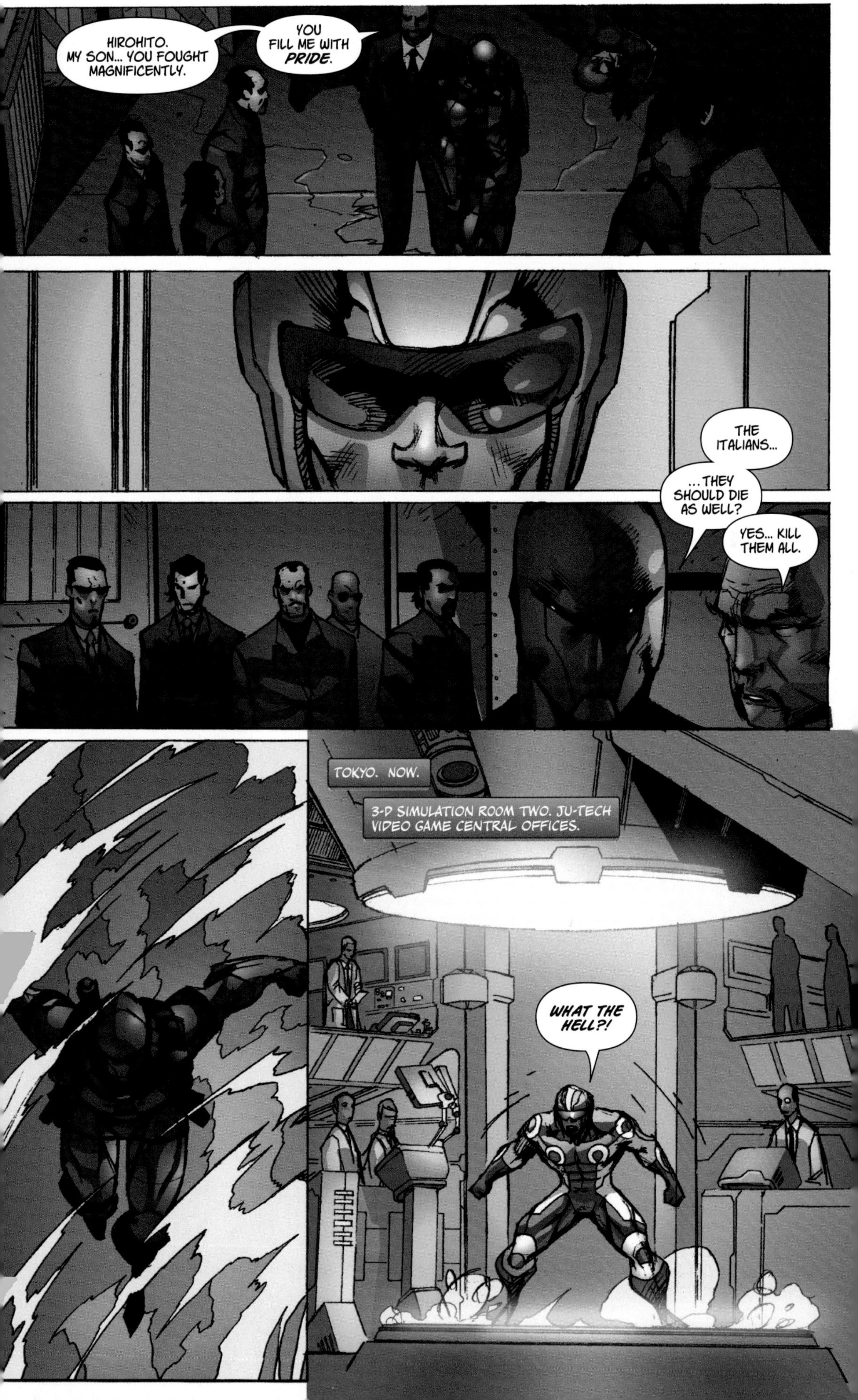
HIROHITO. MY SON... YOU FOUGHT MAGNIFICENTLY.
YOU FILL ME WITH *PRIDE*.
THE ITALIANS...
...THEY SHOULD DIE AS WELL?
YES... KILL THEM ALL.
TOKYO. NOW.
3-D SIMULATION ROOM TWO. JU-TECH VIDEO GAME CENTRAL OFFICES.
WHAT THE HELL?!

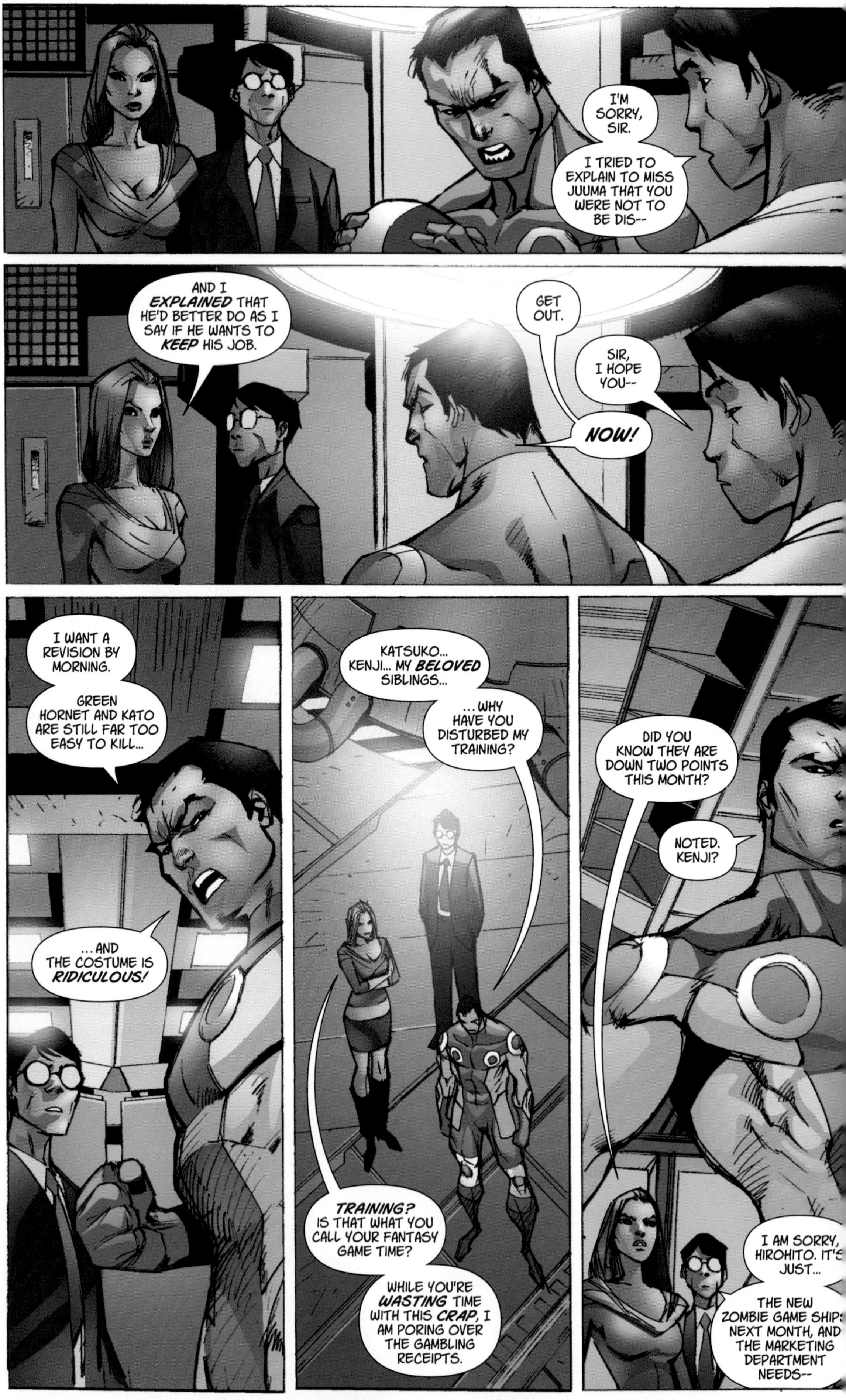
I'M SORRY, SIR.
I TRIED TO EXPLAIN TO MISS JUUMA THAT YOU WERE NOT TO BE DIS--
AND I *EXPLAINED* THAT HE'D BETTER DO AS I SAY IF HE WANTS TO *KEEP* HIS JOB.
GET OUT.
SIR, I HOPE YOU--
NOW!
I WANT A REVISION BY MORNING.
GREEN HORNET AND KATO ARE STILL FAR TOO EASY TO KILL...
...AND THE COSTUME IS *RIDICULOUS!*
KATSUKO... KENJI... MY *BELOVED* SIBLINGS...
...WHY HAVE YOU DISTURBED MY TRAINING?
TRAINING? IS THAT WHAT YOU CALL YOUR FANTASY GAME TIME?
WHILE YOU'RE *WASTING* TIME WITH THIS *CRAP*, I AM PORING OVER THE GAMBLING RECEIPTS.
DID YOU KNOW THEY ARE DOWN TWO POINTS THIS MONTH?
NOTED. KENJI?
I AM SORRY, HIROHITO. IT'S JUST...
THE NEW ZOMBIE GAME SHIPS NEXT MONTH, AND THE MARKETING DEPARTMENT NEEDS--

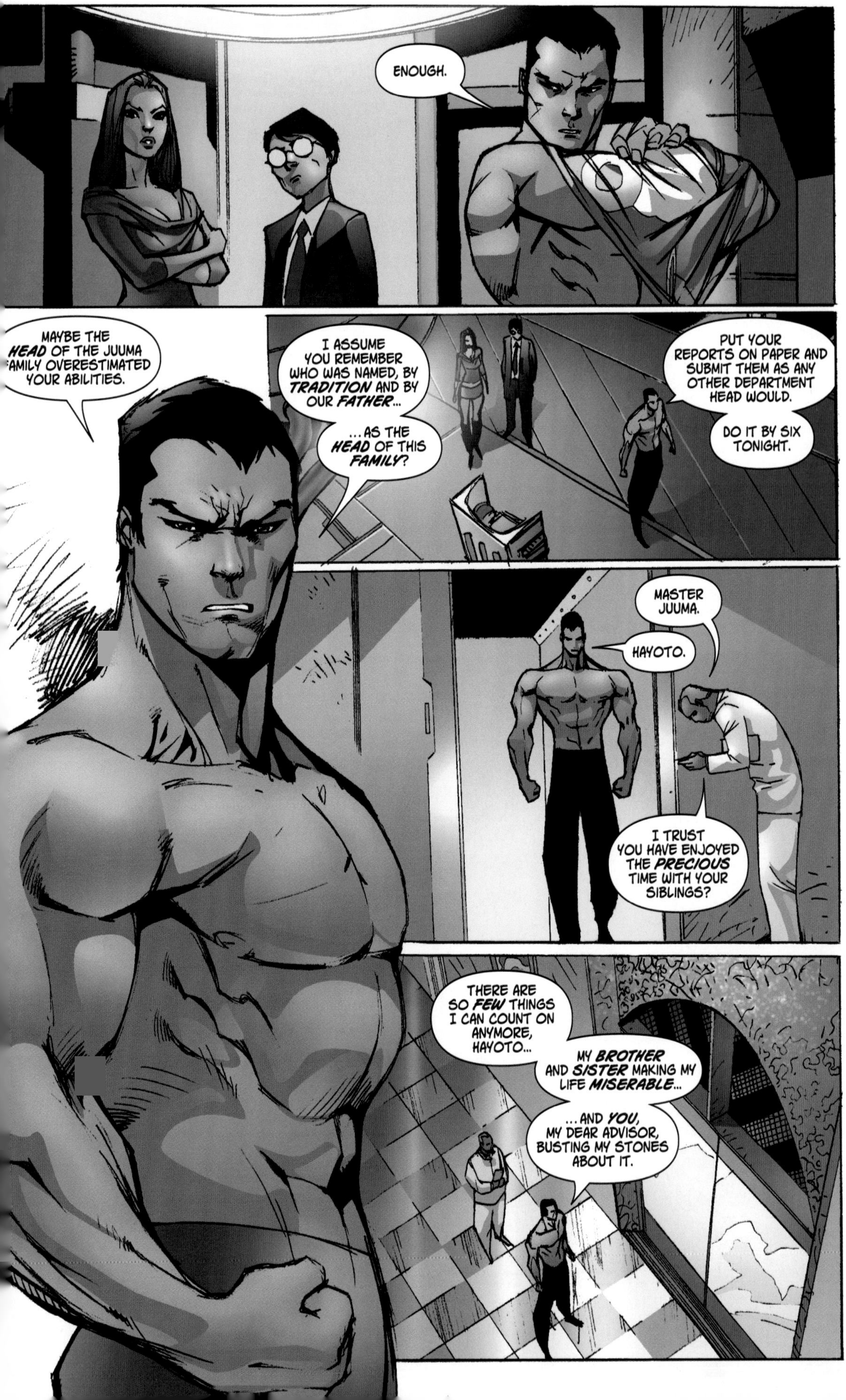
ENOUGH.
MAYBE THE HEAD OF THE JUUMA FAMILY OVERESTIMATED YOUR ABILITIES.
I ASSUME YOU REMEMBER WHO WAS NAMED, BY TRADITION AND BY OUR FATHER...
...AS THE HEAD OF THIS FAMILY?
PUT YOUR REPORTS ON PAPER AND SUBMIT THEM AS ANY OTHER DEPARTMENT HEAD WOULD.
DO IT BY SIX TONIGHT.
MASTER JUUMA.
HAYOTO.
I TRUST YOU HAVE ENJOYED THE PRECIOUS TIME WITH YOUR SIBLINGS?
THERE ARE SO FEW THINGS I CAN COUNT ON ANYMORE, HAYOTO...
MY BROTHER AND SISTER MAKING MY LIFE MISERABLE...
...AND YOU, MY DEAR ADVISOR, BUSTING MY STONES ABOUT IT.

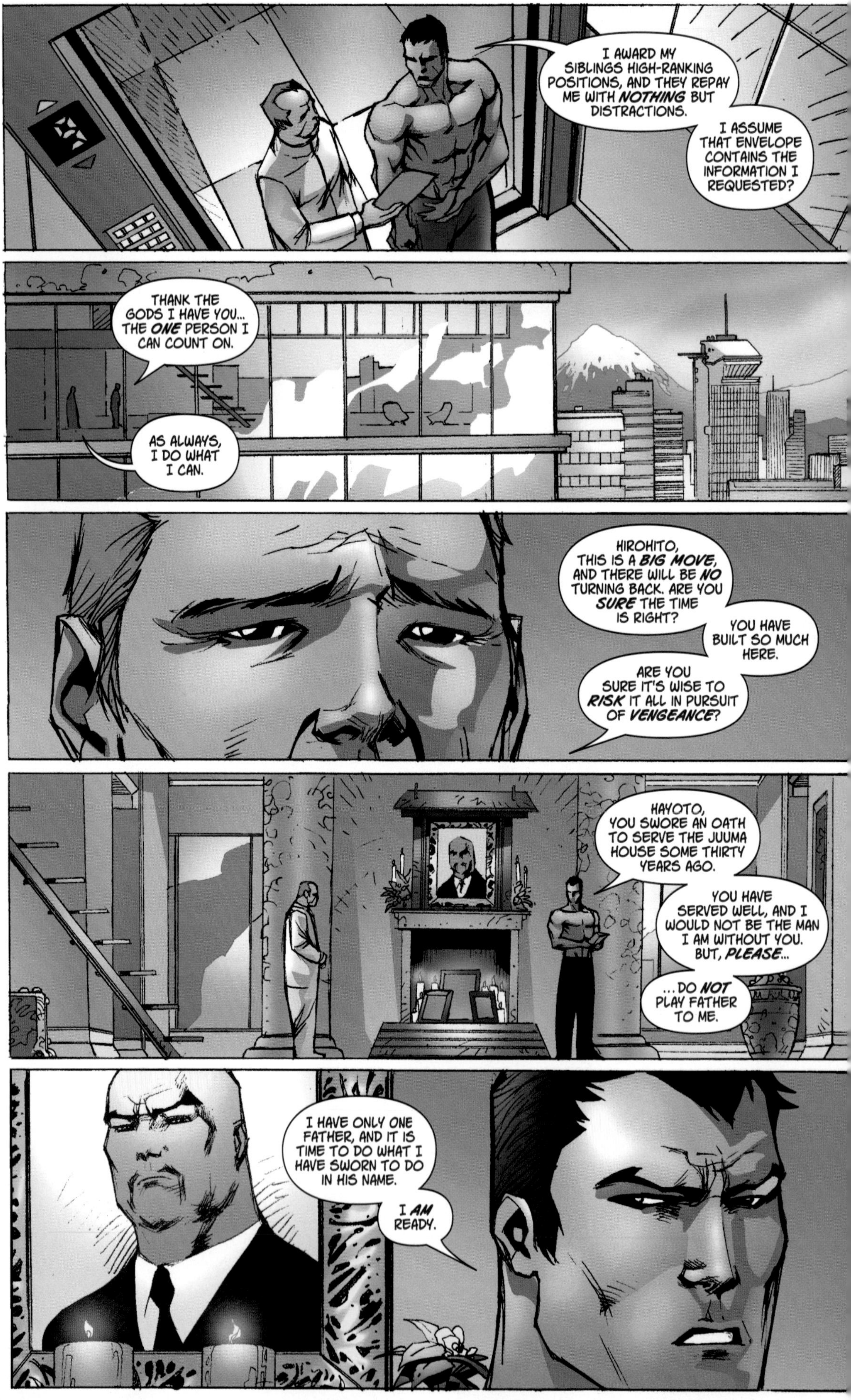
I AWARD MY SIBLINGS HIGH-RANKING POSITIONS, AND THEY REPAY ME WITH NOTHING BUT DISTRACTIONS.
I ASSUME THAT ENVELOPE CONTAINS THE INFORMATION I REQUESTED?
THANK THE GODS I HAVE YOU... THE ONE PERSON I CAN COUNT ON.
AS ALWAYS, I DO WHAT I CAN.
HIROHITO, THIS IS A BIG MOVE, AND THERE WILL BE NO TURNING BACK. ARE YOU SURE THE TIME IS RIGHT?
YOU HAVE BUILT SO MUCH HERE.
ARE YOU SURE IT'S WISE TO RISK IT ALL IN PURSUIT OF VENGEANCE?
HAYOTO, YOU SWORE AN OATH TO SERVE THE JUUMA HOUSE SOME THIRTY YEARS AGO.
YOU HAVE SERVED WELL, AND I WOULD NOT BE THE MAN I AM WITHOUT YOU. BUT, PLEASE...
...DO NOT PLAY FATHER TO ME.
I HAVE ONLY ONE FATHER, AND IT IS TIME TO DO WHAT I HAVE SWORN TO DO IN HIS NAME.
I AM READY.

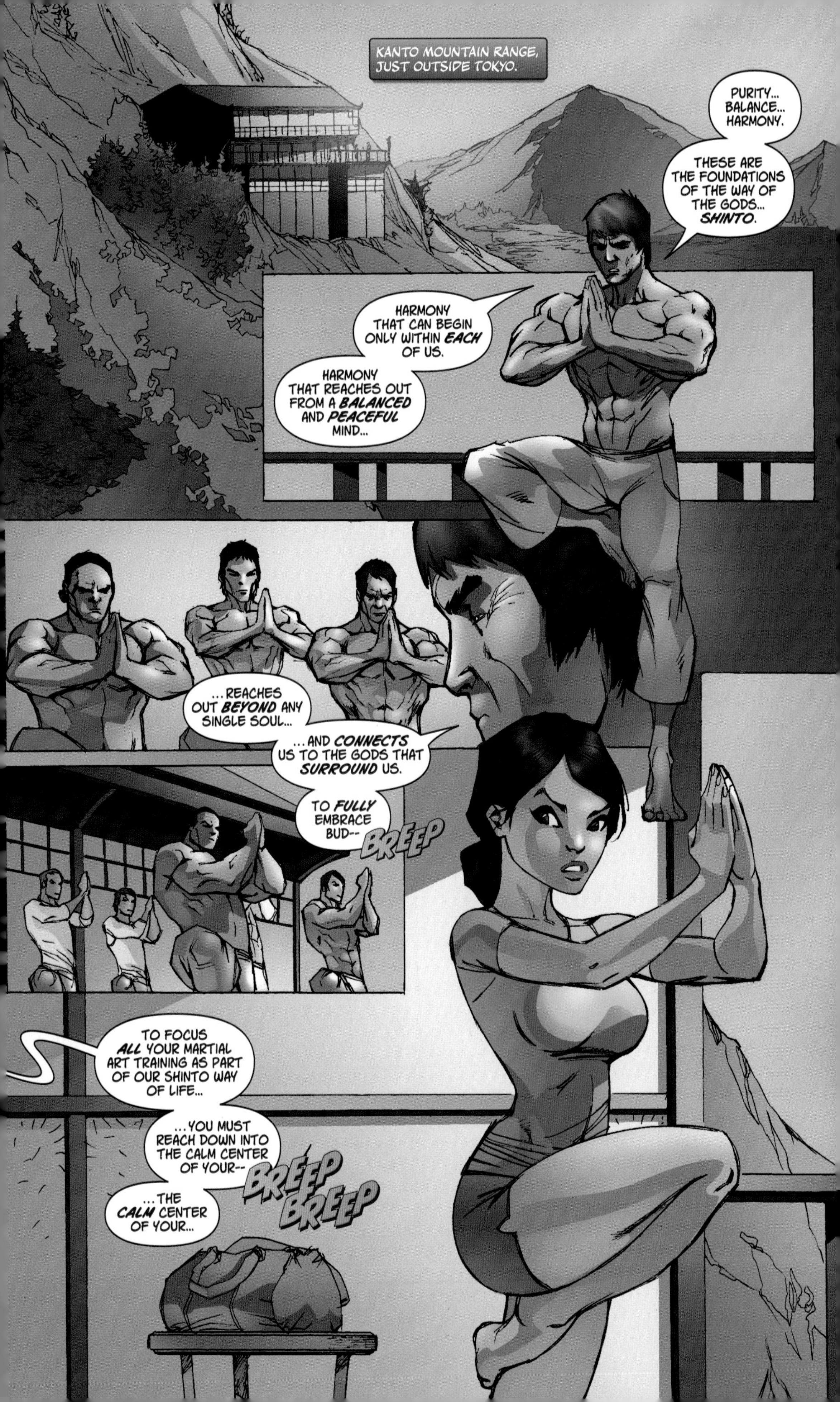

KANTO MOUNTAIN RANGE, JUST OUTSIDE TOKYO.
PURITY... BALANCE... HARMONY.
THESE ARE THE FOUNDATIONS OF THE WAY OF THE GODS... SHINTO.
HARMONY THAT CAN BEGIN ONLY WITHIN EACH OF US.
HARMONY THAT REACHES OUT FROM A BALANCED AND PEACEFUL MIND...
...REACHES OUT BEYOND ANY SINGLE SOUL...
...AND CONNECTS US TO THE GODS THAT SURROUND US.
TO FULLY EMBRACE BUD--
BREEP
TO FOCUS ALL YOUR MARTIAL ART TRAINING AS PART OF OUR SHINTO WAY OF LIFE...
...YOU MUST REACH DOWN INTO THE CALM CENTER OF YOUR--
BREEP BREEP
...THE CALM CENTER OF YOUR...

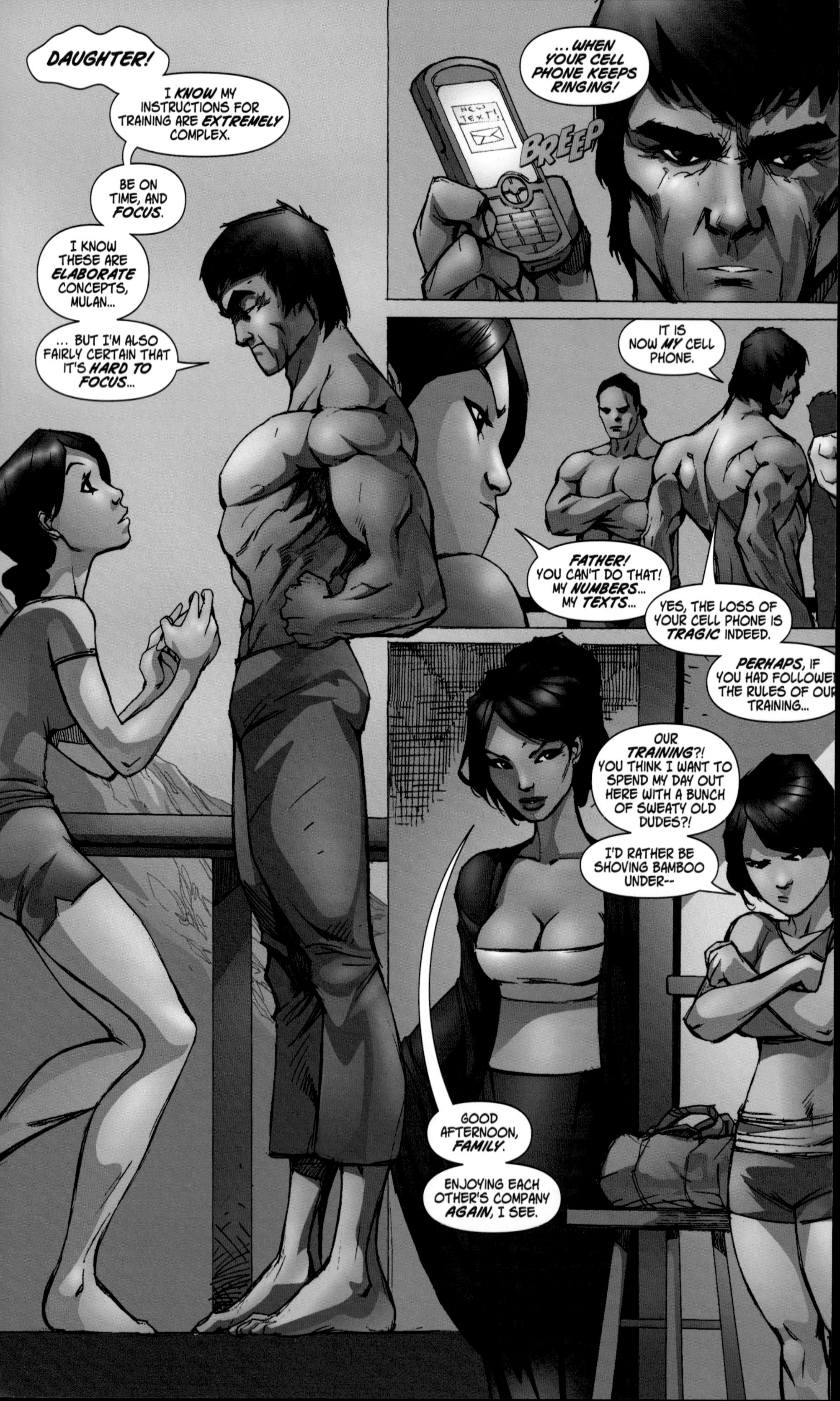
DAUGHTER!
I KNOW MY INSTRUCTIONS FOR TRAINING ARE EXTREMELY COMPLEX.
BE ON TIME, AND FOCUS.
I KNOW THESE ARE ELABORATE CONCEPTS, MULAN...
... BUT I'M ALSO FAIRLY CERTAIN THAT IT'S HARD TO FOCUS...
... WHEN YOUR CELL PHONE KEEPS RINGING!
NEW TEXT!
BREEP
IT IS NOW MY CELL PHONE.
FATHER! YOU CAN'T DO THAT! MY NUMBERS... MY TEXTS...
YES, THE LOSS OF YOUR CELL PHONE IS TRAGIC INDEED.
PERHAPS, IF YOU HAD FOLLOWED THE RULES OF OUR TRAINING...
OUR TRAINING?! YOU THINK I WANT TO SPEND MY DAY OUT HERE WITH A BUNCH OF SWEATY OLD DUDES?!
I'D RATHER BE SHOVING BAMBOO UNDER--
GOOD AFTERNOON, FAMILY.
ENJOYING EACH OTHER'S COMPANY AGAIN, I SEE.

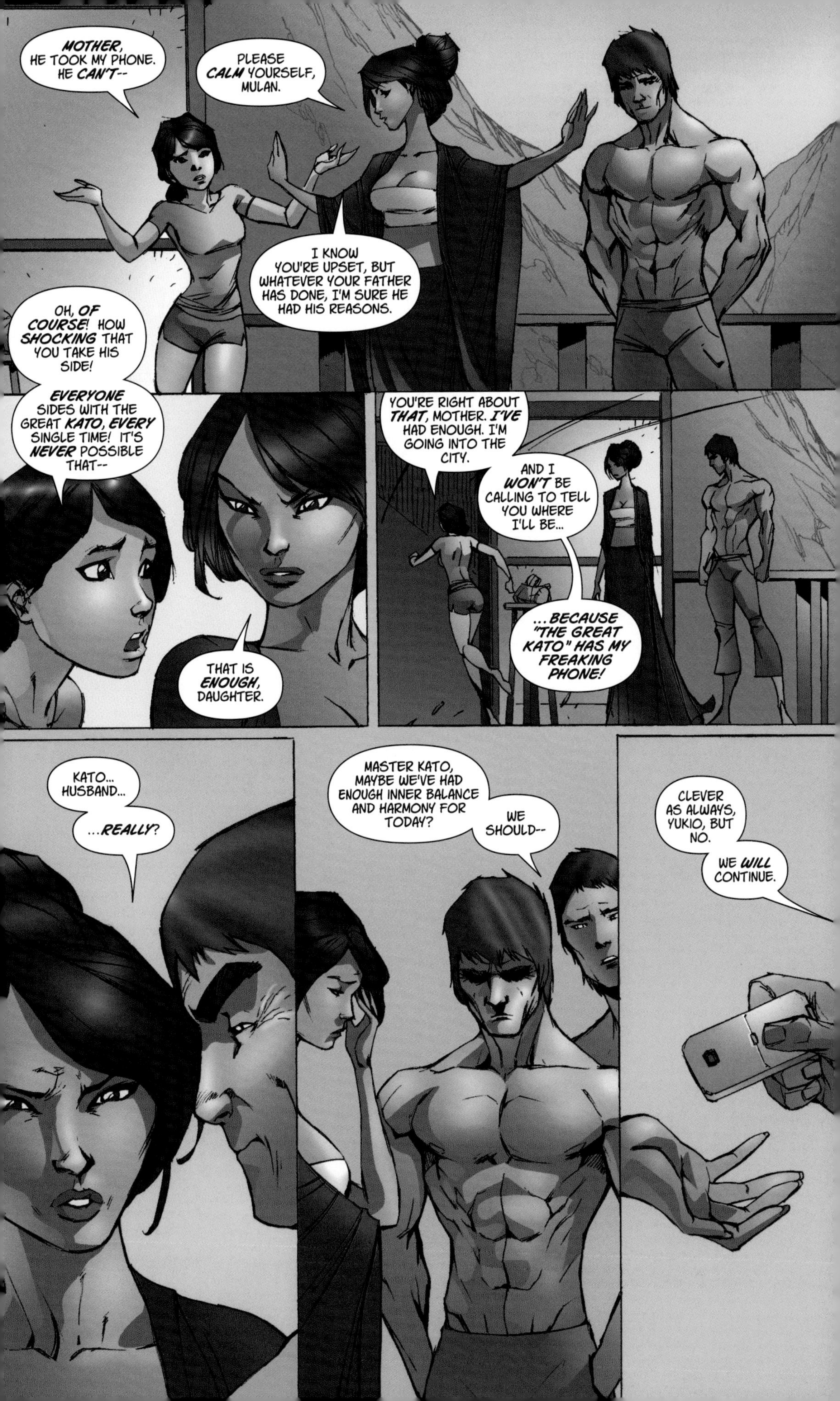

MOTHER, HE TOOK MY PHONE. HE CAN'T--
PLEASE CALM YOURSELF, MULAN.
I KNOW YOU'RE UPSET, BUT WHATEVER YOUR FATHER HAS DONE, I'M SURE HE HAD HIS REASONS.
OH, OF COURSE! HOW SHOCKING THAT YOU TAKE HIS SIDE!
EVERYONE SIDES WITH THE GREAT KATO, EVERY SINGLE TIME! IT'S NEVER POSSIBLE THAT--
THAT IS ENOUGH, DAUGHTER.
YOU'RE RIGHT ABOUT THAT, MOTHER. I'VE HAD ENOUGH. I'M GOING INTO THE CITY.
AND I WON'T BE CALLING TO TELL YOU WHERE I'LL BE...
...BECAUSE "THE GREAT KATO" HAS MY FREAKING PHONE!
KATO... HUSBAND...
...REALLY?
MASTER KATO, MAYBE WE'VE HAD ENOUGH INNER BALANCE AND HARMONY FOR TODAY?
WE SHOULD--
CLEVER AS ALWAYS, YUKIO, BUT NO.
WE WILL CONTINUE.

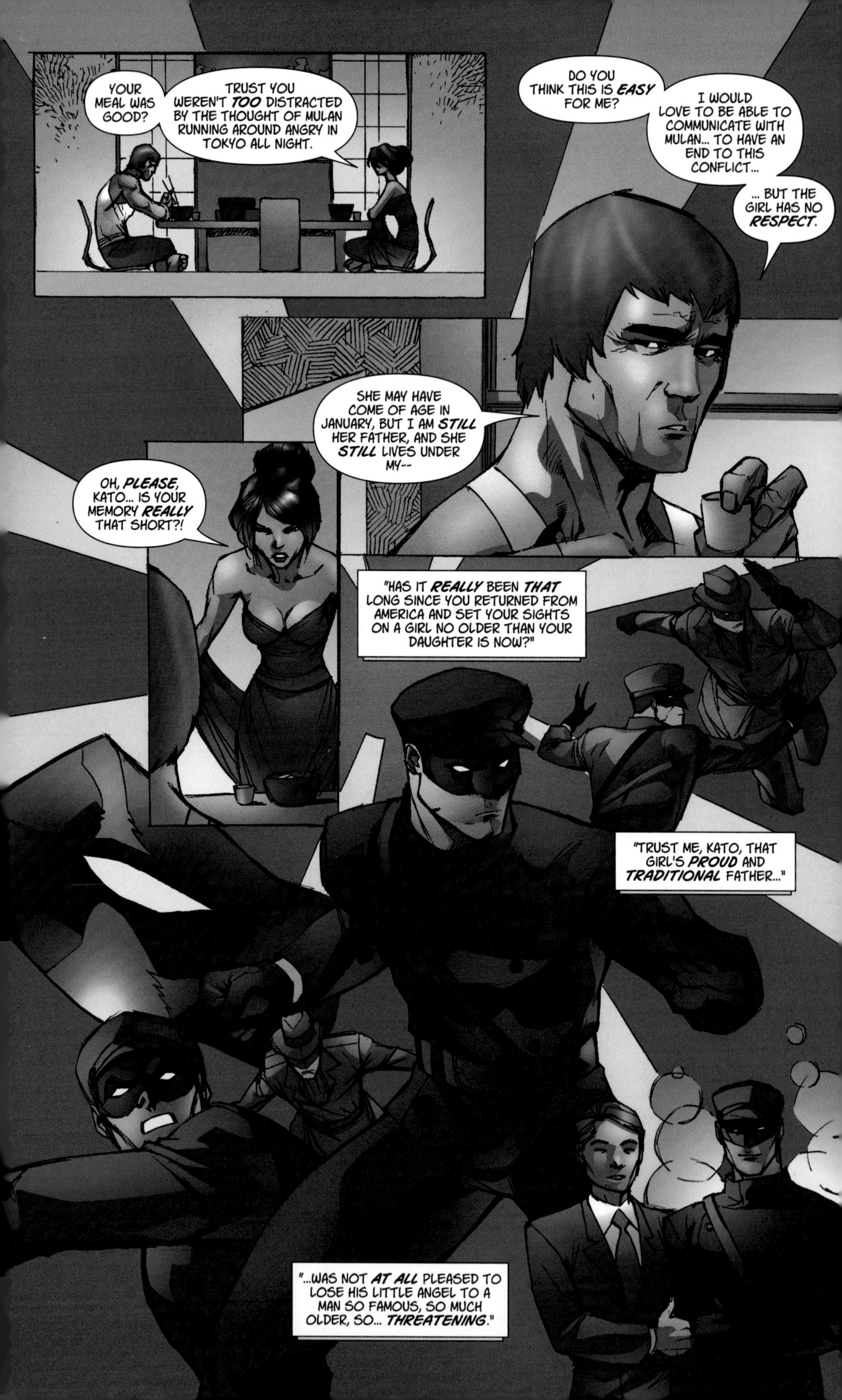

YOUR MEAL WAS GOOD?
TRUST YOU WEREN'T TOO DISTRACTED BY THE THOUGHT OF MULAN RUNNING AROUND ANGRY IN TOKYO ALL NIGHT.
DO YOU THINK THIS IS EASY FOR ME?
I WOULD LOVE TO BE ABLE TO COMMUNICATE WITH MULAN... TO HAVE AN END TO THIS CONFLICT...
... BUT THE GIRL HAS NO RESPECT.
SHE MAY HAVE COME OF AGE IN JANUARY, BUT I AM STILL HER FATHER, AND SHE STILL LIVES UNDER MY--
OH, PLEASE, KATO... IS YOUR MEMORY REALLY THAT SHORT?!
"HAS IT REALLY BEEN THAT LONG SINCE YOU RETURNED FROM AMERICA AND SET YOUR SIGHTS ON A GIRL NO OLDER THAN YOUR DAUGHTER IS NOW?"
"TRUST ME, KATO, THAT GIRL'S PROUD AND TRADITIONAL FATHER..."
"...WAS NOT AT ALL PLEASED TO LOSE HIS LITTLE ANGEL TO A MAN SO FAMOUS, SO MUCH OLDER, SO... THREATENING."

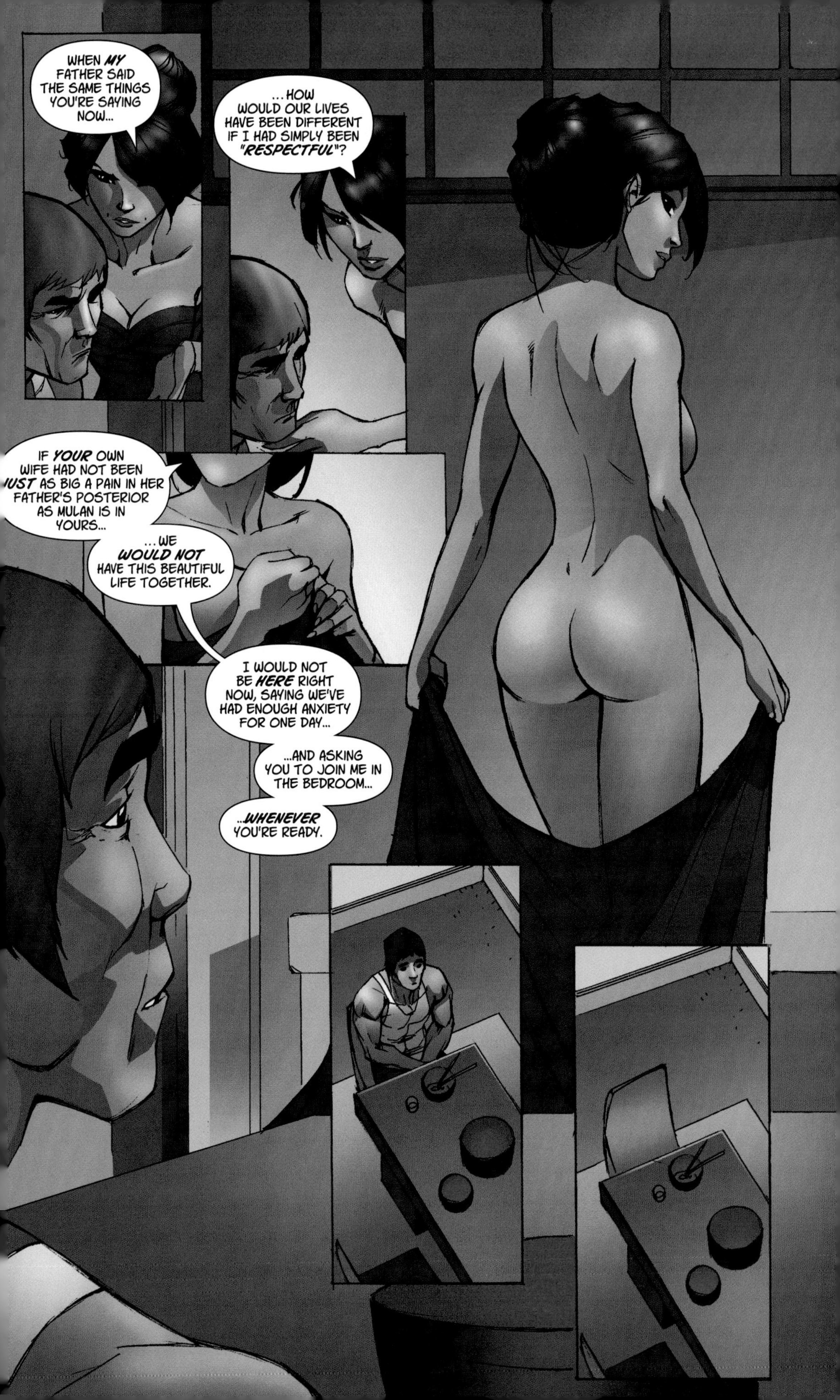
WHEN *MY* FATHER SAID THE SAME THINGS YOU'RE SAYING NOW...
...HOW WOULD OUR LIVES HAVE BEEN DIFFERENT IF I HAD SIMPLY BEEN "*RESPECTFUL*"?
IF *YOUR* OWN WIFE HAD NOT BEEN *JUST* AS BIG A PAIN IN HER FATHER'S POSTERIOR AS MULAN IS IN YOURS...
...WE *WOULD NOT* HAVE THIS BEAUTIFUL LIFE TOGETHER.
I WOULD NOT BE *HERE* RIGHT NOW, SAYING WE'VE HAD ENOUGH ANXIETY FOR ONE DAY...
...AND ASKING YOU TO JOIN ME IN THE BEDROOM...
...*WHENEVER* YOU'RE READY.

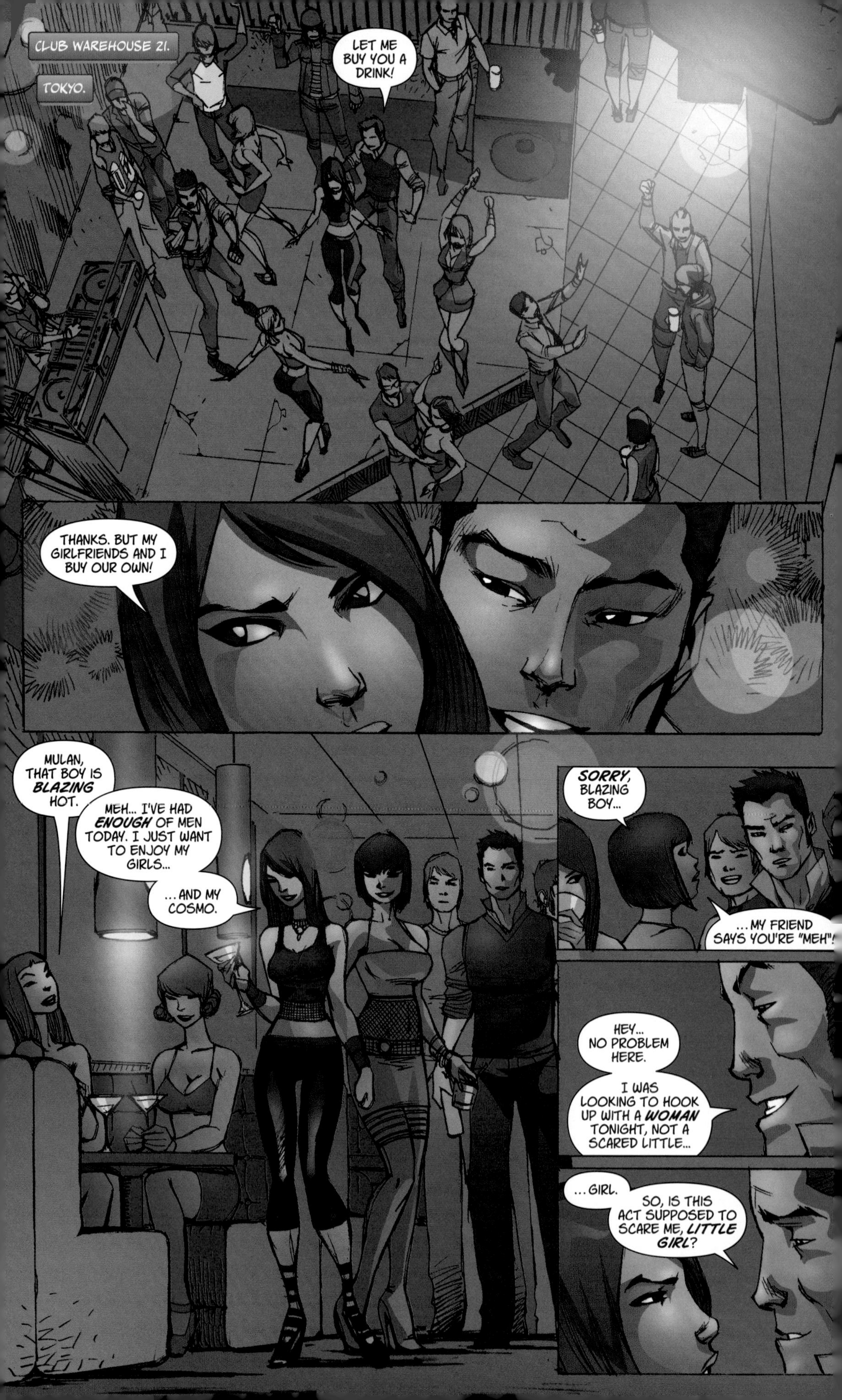
CLUB WAREHOUSE 21.
TOKYO.
LET ME BUY YOU A DRINK!
THANKS. BUT MY GIRLFRIENDS AND I BUY OUR OWN!
MULAN, THAT BOY IS **BLAZING** HOT.
MEH... I'VE HAD **ENOUGH** OF MEN TODAY. I JUST WANT TO ENJOY MY GIRLS...
...AND MY COSMO.
SORRY, BLAZING BOY...
...MY FRIEND SAYS YOU'RE "MEH"!
HEY... NO PROBLEM HERE.
I WAS LOOKING TO HOOK UP WITH A **WOMAN** TONIGHT, NOT A SCARED LITTLE...
...GIRL.
SO, IS THIS ACT SUPPOSED TO SCARE ME, **LITTLE GIRL**?

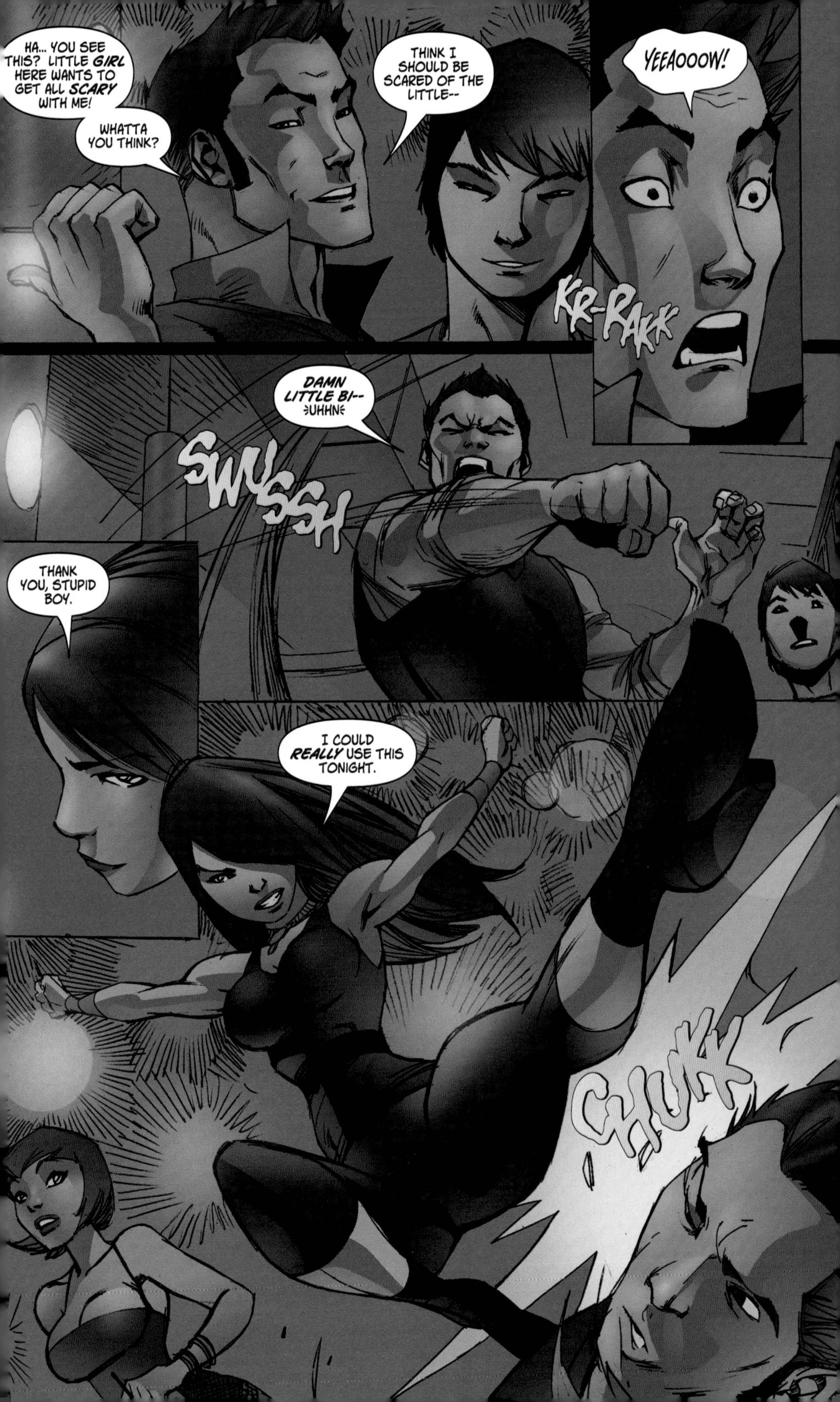
HA... YOU SEE THIS? LITTLE GIRL HERE WANTS TO GET ALL SCARY WITH ME!
WHATTA YOU THINK?
THINK I SHOULD BE SCARED OF THE LITTLE--
YEEAOOOW!
KR-RAKK
DAMN LITTLE BI-- UHHN
SWUSSH
THANK YOU, STUPID BOY.
I COULD REALLY USE THIS TONIGHT.
CHUKK

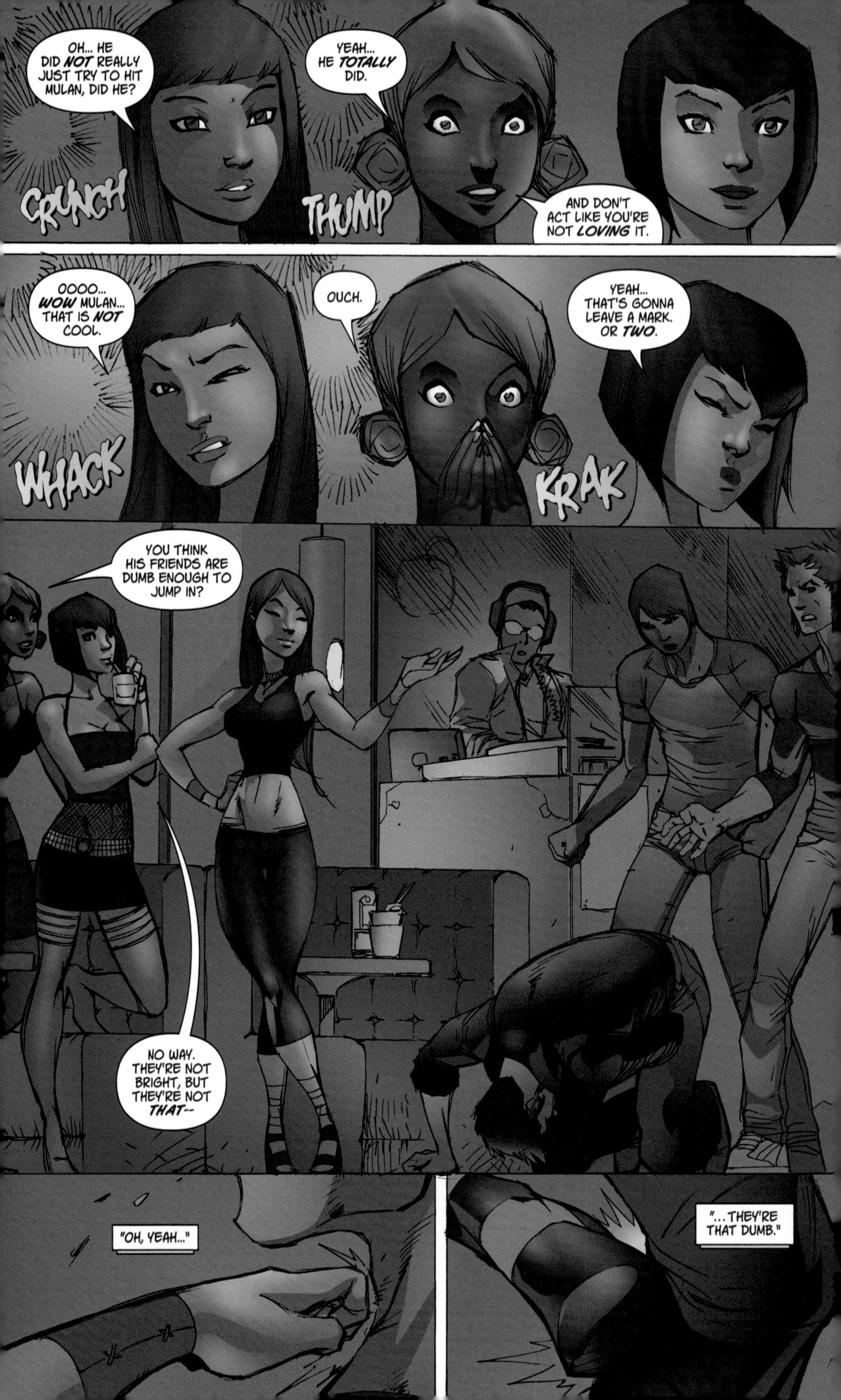
OH... HE DID NOT REALLY JUST TRY TO HIT MULAN, DID HE?
YEAH... HE TOTALLY DID.
CRUNCH
THUMP
AND DON'T ACT LIKE YOU'RE NOT LOVING IT.
OOOO... WOW MULAN... THAT IS NOT COOL.
OUCH.
YEAH... THAT'S GONNA LEAVE A MARK. OR TWO.
WHACK
KRAK
YOU THINK HIS FRIENDS ARE DUMB ENOUGH TO JUMP IN?
NO WAY. THEY'RE NOT BRIGHT, BUT THEY'RE NOT THAT--
"OH, YEAH..."
"...THEY'RE THAT DUMB."

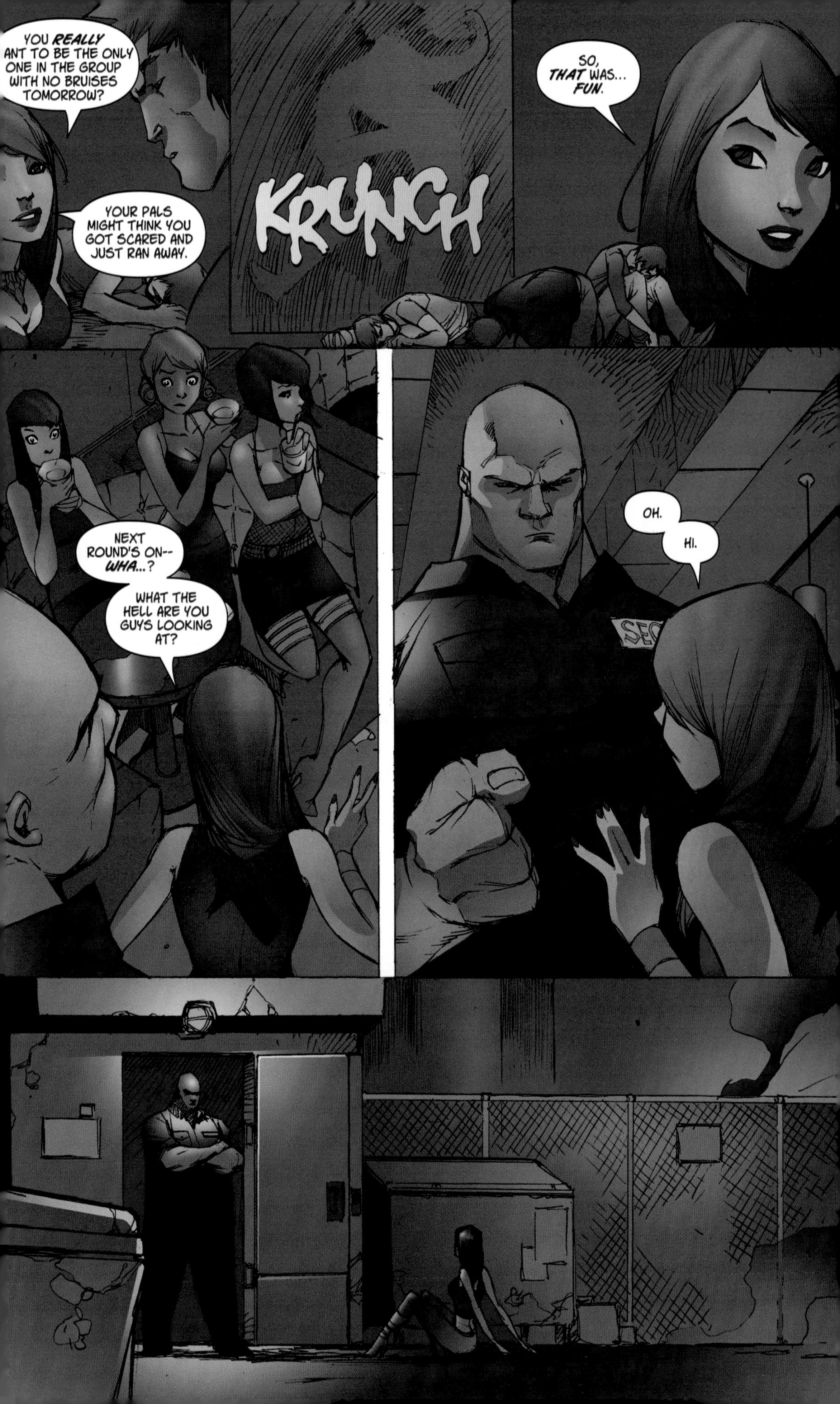
YOU REALLY ANT TO BE THE ONLY ONE IN THE GROUP WITH NO BRUISES TOMORROW?
YOUR PALS MIGHT THINK YOU GOT SCARED AND JUST RAN AWAY.
KRUNCH
SO, THAT WAS... FUN.
NEXT ROUND'S ON-- WHA...?
WHAT THE HELL ARE YOU GUYS LOOKING AT?
SEC
OH.
HI.

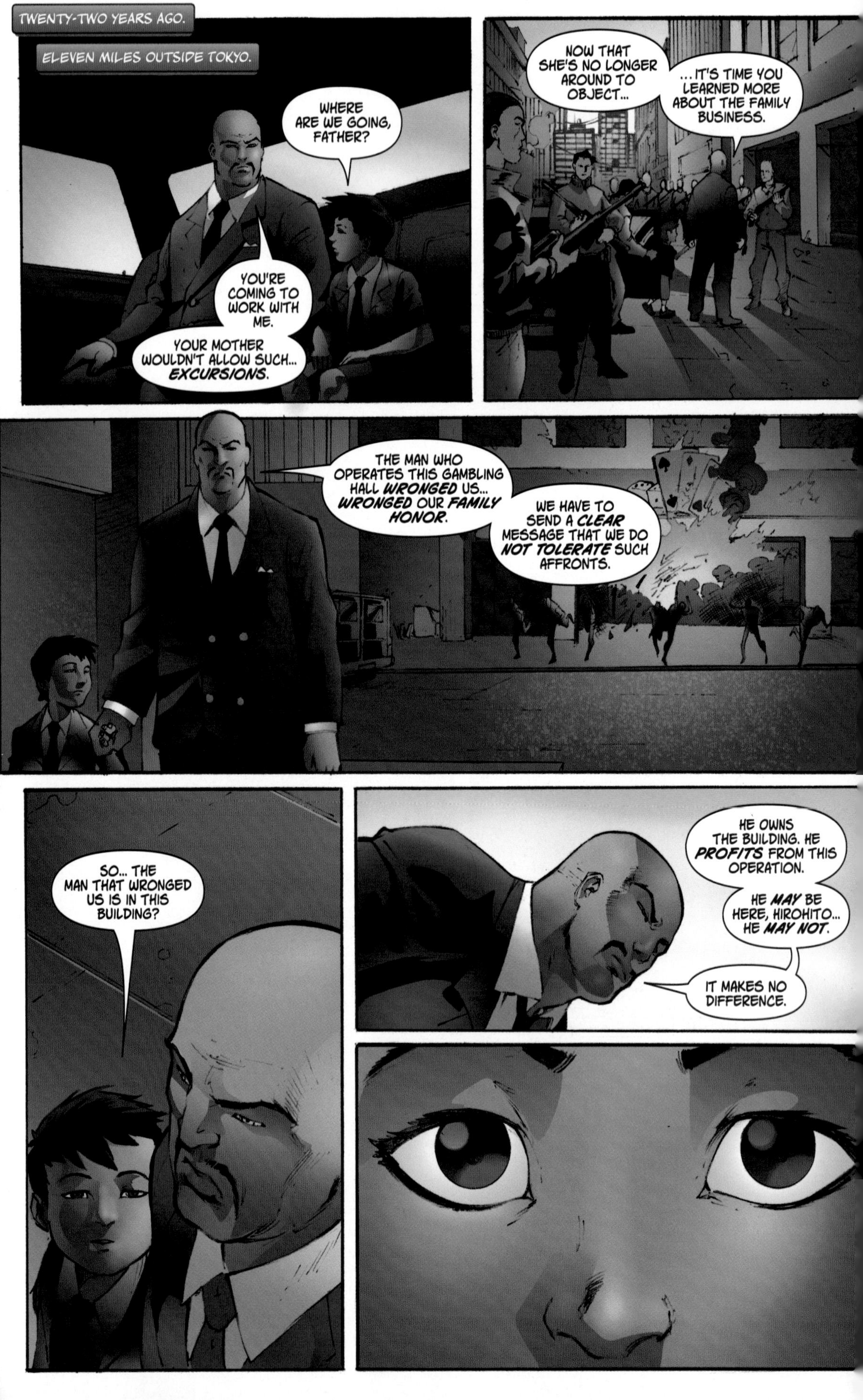

TWENTY-TWO YEARS AGO.
ELEVEN MILES OUTSIDE TOKYO.
WHERE ARE WE GOING, FATHER?
YOU'RE COMING TO WORK WITH ME.
YOUR MOTHER WOULDN'T ALLOW SUCH... EXCURSIONS.
NOW THAT SHE'S NO LONGER AROUND TO OBJECT...
...IT'S TIME YOU LEARNED MORE ABOUT THE FAMILY BUSINESS.
THE MAN WHO OPERATES THIS GAMBLING HALL WRONGED US... WRONGED OUR FAMILY HONOR.
WE HAVE TO SEND A CLEAR MESSAGE THAT WE DO NOT TOLERATE SUCH AFFRONTS.
SO... THE MAN THAT WRONGED US IS IN THIS BUILDING?
HE OWNS THE BUILDING. HE PROFITS FROM THIS OPERATION.
HE MAY BE HERE, HIROHITO... HE MAY NOT.
IT MAKES NO DIFFERENCE.

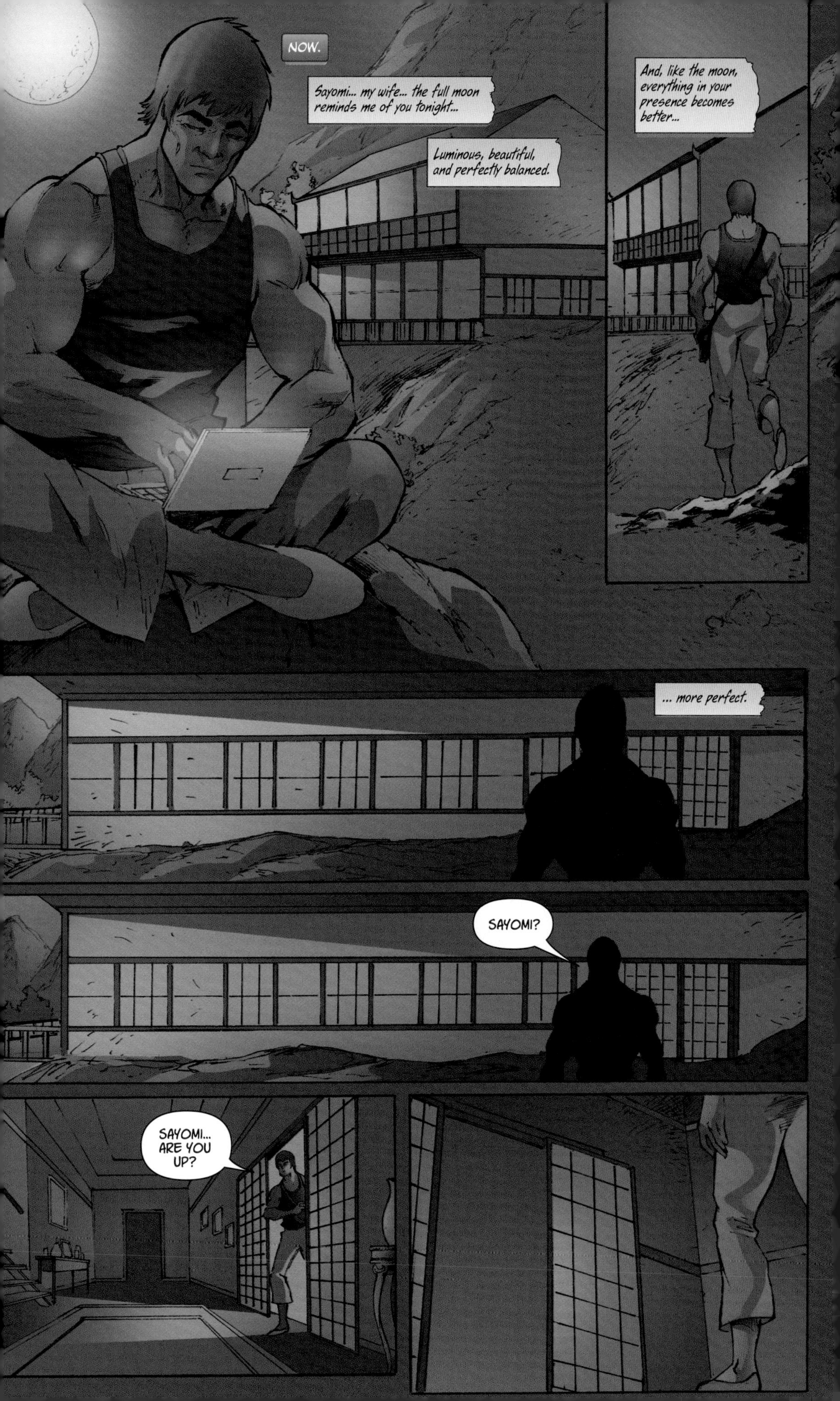
NOW.
Sayomi... my wife... the full moon reminds me of you tonight...
Luminous, beautiful, and perfectly balanced.
And, like the moon, everything in your presence becomes better...
... more perfect.
SAYOMI?
SAYOMI... ARE YOU UP?

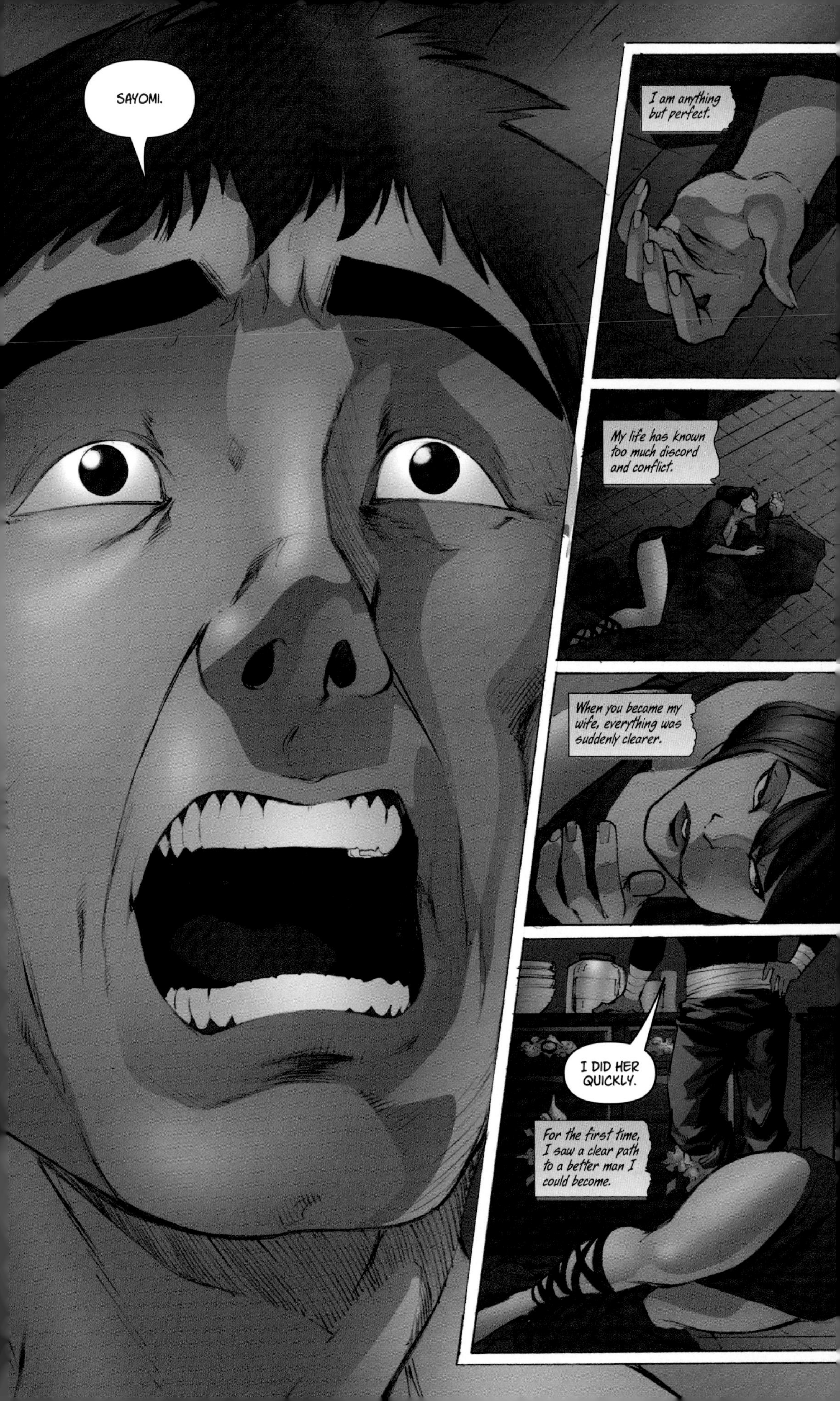
SAYOMI.
I am anything but perfect.
My life has known too much discord and conflict.
When you became my wife, everything was suddenly clearer.
I DID HER QUICKLY.
For the first time, I saw a clear path to a better man I could become.

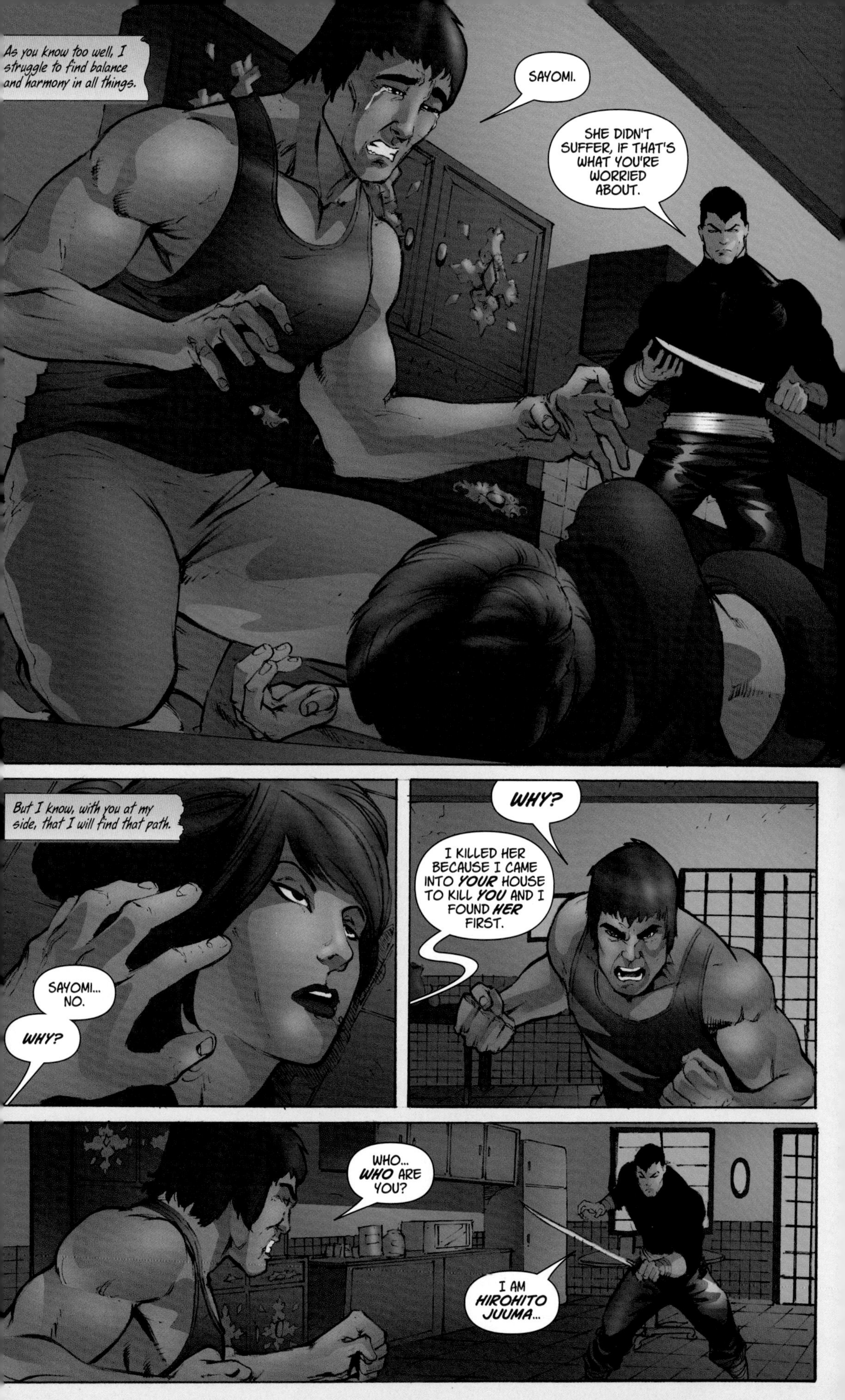

As you know too well, I struggle to find balance and harmony in all things.
SAYOMI.
SHE DIDN'T SUFFER, IF THAT'S WHAT YOU'RE WORRIED ABOUT.
But I know, with you at my side, that I will find that path.
SAYOMI... NO.
WHY?
WHY?
I KILLED HER BECAUSE I CAME INTO YOUR HOUSE TO KILL YOU AND I FOUND HER FIRST.
WHO... WHO ARE YOU?
I AM HIROHITO JUUMA...

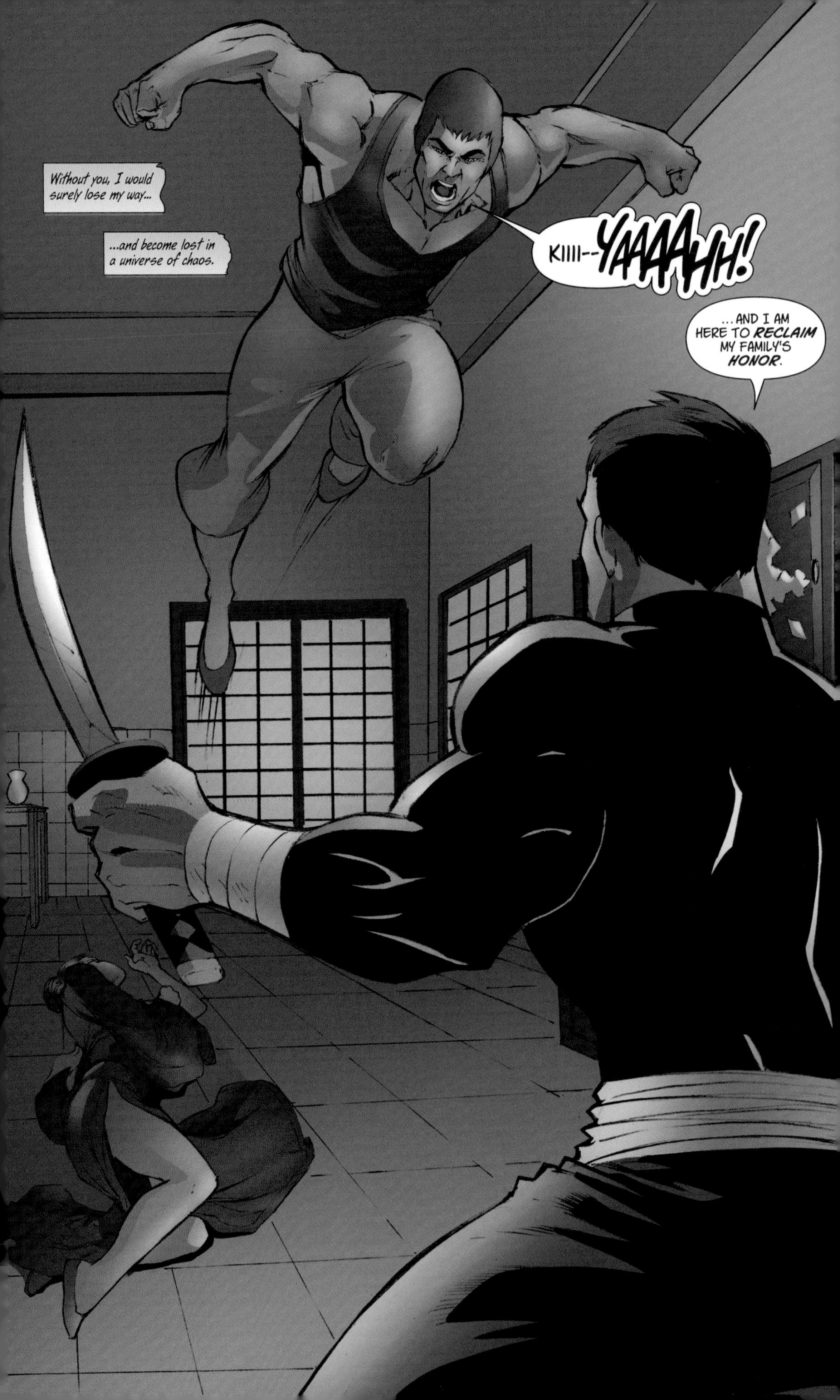

Without you, I would surely lose my way...
...and become lost in a universe of chaos.
KIIII--YAAAAHH!
...AND I AM HERE TO RECLAIM MY FAMILY'S HONOR.

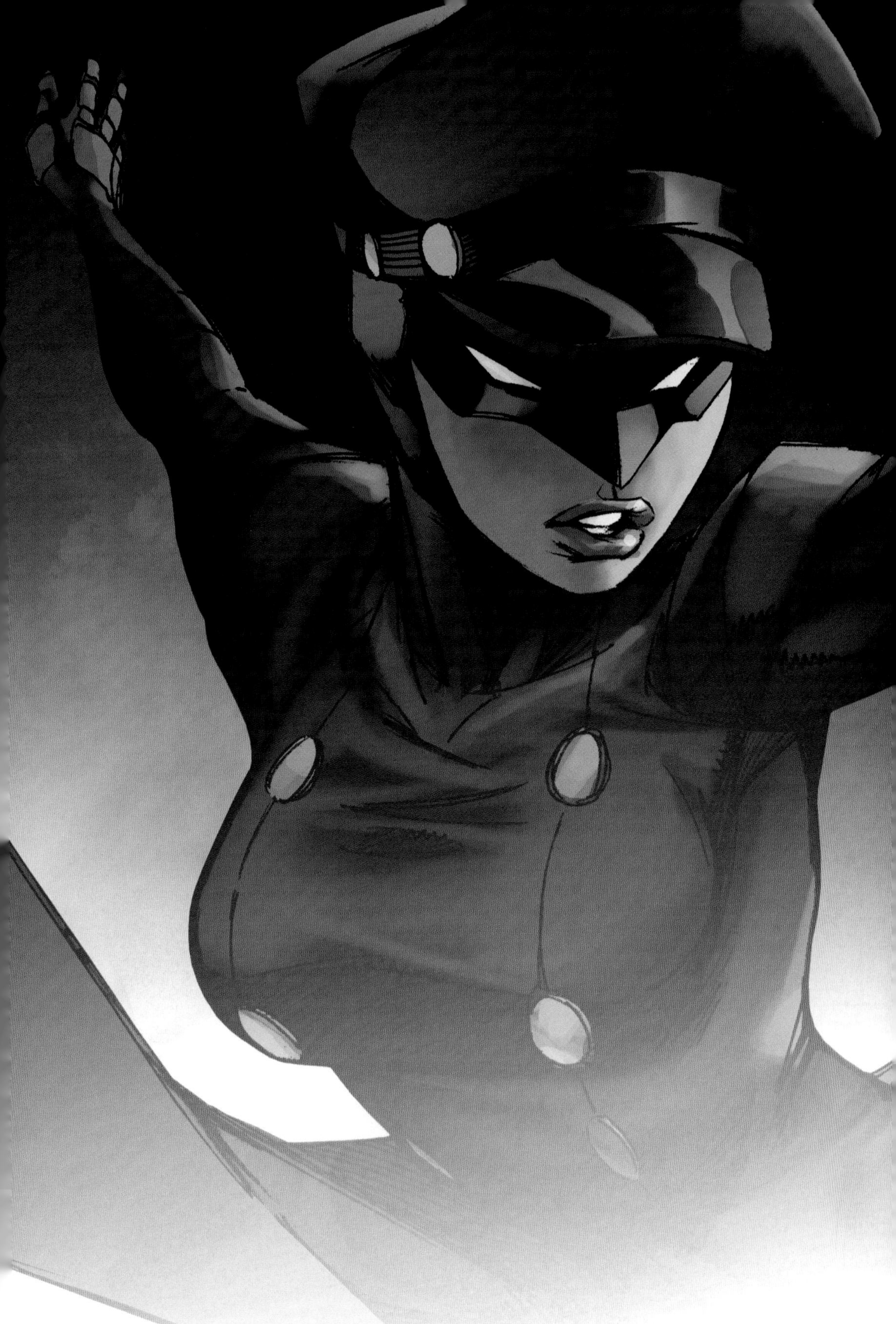

Issue TWO

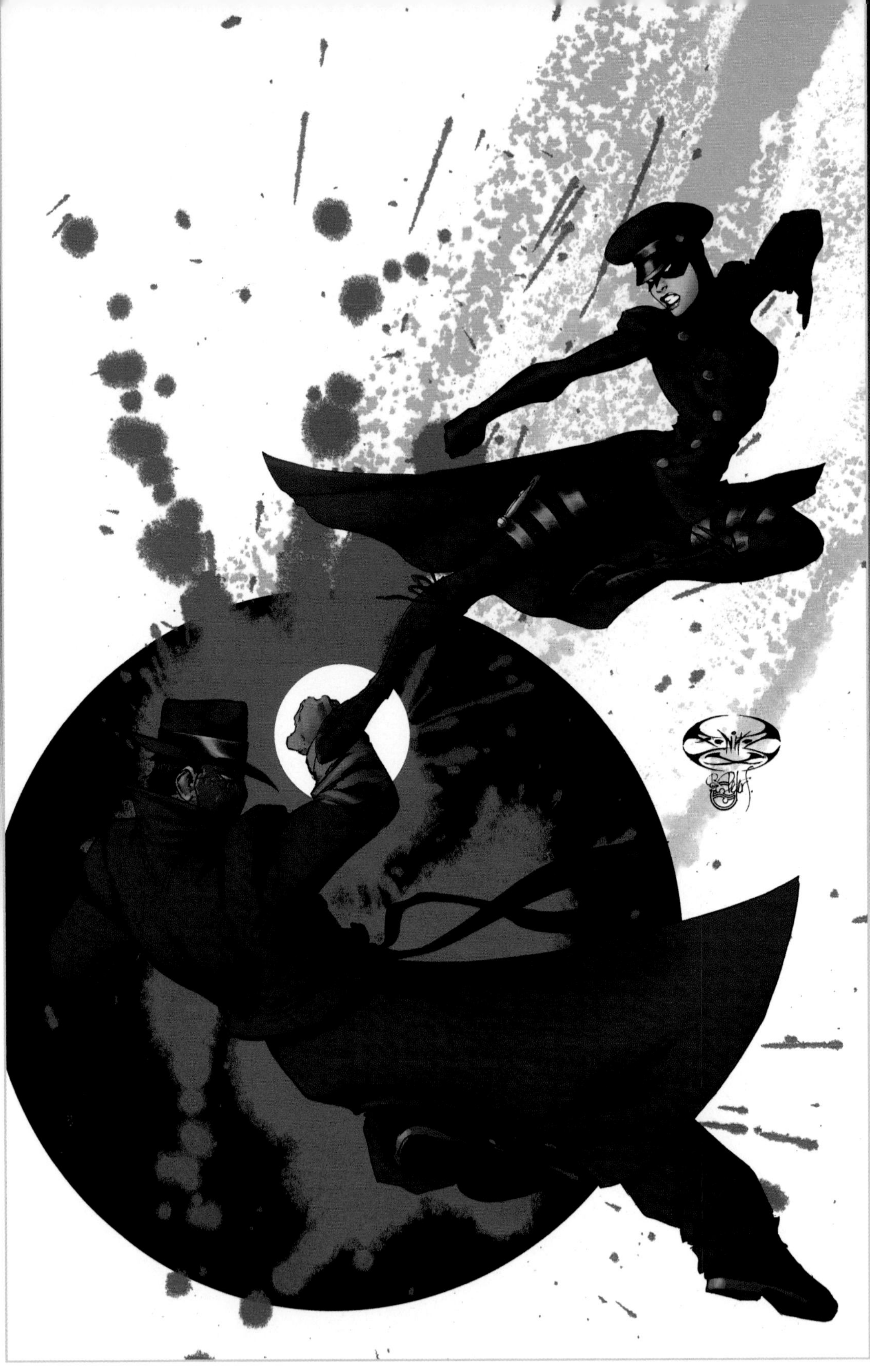

Issue two cover by **JOE BENITEZ**

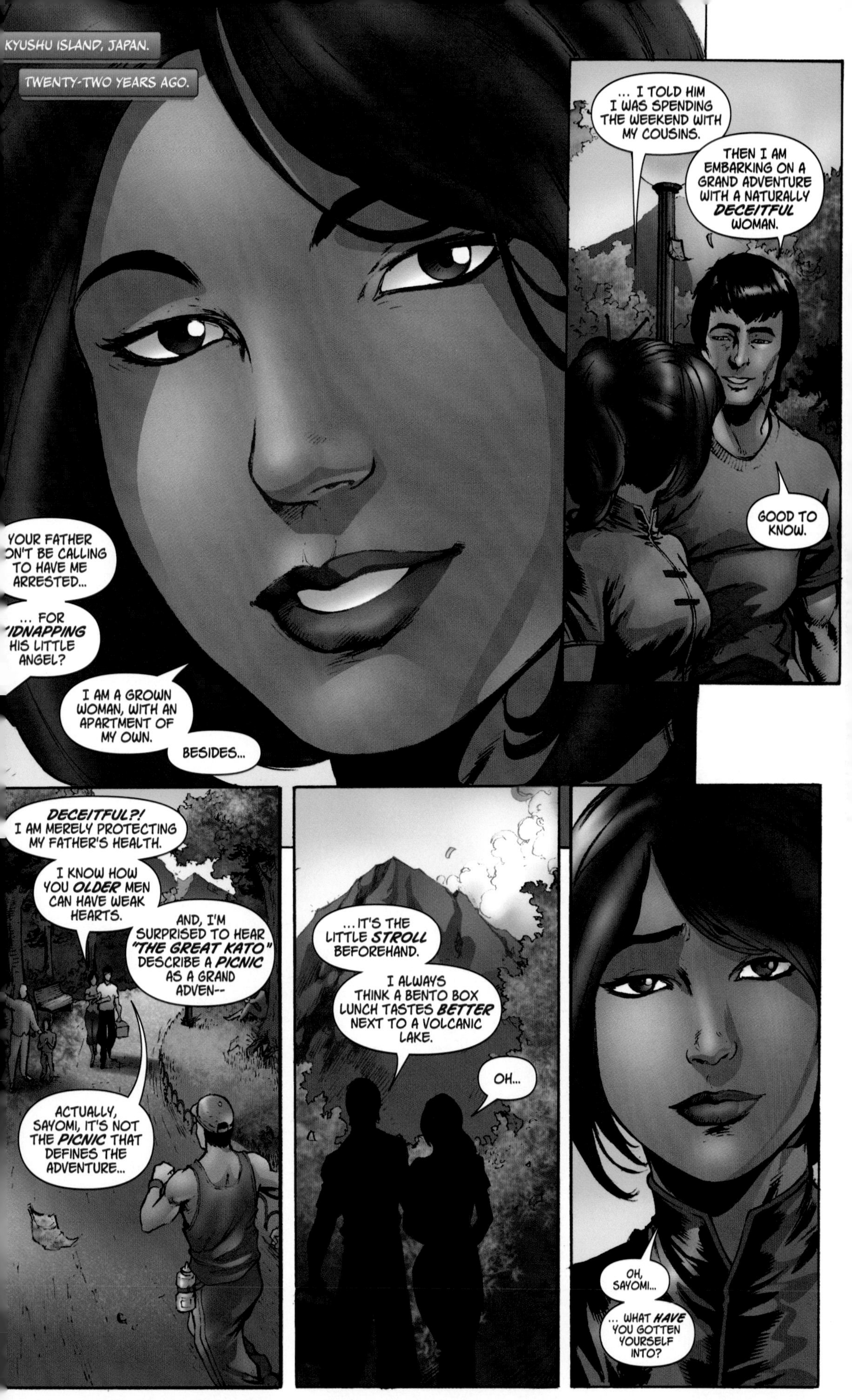

KYUSHU ISLAND, JAPAN.
TWENTY-TWO YEARS AGO.
YOUR FATHER ON'T BE CALLING TO HAVE ME ARRESTED...
... FOR IDNAPPING HIS LITTLE ANGEL?
I AM A GROWN WOMAN, WITH AN APARTMENT OF MY OWN.
BESIDES...
... I TOLD HIM I WAS SPENDING THE WEEKEND WITH MY COUSINS.
THEN I AM EMBARKING ON A GRAND ADVENTURE WITH A NATURALLY DECEITFUL WOMAN.
GOOD TO KNOW.
DECEITFUL?! I AM MERELY PROTECTING MY FATHER'S HEALTH.
I KNOW HOW YOU OLDER MEN CAN HAVE WEAK HEARTS.
AND, I'M SURPRISED TO HEAR "THE GREAT KATO" DESCRIBE A PICNIC AS A GRAND ADVEN--
ACTUALLY, SAYOMI, IT'S NOT THE PICNIC THAT DEFINES THE ADVENTURE...
...IT'S THE LITTLE STROLL BEFOREHAND.
I ALWAYS THINK A BENTO BOX LUNCH TASTES BETTER NEXT TO A VOLCANIC LAKE.
OH...
OH, SAYOMI...
... WHAT HAVE YOU GOTTEN YOURSELF INTO?

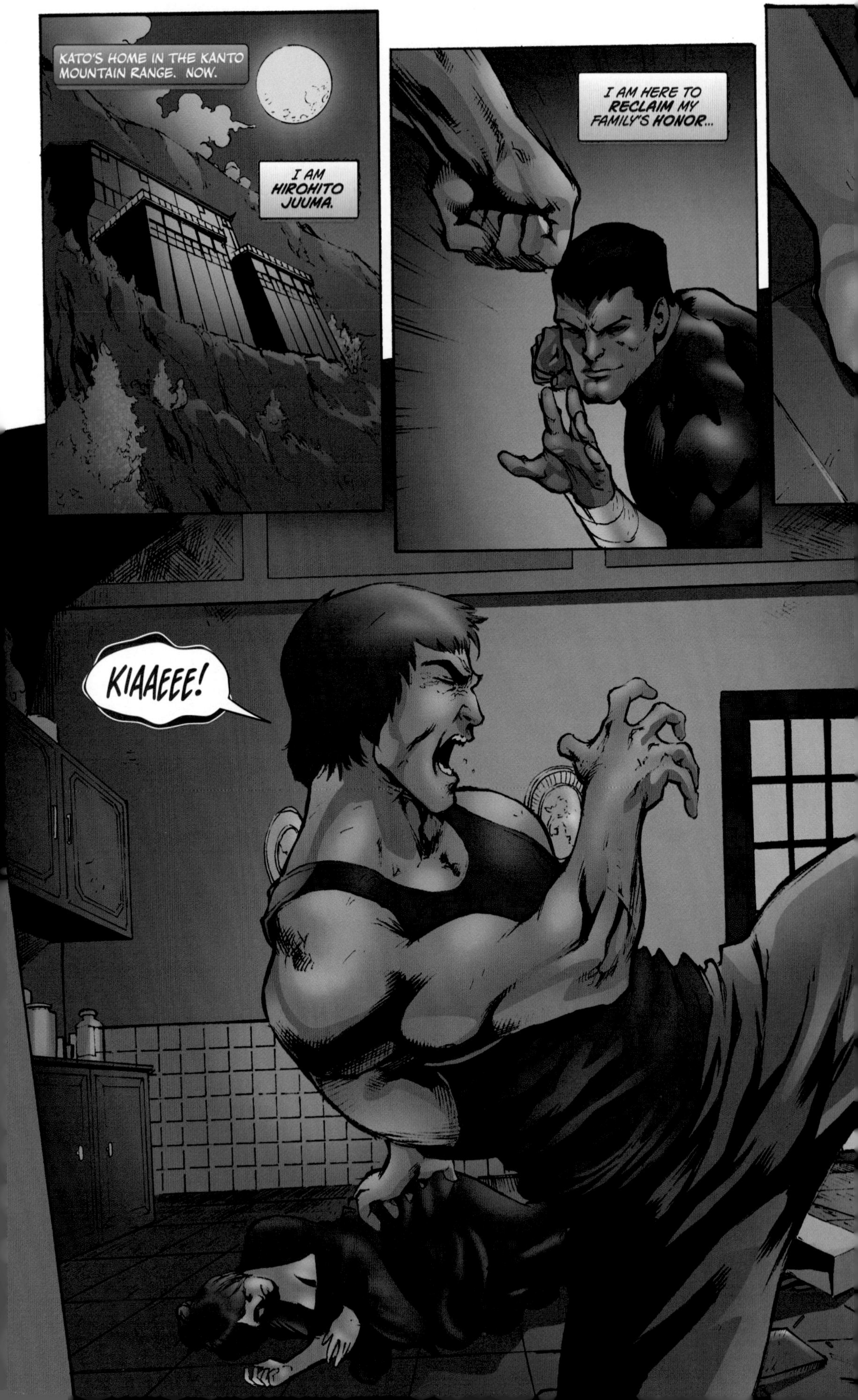

KATO'S HOME IN THE KANTO MOUNTAIN RANGE. NOW.
I AM HIROHITO JUUMA.
I AM HERE TO RECLAIM MY FAMILY'S HONOR...
KIAAEEE!

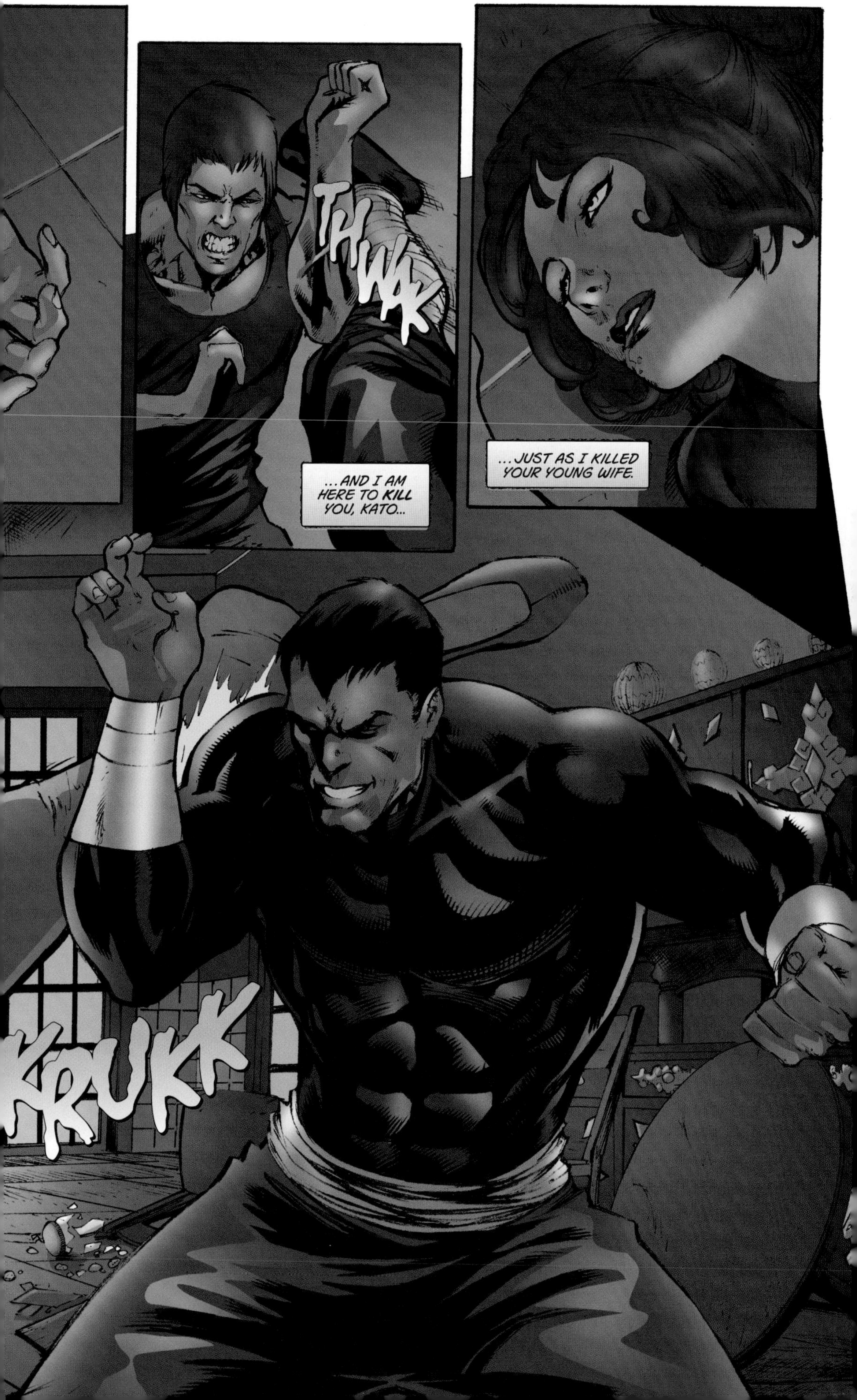
THWAK
...AND I AM HERE TO KILL YOU, KATO...
...JUST AS I KILLED YOUR YOUNG WIFE.
KRUKK

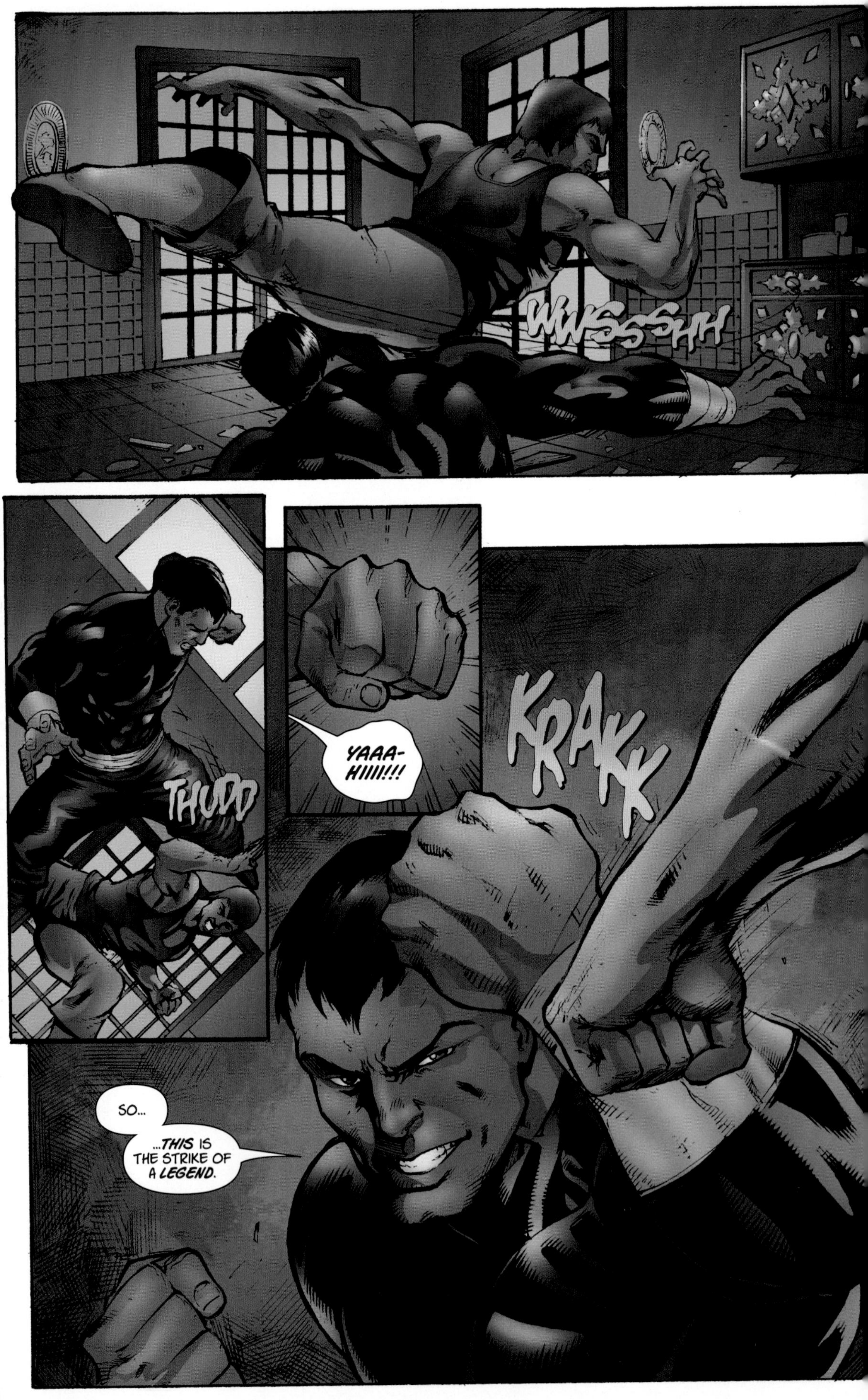

WWSSSHH
THUDD
YAAA-HIIII!!!
KRAKK
SO...
...THIS IS THE STRIKE OF A LEGEND.

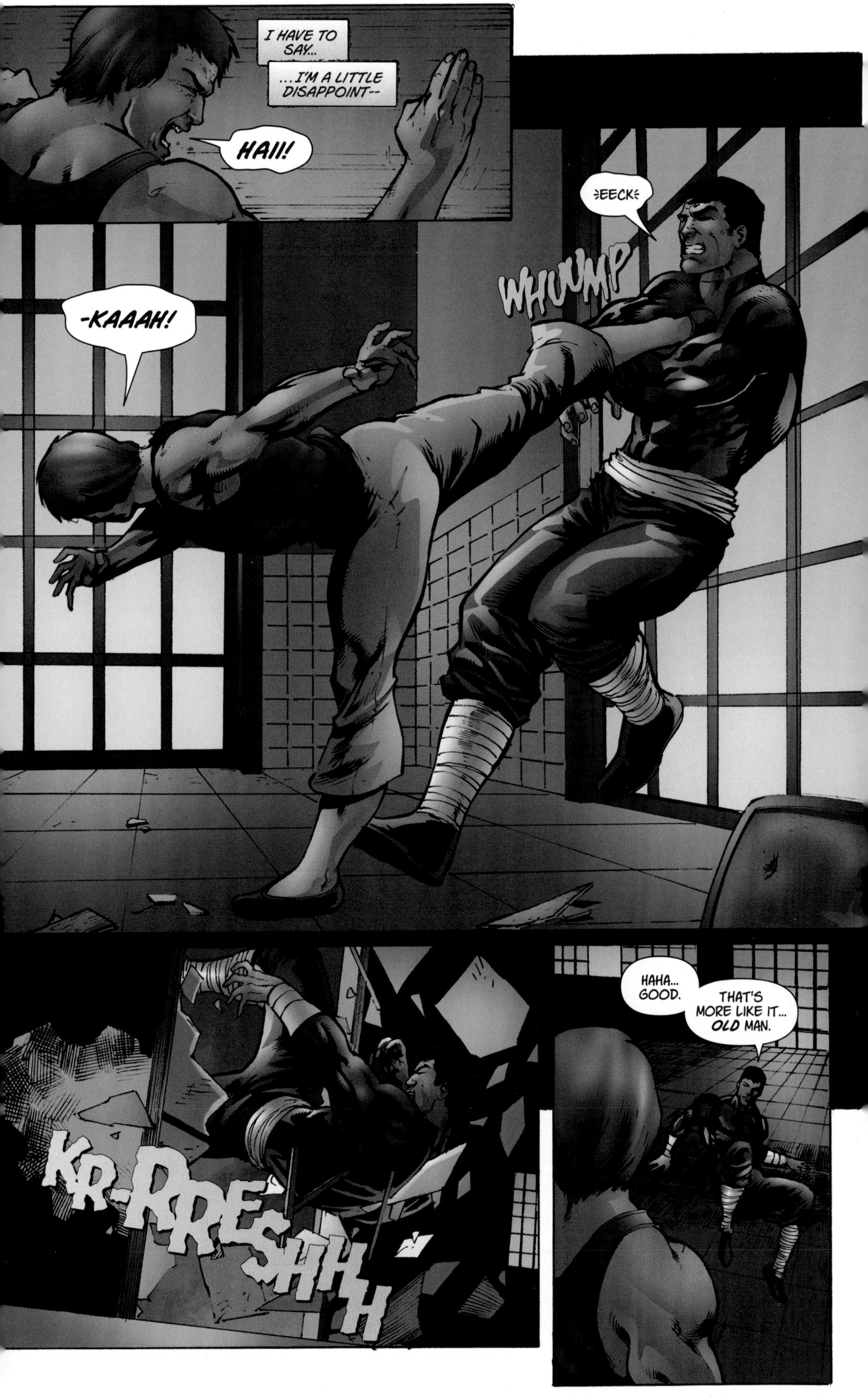
I HAVE TO SAY...
...I'M A LITTLE DISAPPOINT--
HAII!
-KAAAH!
EECK
WHUUMP
KR-RRESHHH
HAHA... GOOD.
THAT'S MORE LIKE IT... OLD MAN.

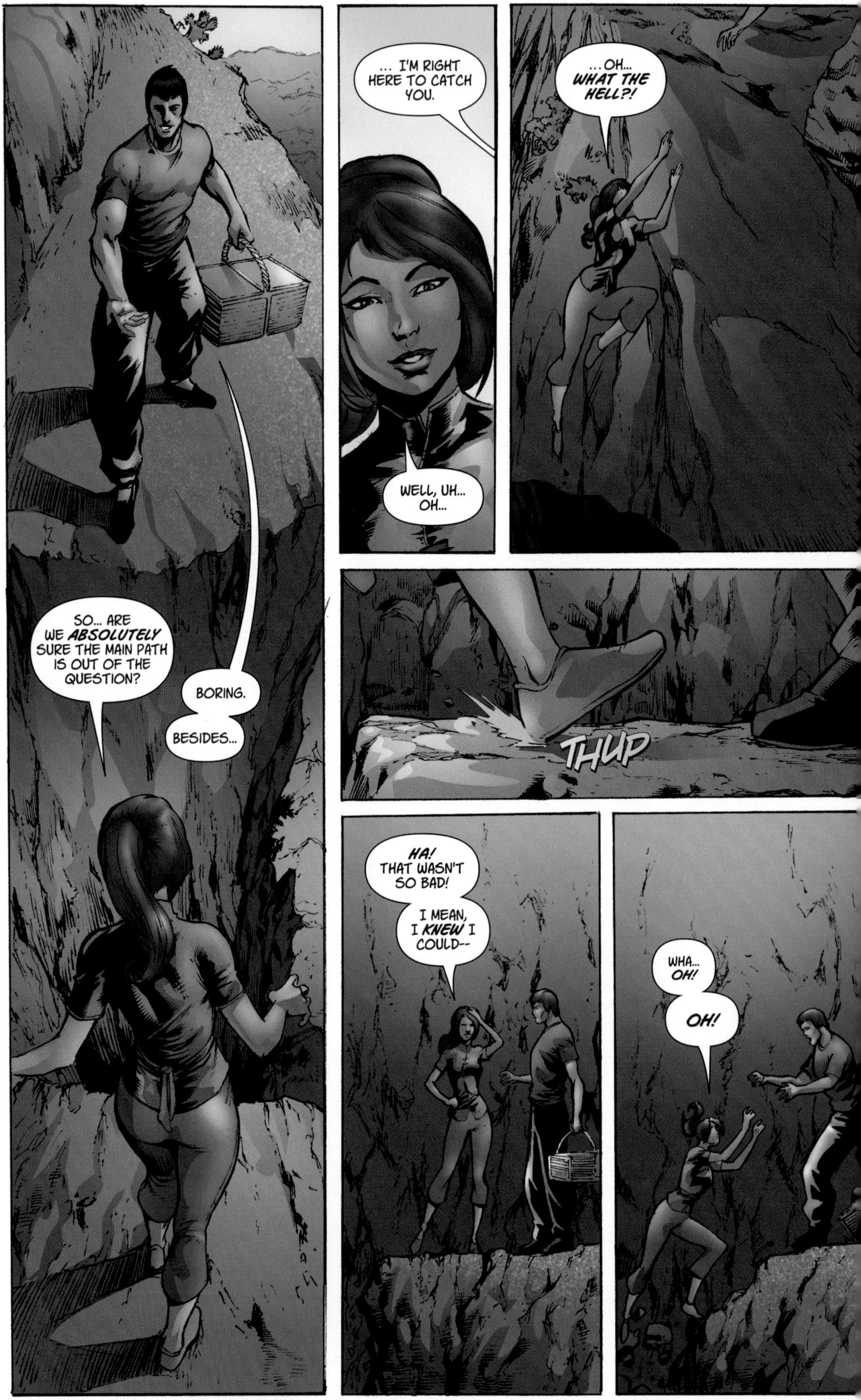

SO... ARE WE ABSOLUTELY SURE THE MAIN PATH IS OUT OF THE QUESTION?
BORING.
BESIDES...
... I'M RIGHT HERE TO CATCH YOU.
WELL, UH... OH...
...OH... WHAT THE HELL?!
THUP
HA! THAT WASN'T SO BAD!
I MEAN, I KNEW I COULD--
WHA... OH!
OH!

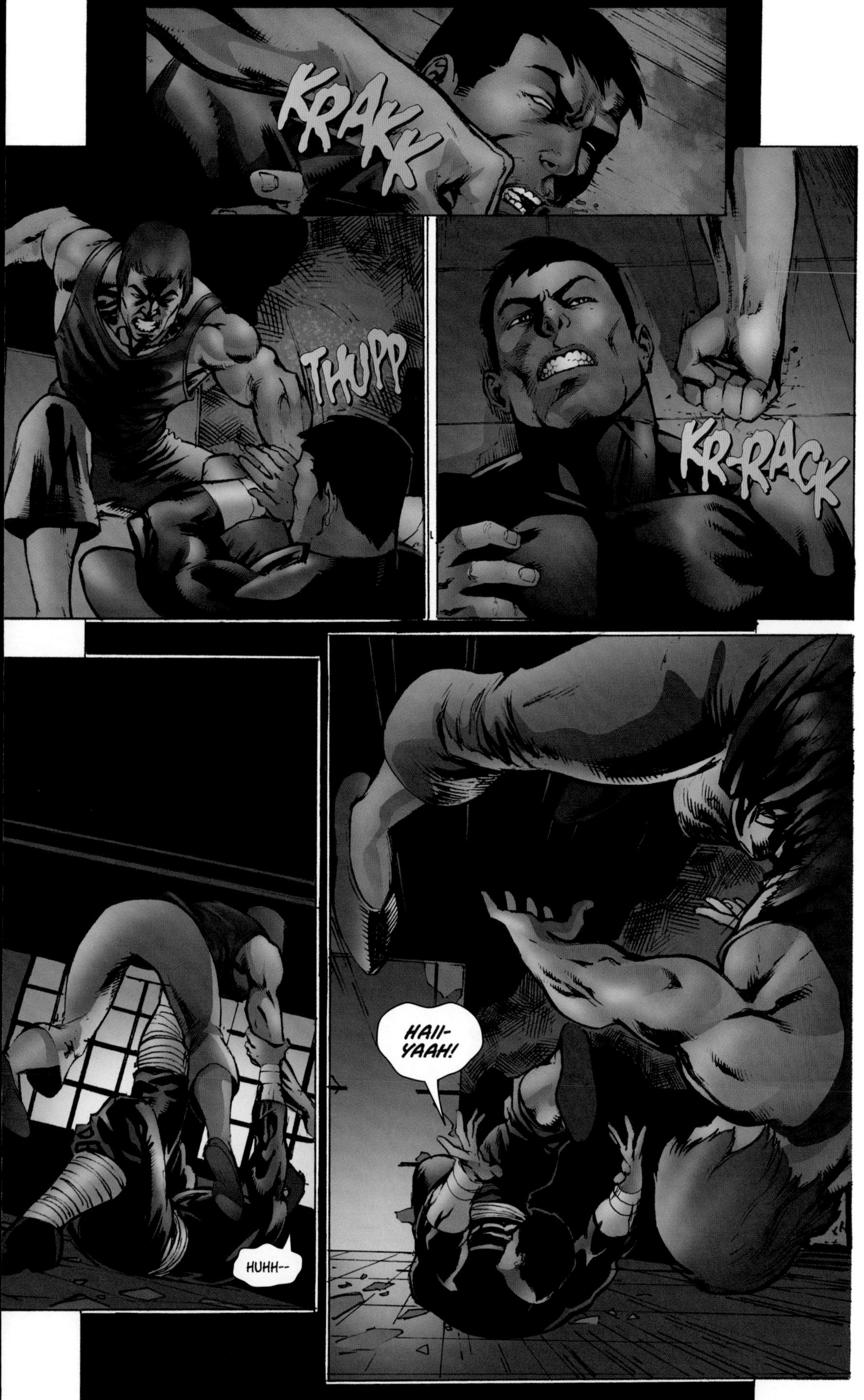
KRAKK
THUPP
KR-RACK
HUHH--
HAII-YAAH!

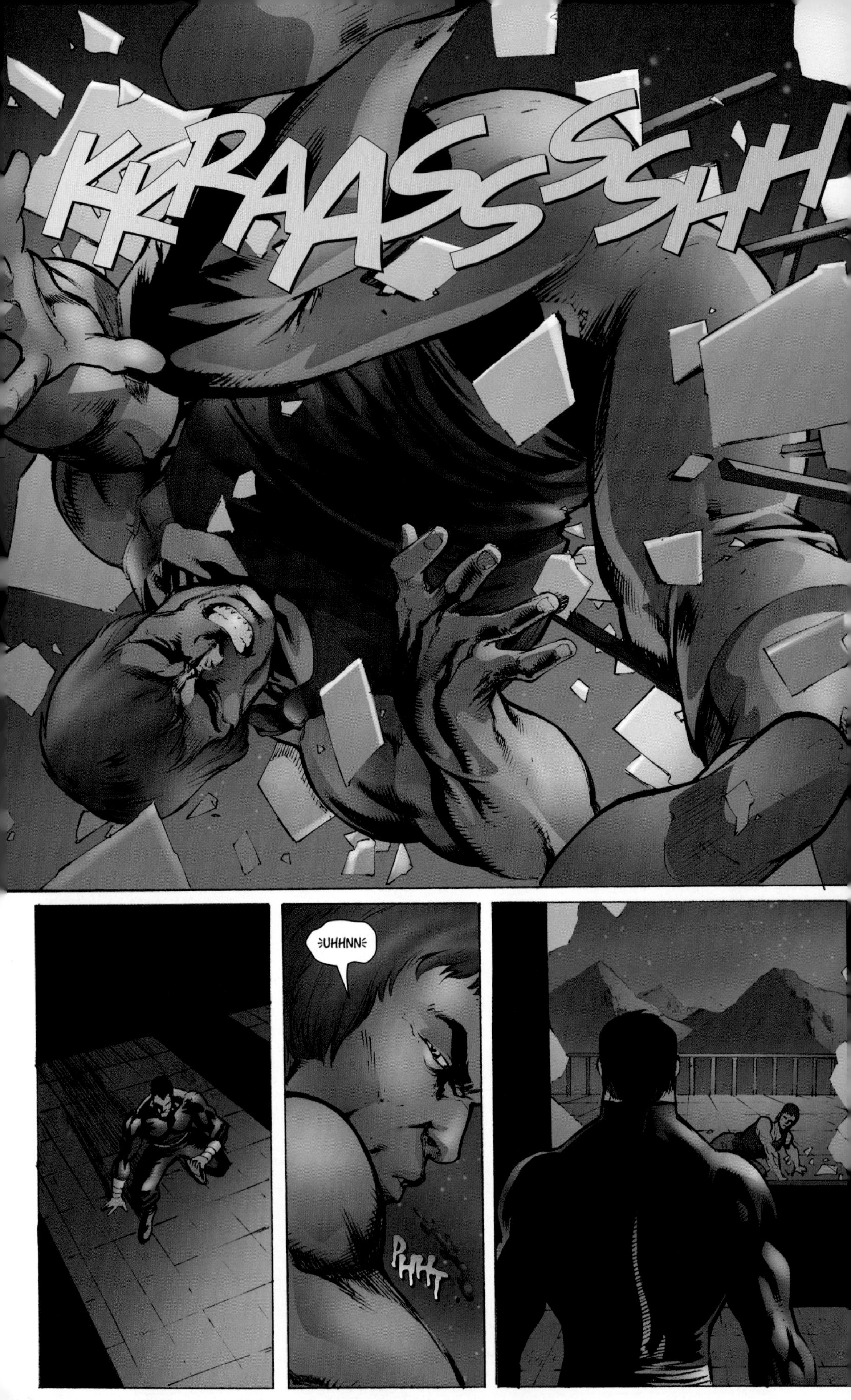

KKRAASSSSH!
UHHNN
PHHT

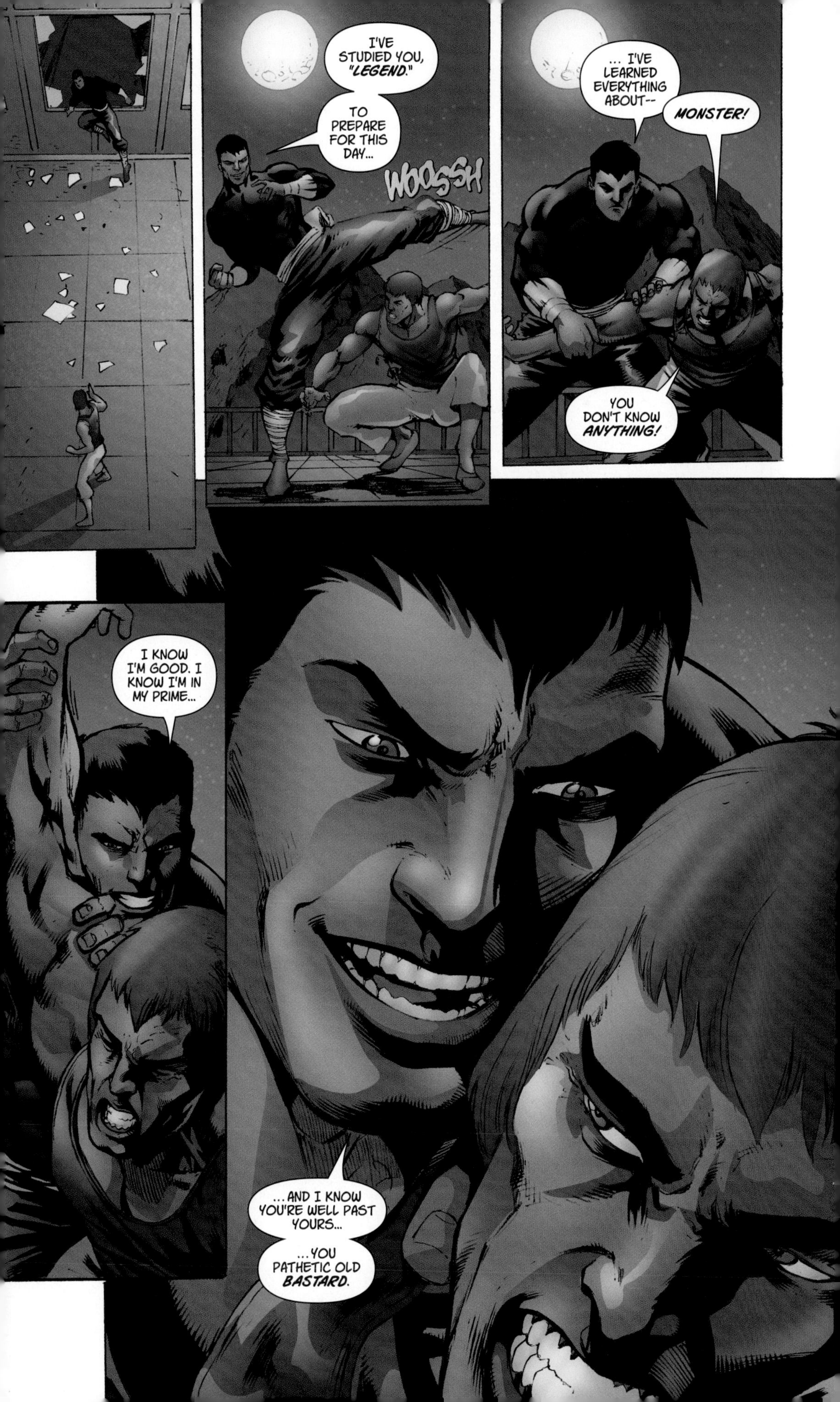
I'VE STUDIED YOU, "LEGEND."
TO PREPARE FOR THIS DAY...
WOOSSH
... I'VE LEARNED EVERYTHING ABOUT--
MONSTER!
YOU DON'T KNOW ANYTHING!
I KNOW I'M GOOD. I KNOW I'M IN MY PRIME...
...AND I KNOW YOU'RE WELL PAST YOURS...
...YOU PATHETIC OLD BASTARD.

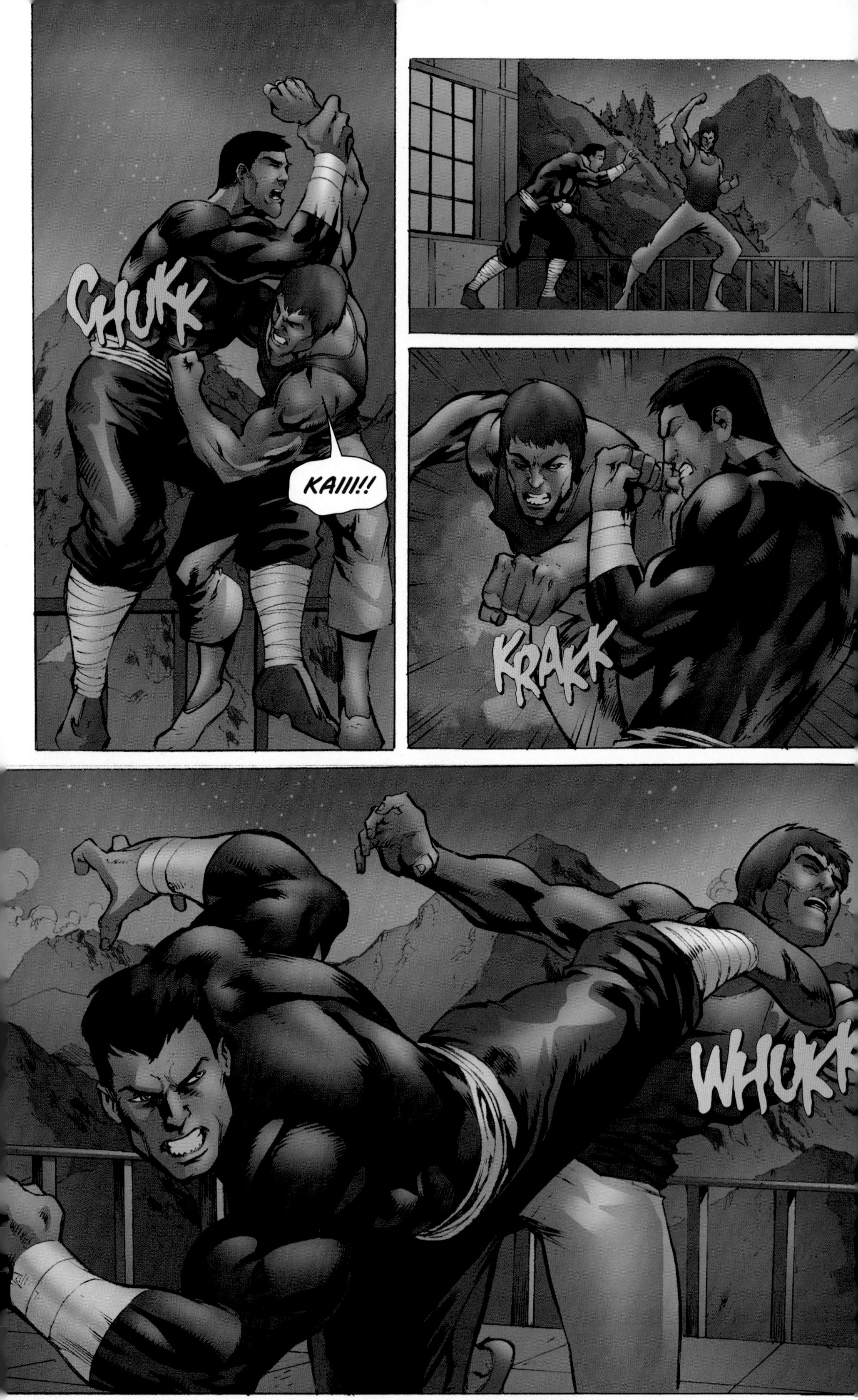
CHUKK
KAIII!!
KRAKK
WHUKK

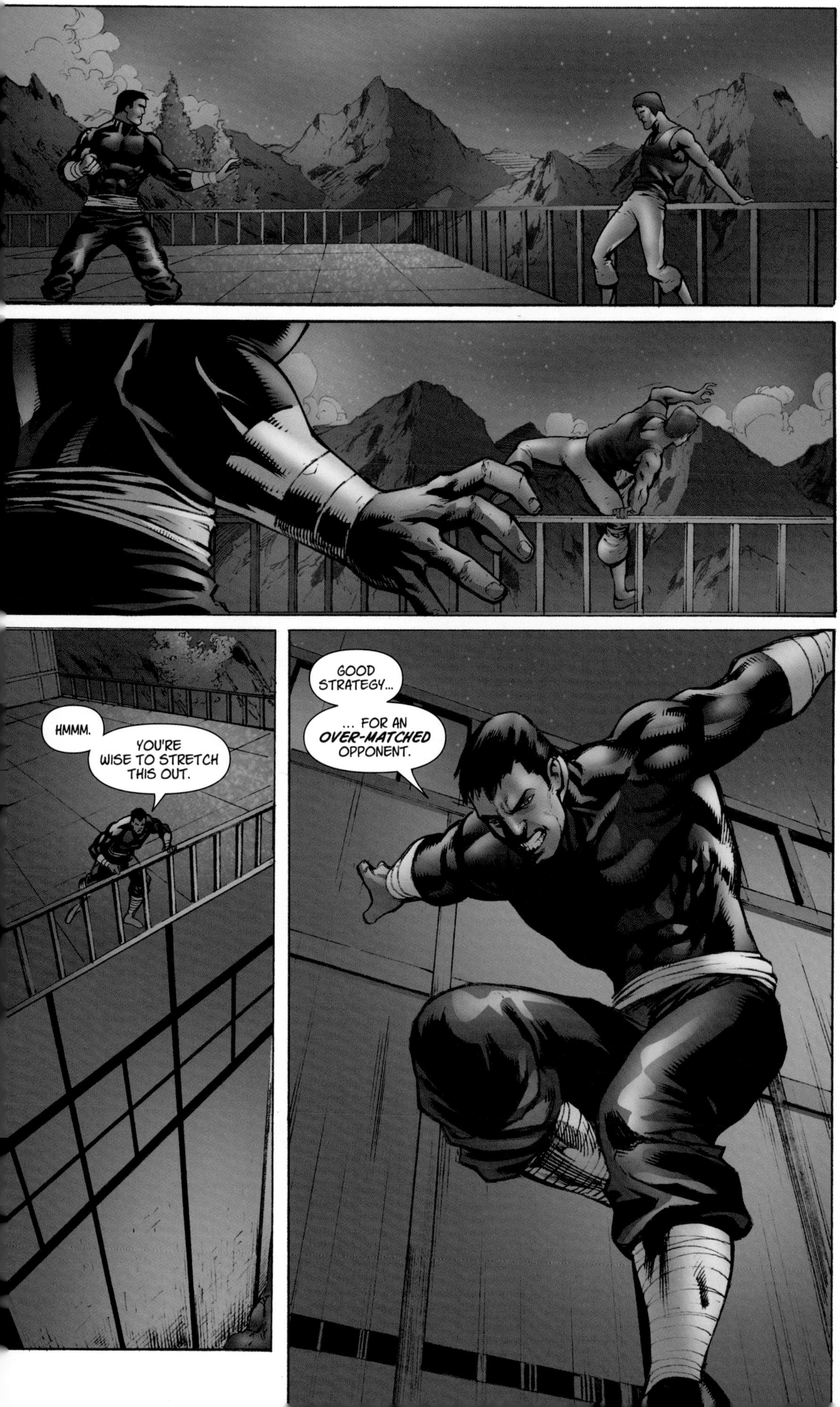
HMMM.
YOU'RE WISE TO STRETCH THIS OUT.
GOOD STRATEGY...
... FOR AN *OVER-MATCHED* OPPONENT.

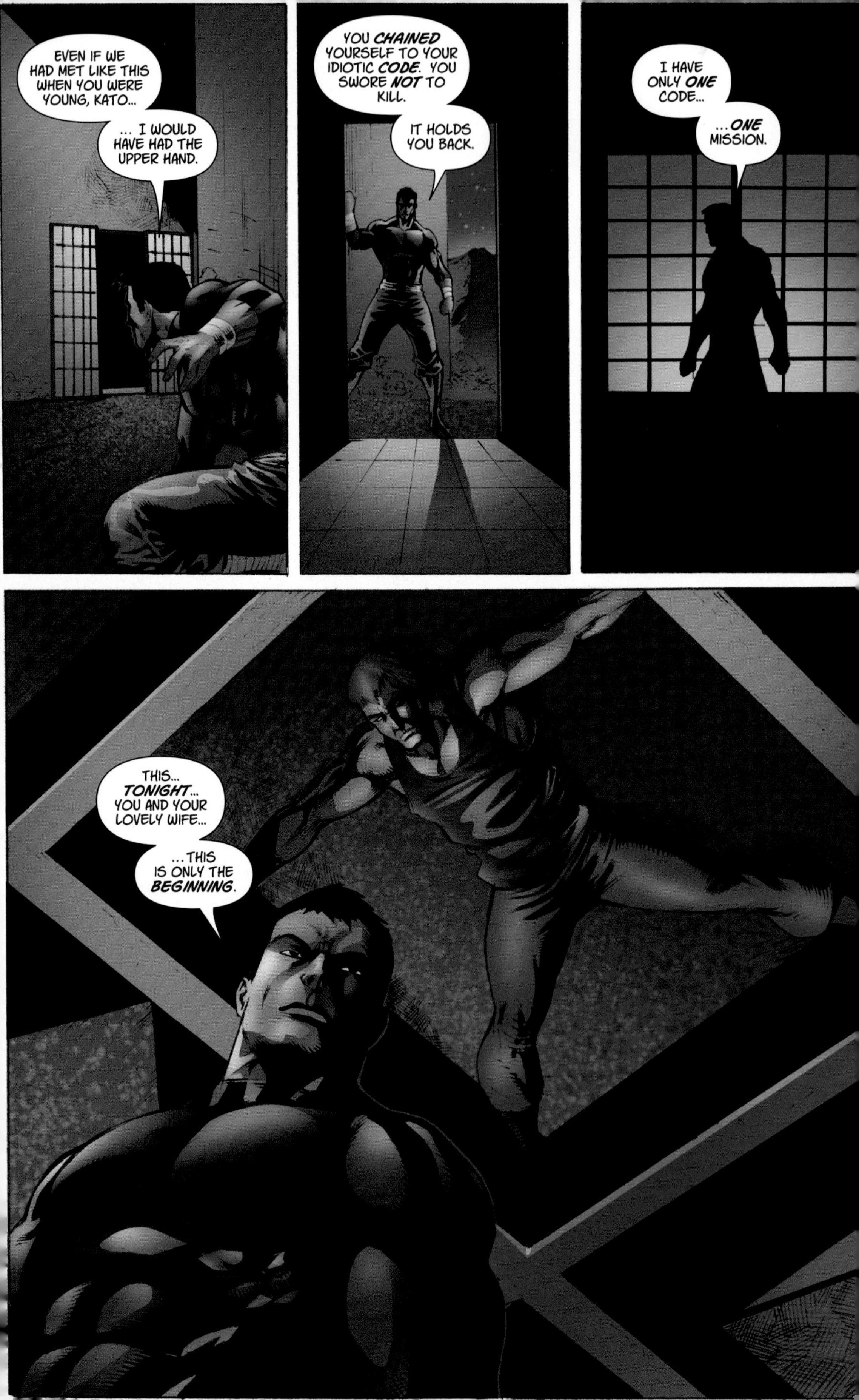
EVEN IF WE HAD MET LIKE THIS WHEN YOU WERE YOUNG, KATO...
... I WOULD HAVE HAD THE UPPER HAND.
YOU **CHAINED** YOURSELF TO YOUR IDIOTIC **CODE**. YOU SWORE **NOT** TO KILL.
IT HOLDS YOU BACK.
I HAVE ONLY **ONE** CODE...
...**ONE** MISSION.
THIS... **TONIGHT**... YOU AND YOUR LOVELY WIFE...
...THIS IS ONLY THE **BEGINNING**.

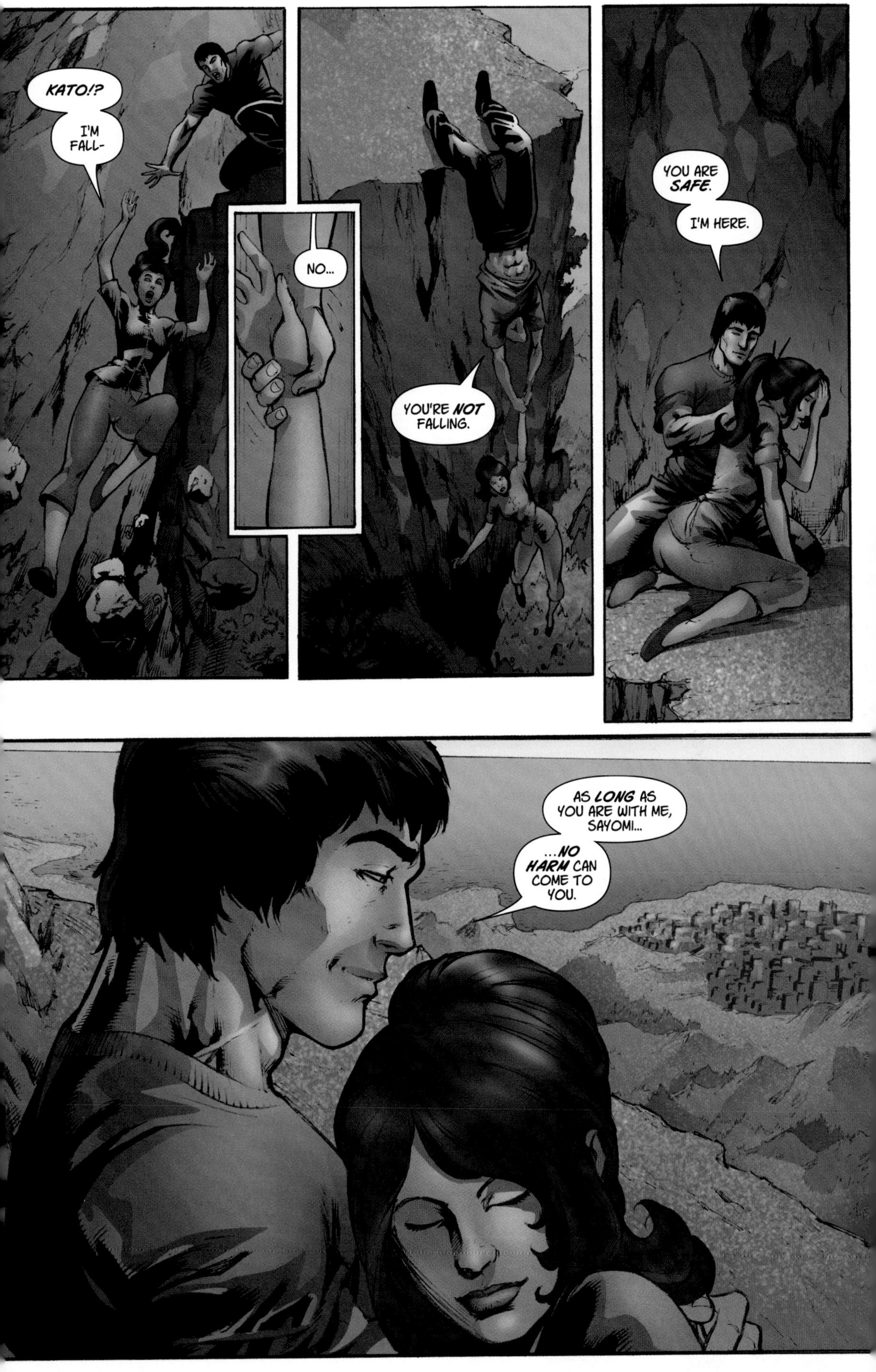
KATO!?
I'M FALL-
NO...
YOU'RE NOT FALLING.
YOU ARE SAFE.
I'M HERE.
AS LONG AS YOU ARE WITH ME, SAYOMI...
...NO HARM CAN COME TO YOU.

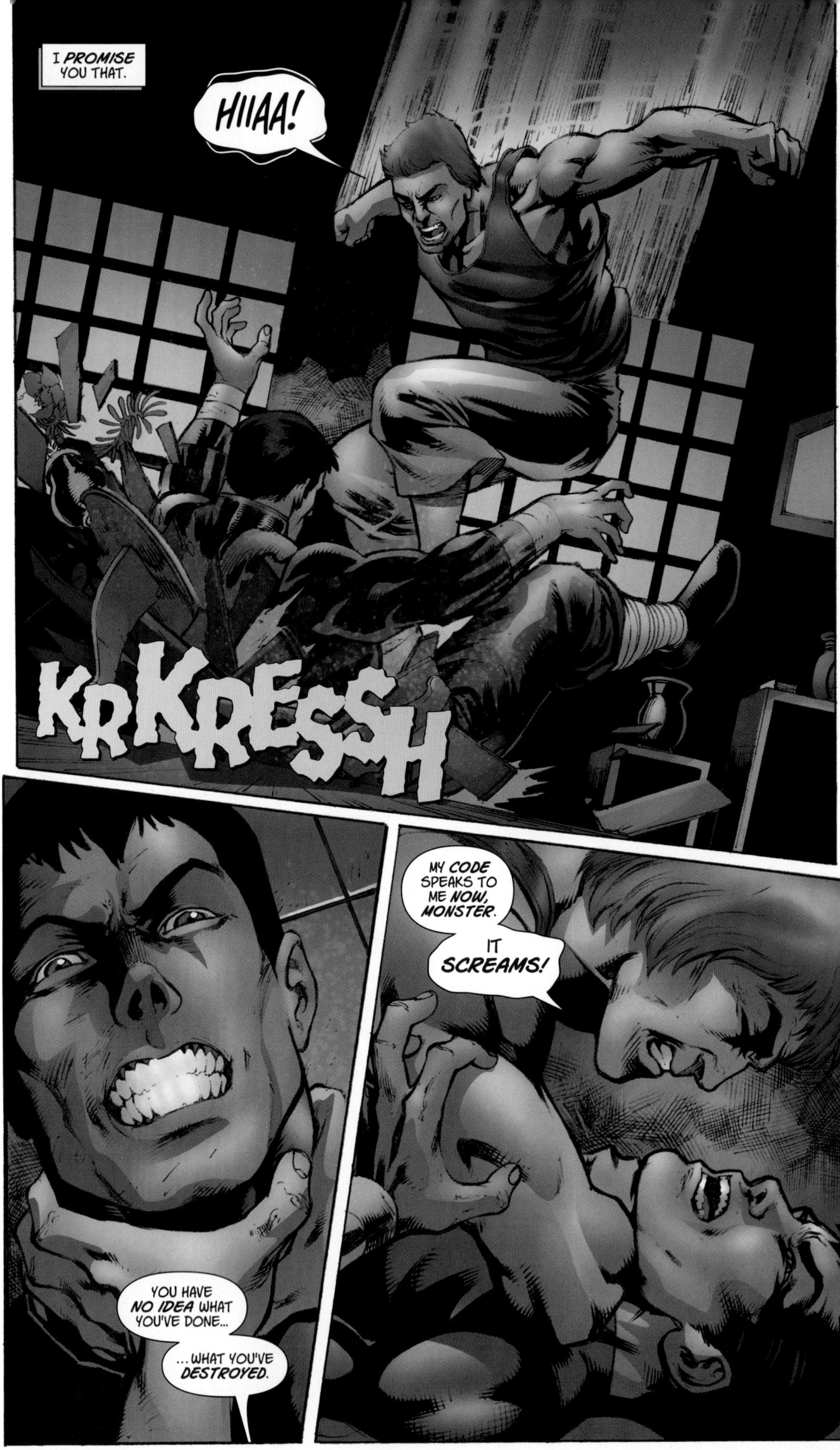

I PROMISE YOU THAT.
HIIAA!
KRKRESSH
YOU HAVE NO IDEA WHAT YOU'VE DONE...
...WHAT YOU'VE DESTROYED.
MY CODE SPEAKS TO ME NOW, MONSTER.
IT SCREAMS!

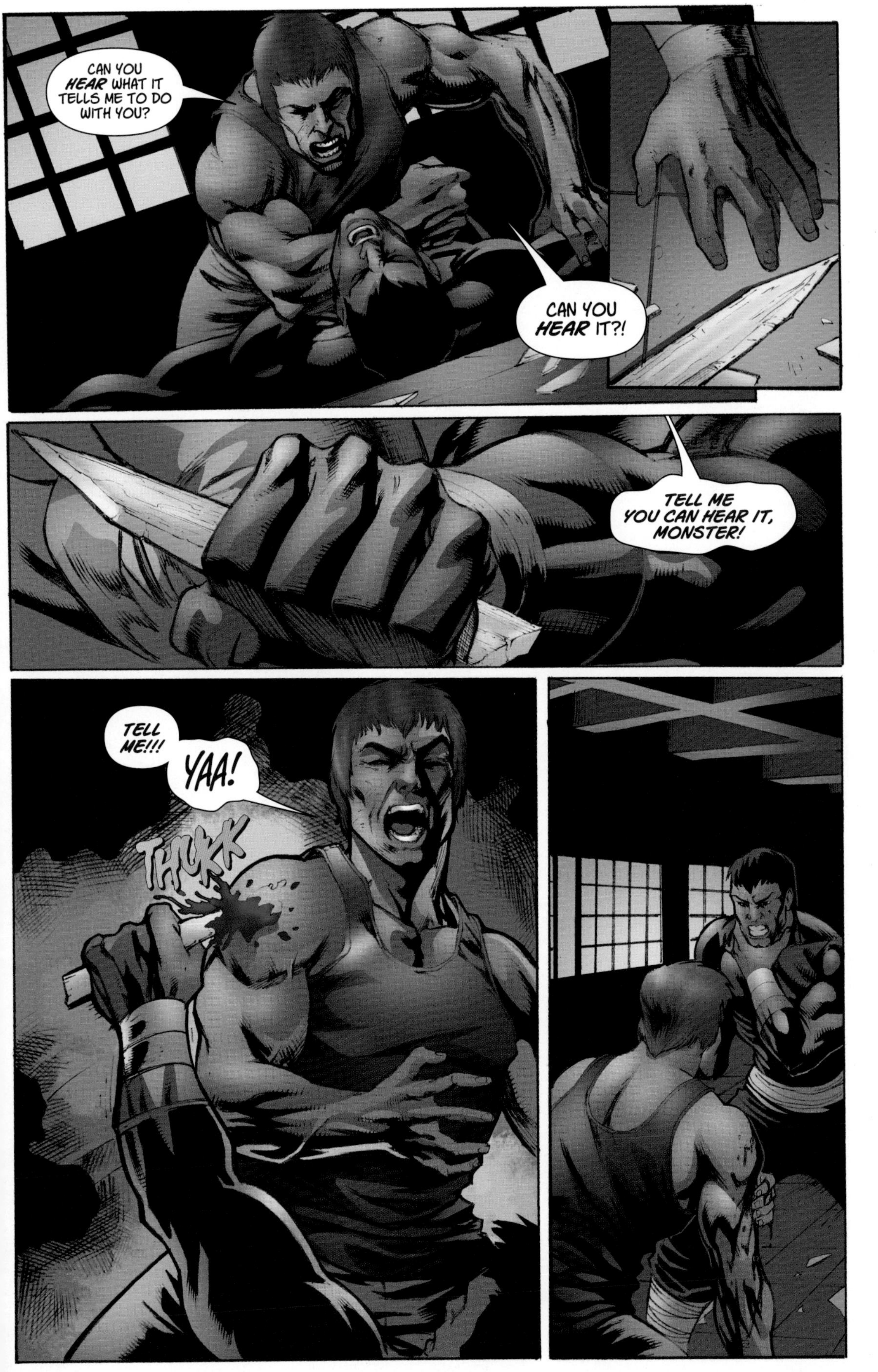
CAN YOU HEAR WHAT IT TELLS ME TO DO WITH YOU?
CAN YOU HEAR IT?!
TELL ME YOU CAN HEAR IT, MONSTER!
TELL ME!!!
YAA!
THUKK

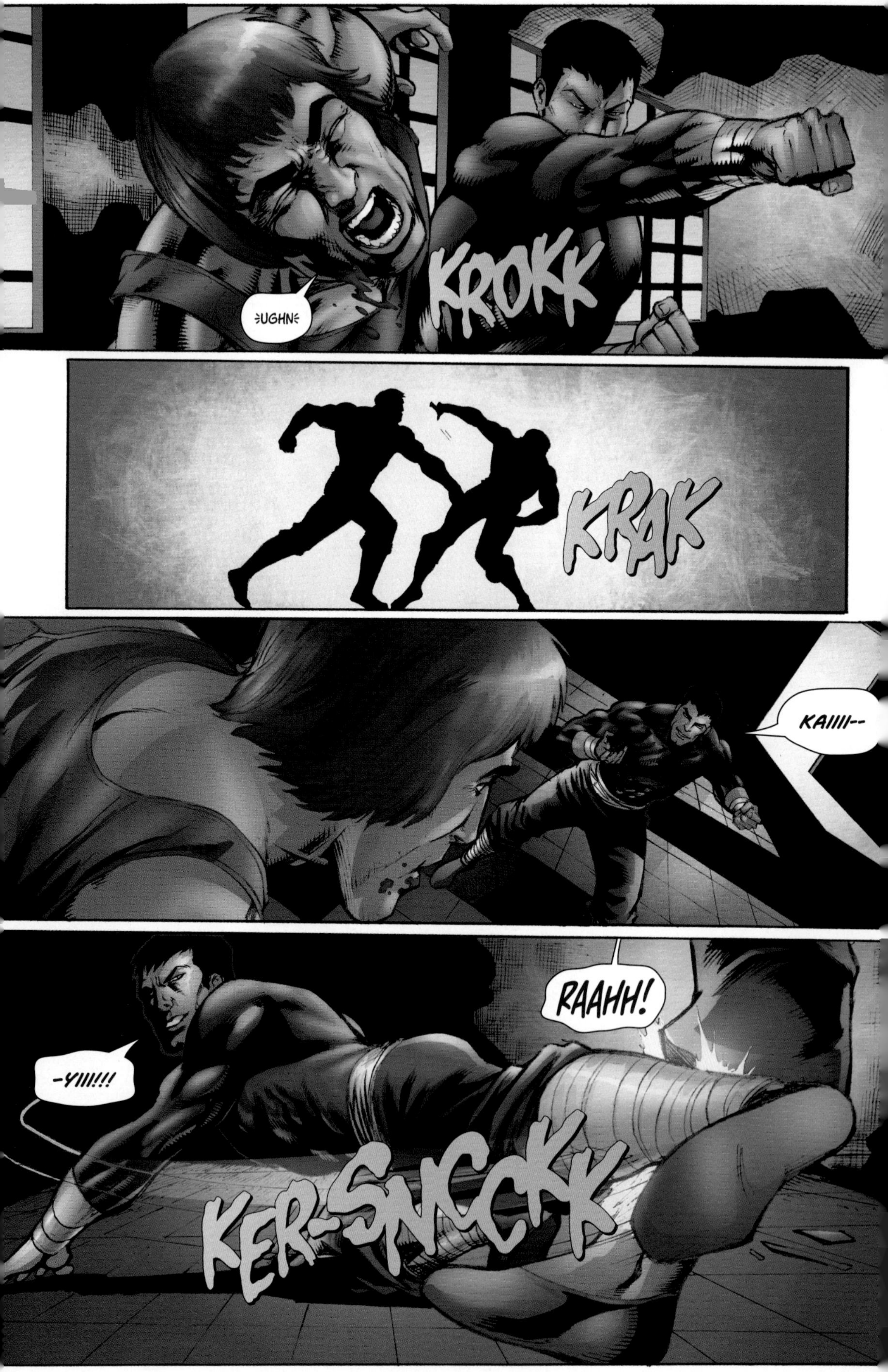
UGHN
KROKK
KRAK
KAIIII--
RAAHH!
-YIIII!!!
KER-SNCCKK

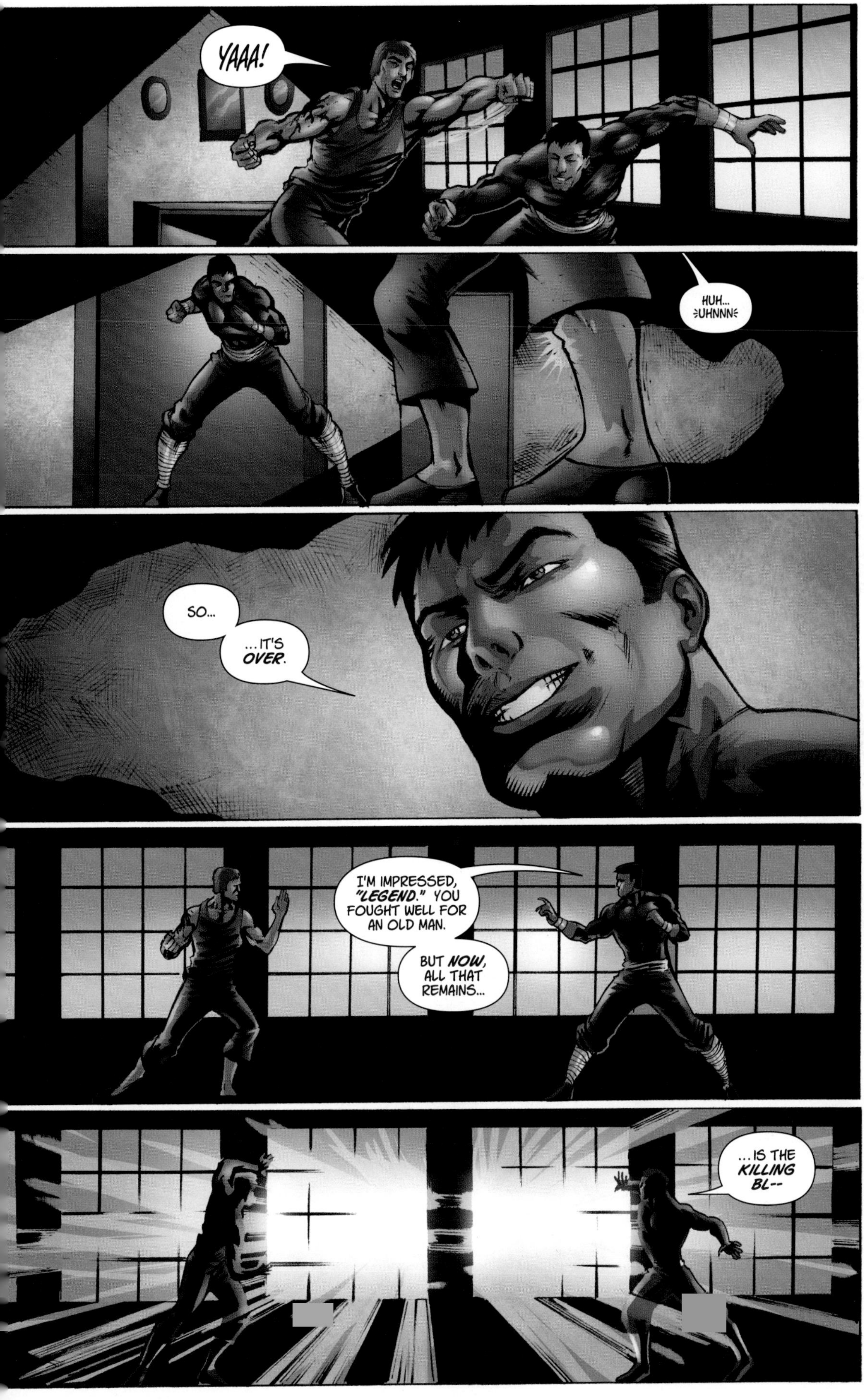
YAAA!
HUH... UHNNN
SO...
...IT'S OVER.
I'M IMPRESSED, "LEGEND." YOU FOUGHT WELL FOR AN OLD MAN.
BUT NOW, ALL THAT REMAINS...
...IS THE KILLING BL--

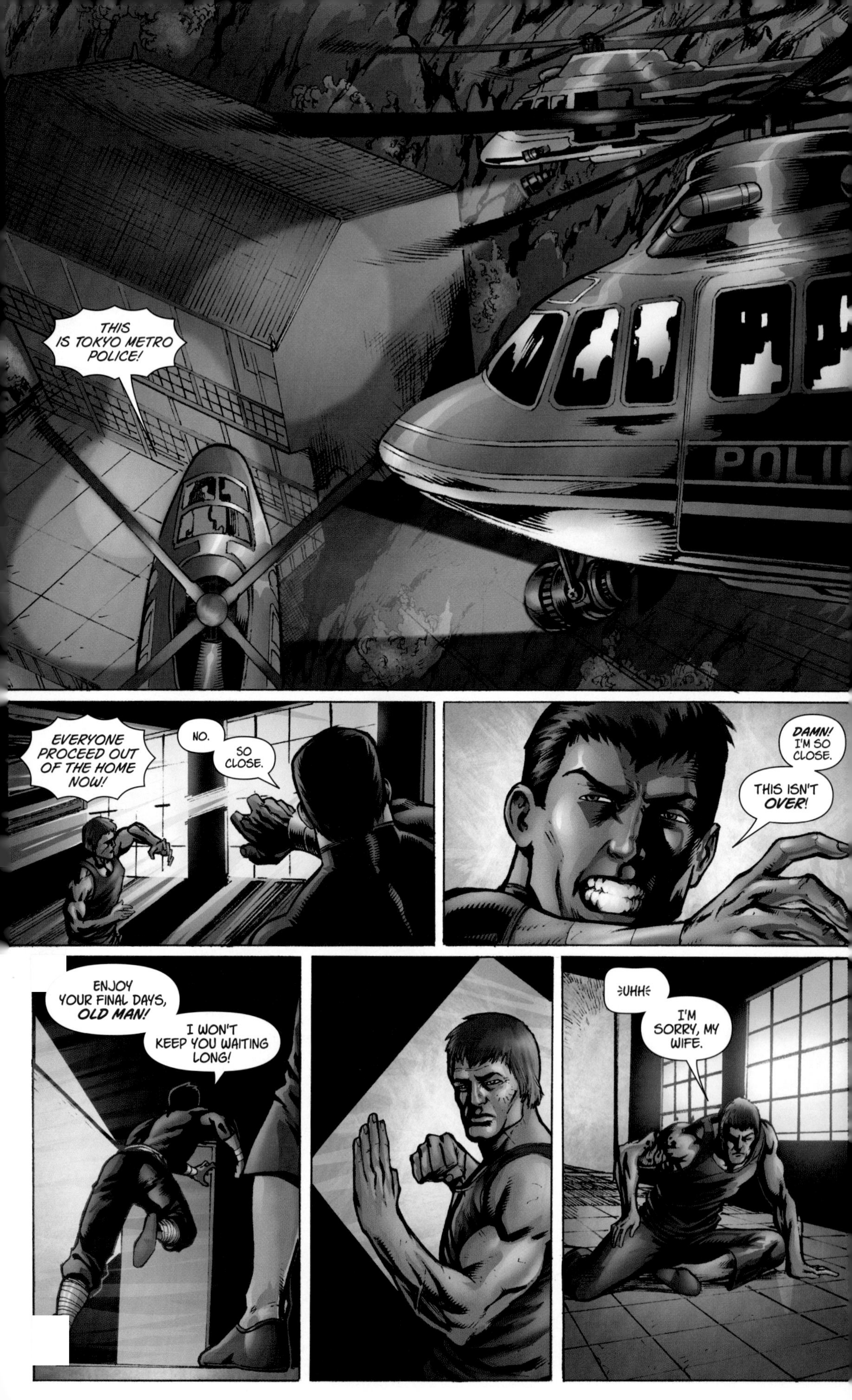
THIS IS TOKYO METRO POLICE!
POLIC
EVERYONE PROCEED OUT OF THE HOME NOW!
NO.
SO CLOSE.
DAMN! I'M SO CLOSE.
THIS ISN'T OVER!
ENJOY YOUR FINAL DAYS, OLD MAN!
I WON'T KEEP YOU WAITING LONG!
UHH
I'M SORRY, MY WIFE.

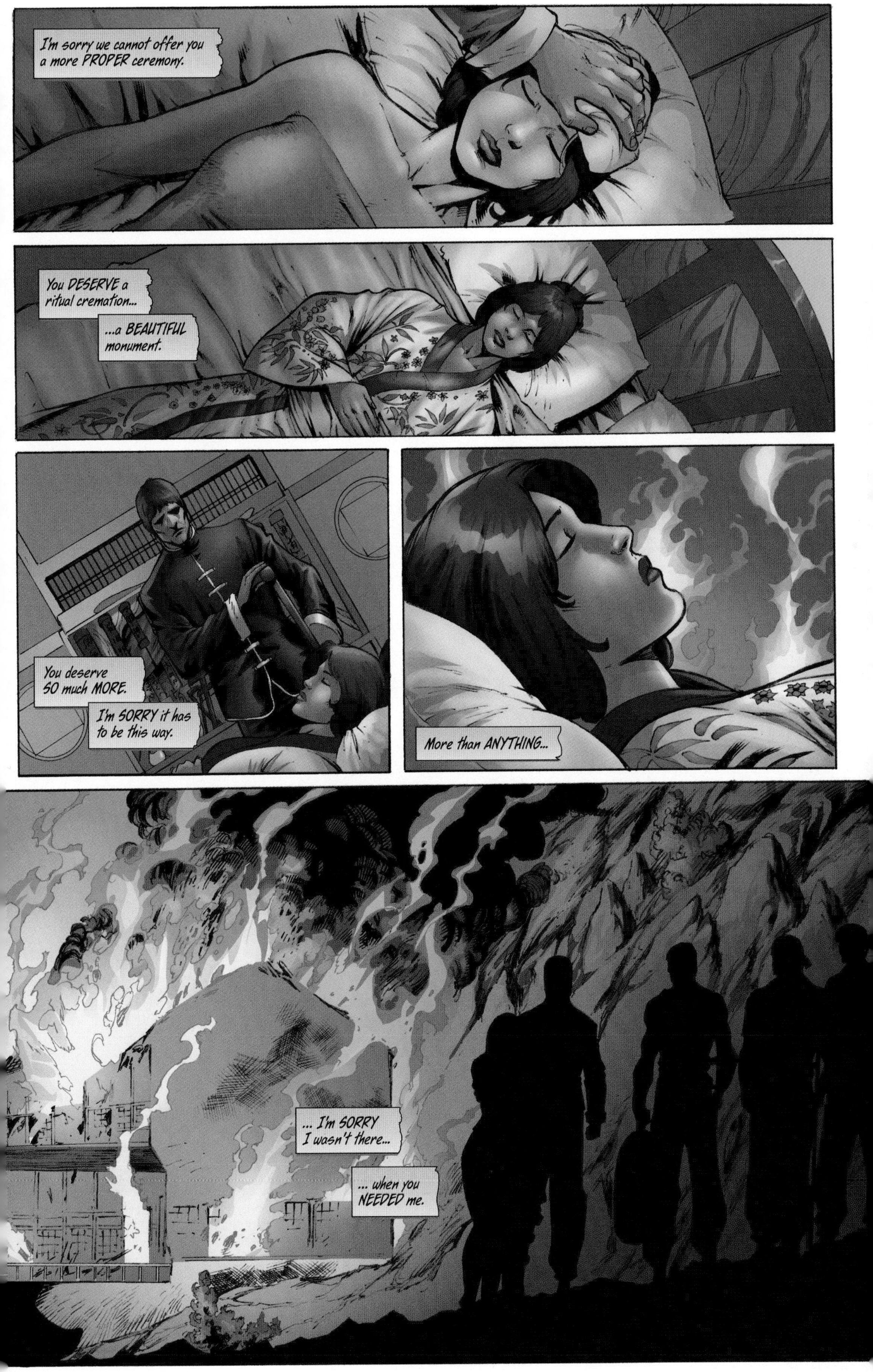
I'm sorry we cannot offer you a more PROPER ceremony.
You DESERVE a ritual cremation...
...a BEAUTIFUL monument.
You deserve SO much MORE.
I'm SORRY it has to be this way.
More than ANYTHING...
... I'm SORRY I wasn't there...
... when you NEEDED me.

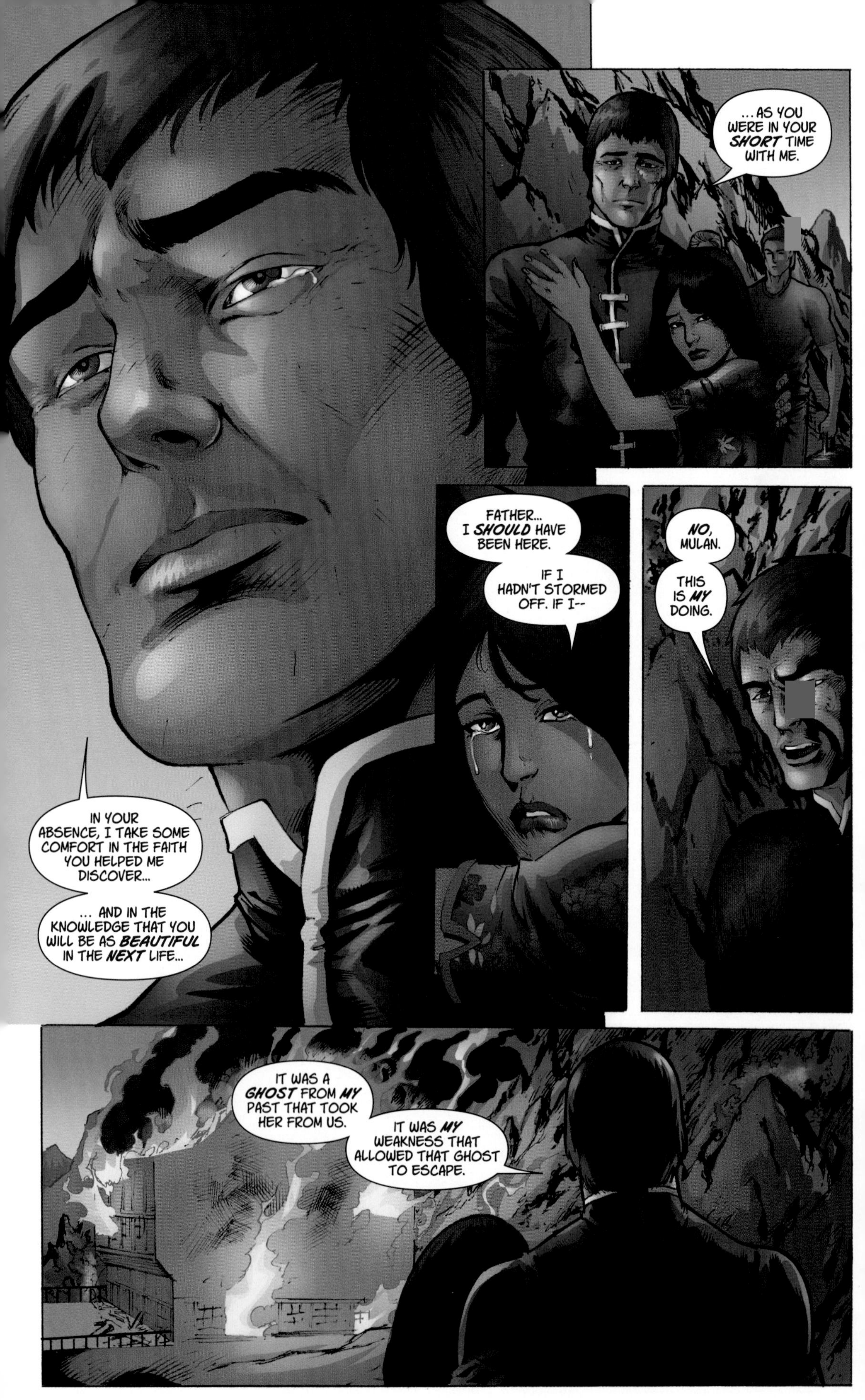

IN YOUR ABSENCE, I TAKE SOME COMFORT IN THE FAITH YOU HELPED ME DISCOVER...
... AND IN THE KNOWLEDGE THAT YOU WILL BE AS *BEAUTIFUL* IN THE *NEXT* LIFE...
...AS YOU WERE IN YOUR *SHORT* TIME WITH ME.
FATHER... I *SHOULD* HAVE BEEN HERE.
IF I HADN'T STORMED OFF. IF I--
NO, MULAN.
THIS IS *MY* DOING.
IT WAS A *GHOST* FROM *MY* PAST THAT TOOK HER FROM US.
IT WAS *MY* WEAKNESS THAT ALLOWED THAT GHOST TO ESCAPE.

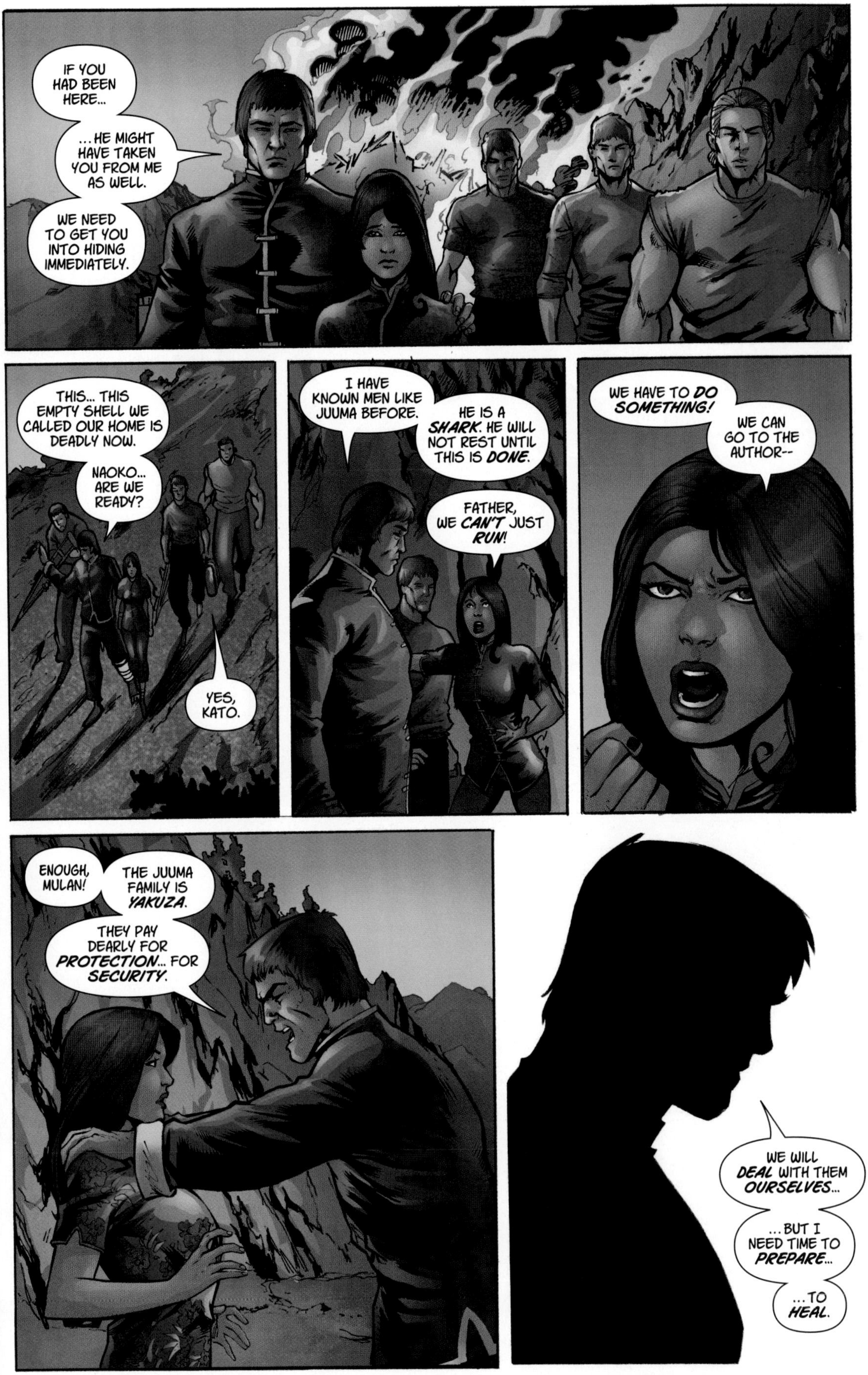
IF YOU HAD BEEN HERE...
...HE MIGHT HAVE TAKEN YOU FROM ME AS WELL.
WE NEED TO GET YOU INTO HIDING IMMEDIATELY.
THIS... THIS EMPTY SHELL WE CALLED OUR HOME IS DEADLY NOW.
NAOKO... ARE WE READY?
YES, KATO.
I HAVE KNOWN MEN LIKE JUUMA BEFORE.
HE IS A SHARK. HE WILL NOT REST UNTIL THIS IS DONE.
FATHER, WE CAN'T JUST RUN!
WE HAVE TO DO SOMETHING!
WE CAN GO TO THE AUTHOR--
ENOUGH, MULAN!
THE JUUMA FAMILY IS YAKUZA.
THEY PAY DEARLY FOR PROTECTION... FOR SECURITY.
WE WILL DEAL WITH THEM OURSELVES...
...BUT I NEED TIME TO PREPARE...
...TO HEAL.

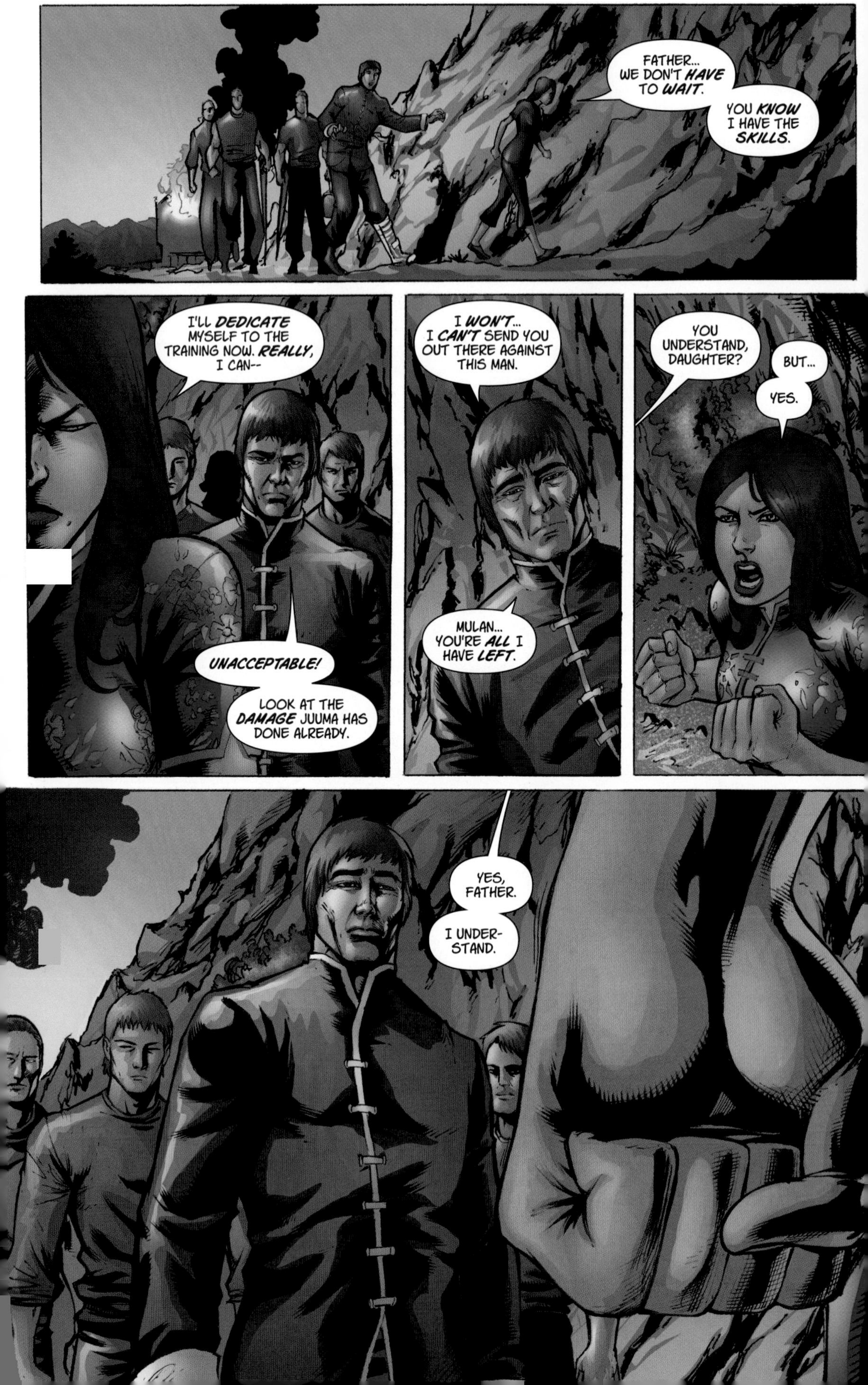
FATHER... WE DON'T HAVE TO WAIT.
YOU KNOW I HAVE THE SKILLS.
I'LL DEDICATE MYSELF TO THE TRAINING NOW. REALLY, I CAN--
UNACCEPTABLE!
LOOK AT THE DAMAGE JUUMA HAS DONE ALREADY.
I WON'T... I CAN'T SEND YOU OUT THERE AGAINST THIS MAN.
MULAN... YOU'RE ALL I HAVE LEFT.
YOU UNDERSTAND, DAUGHTER?
BUT...
YES.
YES, FATHER.
I UNDER-STAND.

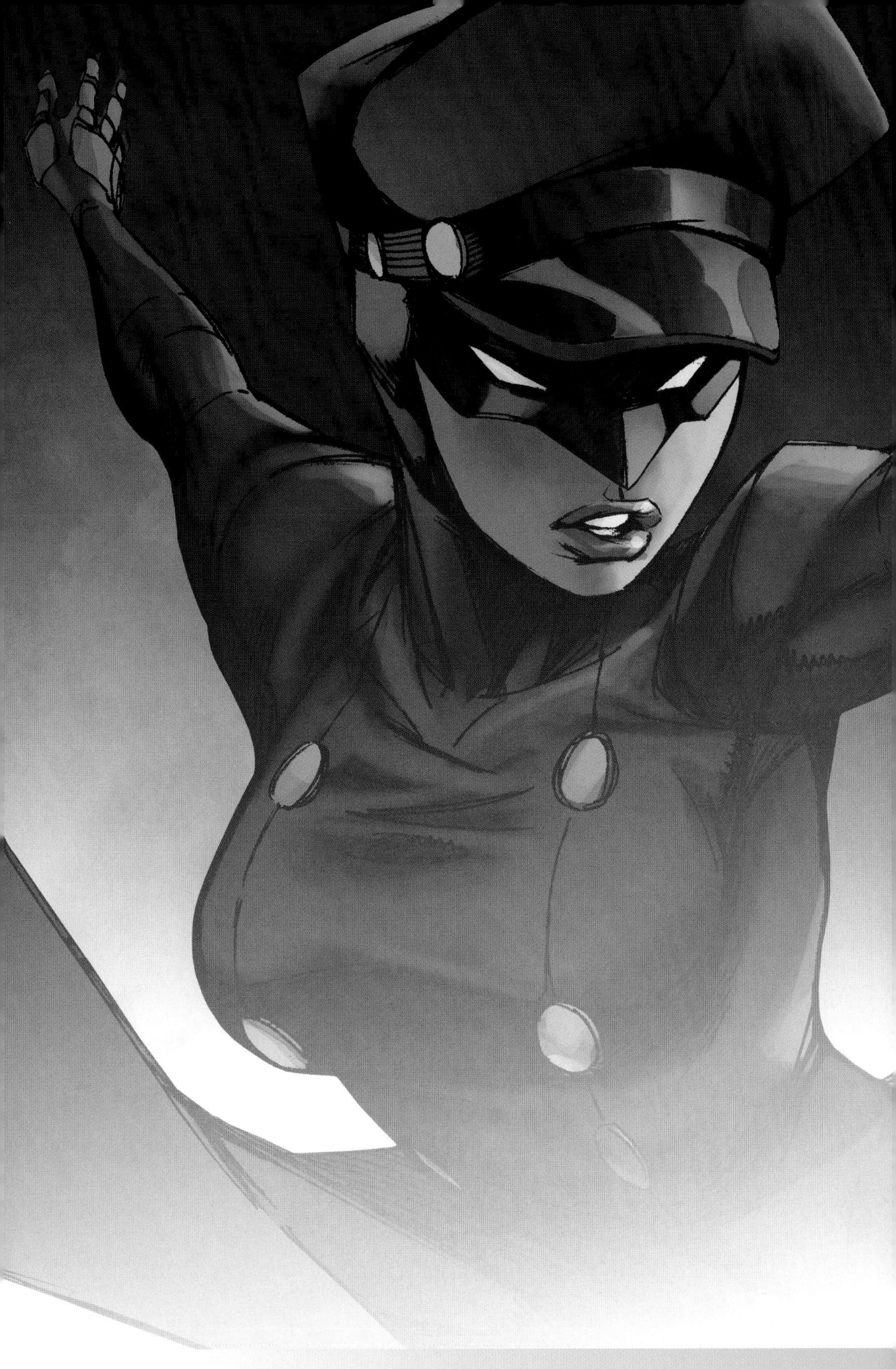

Issue THREE

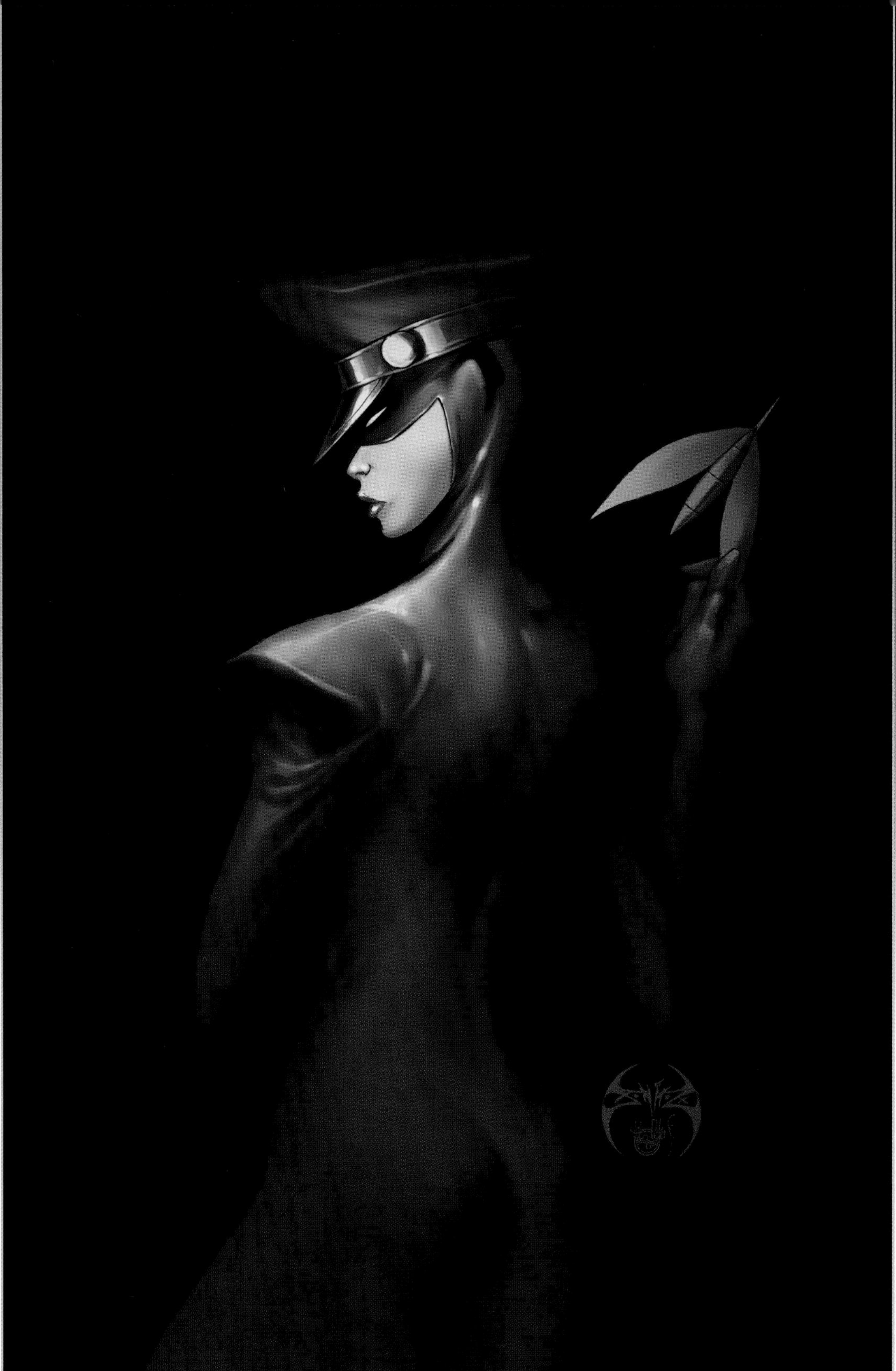

Issue three cover by **JOE BENITEZ**

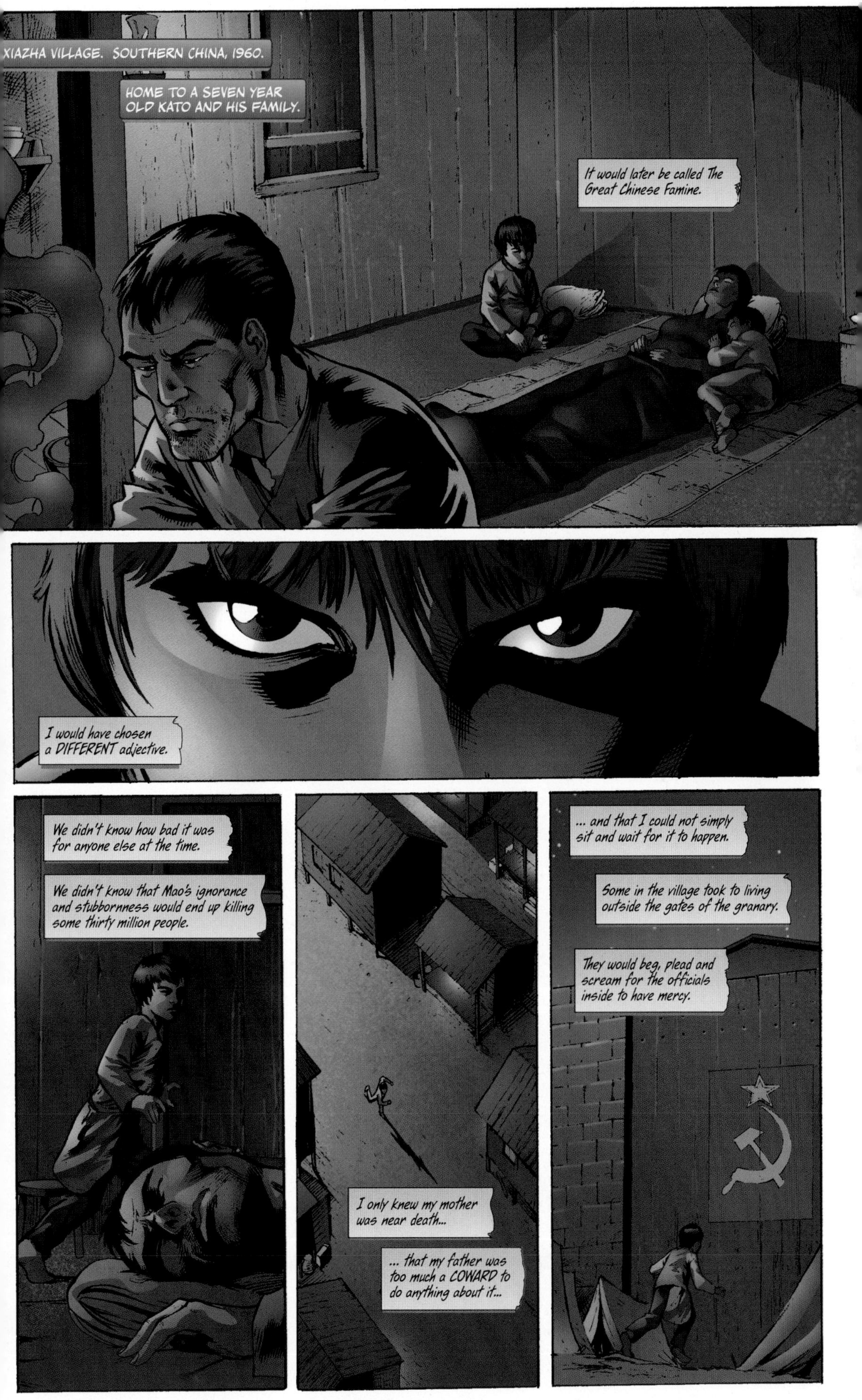
XIAZHA VILLAGE. SOUTHERN CHINA, 1960.
HOME TO A SEVEN YEAR OLD KATO AND HIS FAMILY.
It would later be called The Great Chinese Famine.
I would have chosen a DIFFERENT adjective.
We didn't know how bad it was for anyone else at the time.
We didn't know that Mao's ignorance and stubbornness would end up killing some thirty million people.
I only knew my mother was near death...
... that my father was too much a COWARD to do anything about it...
... and that I could not simply sit and wait for it to happen.
Some in the village took to living outside the gates of the granary.
They would beg, plead and scream for the officials inside to have mercy.

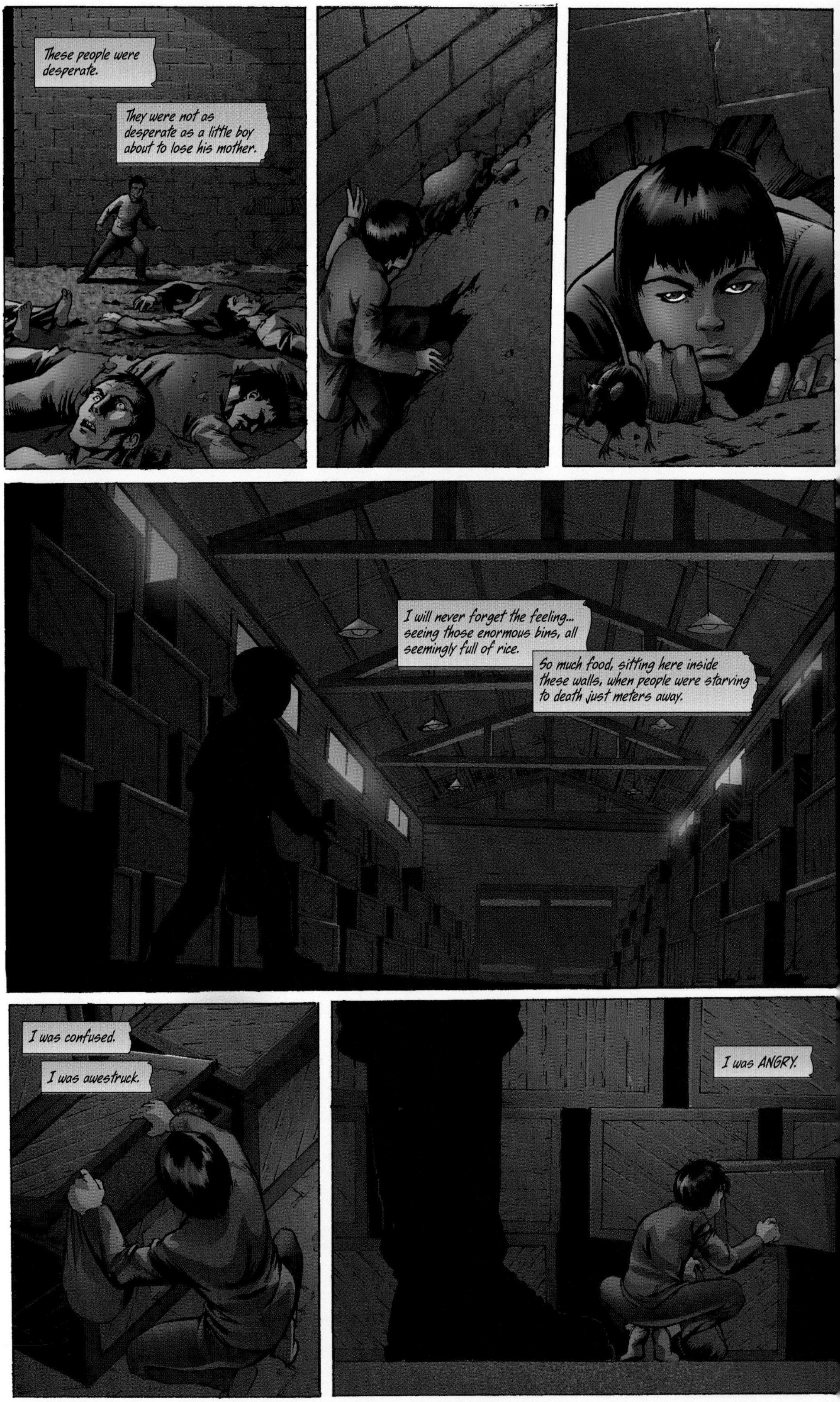

These people were desperate.
They were not as desperate as a little boy about to lose his mother.
I will never forget the feeling... seeing those enormous bins, all seemingly full of rice.
So much food, sitting here inside these walls, when people were starving to death just meters away.
I was confused.
I was awestruck.
I was ANGRY.

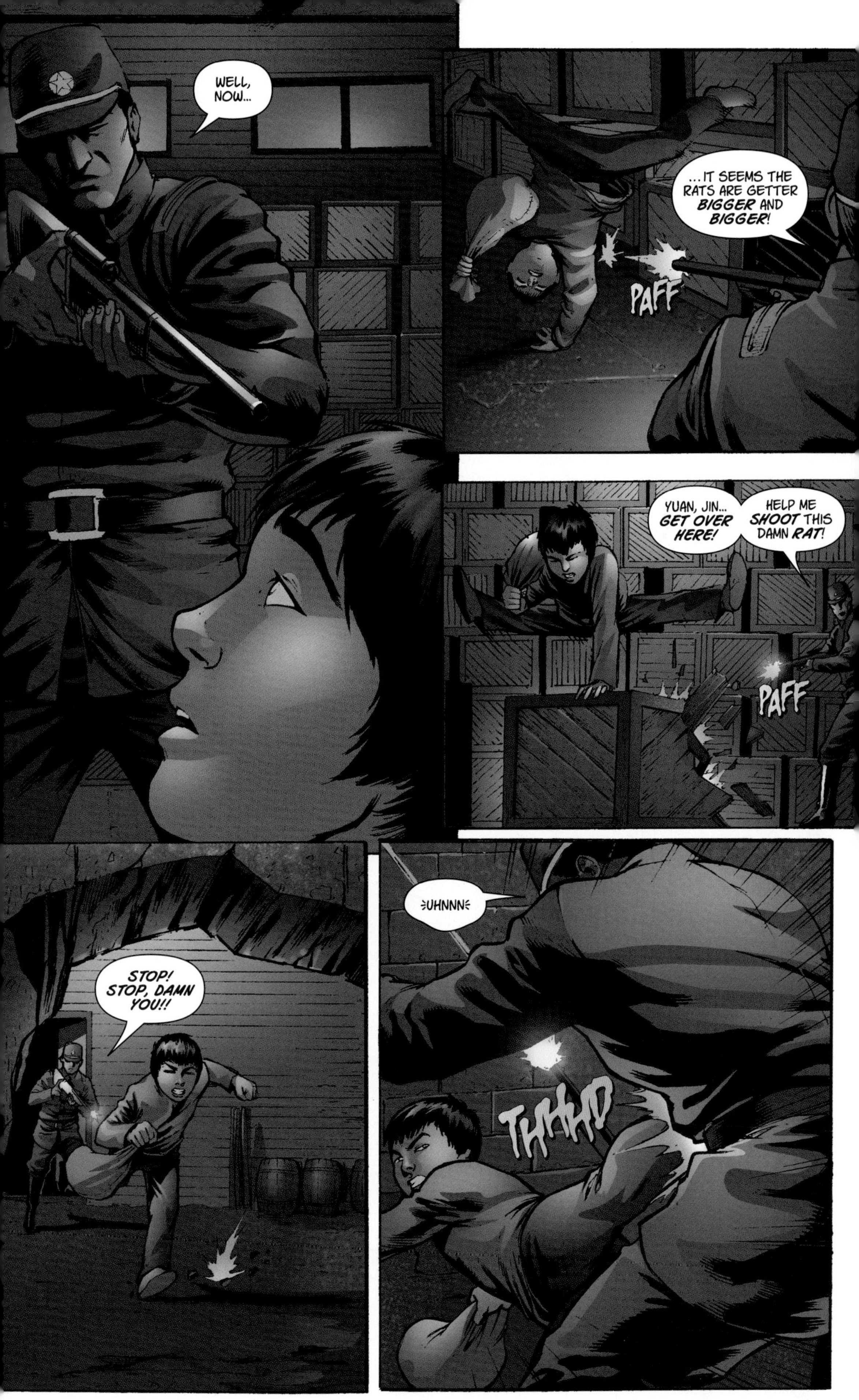

WELL, NOW...
...IT SEEMS THE RATS ARE GETTER BIGGER AND BIGGER!
PAFF
YUAN, JIN... GET OVER HERE!
HELP ME SHOOT THIS DAMN RAT!
PAFF
STOP! STOP, DAMN YOU!!
UHNNN
THHHD

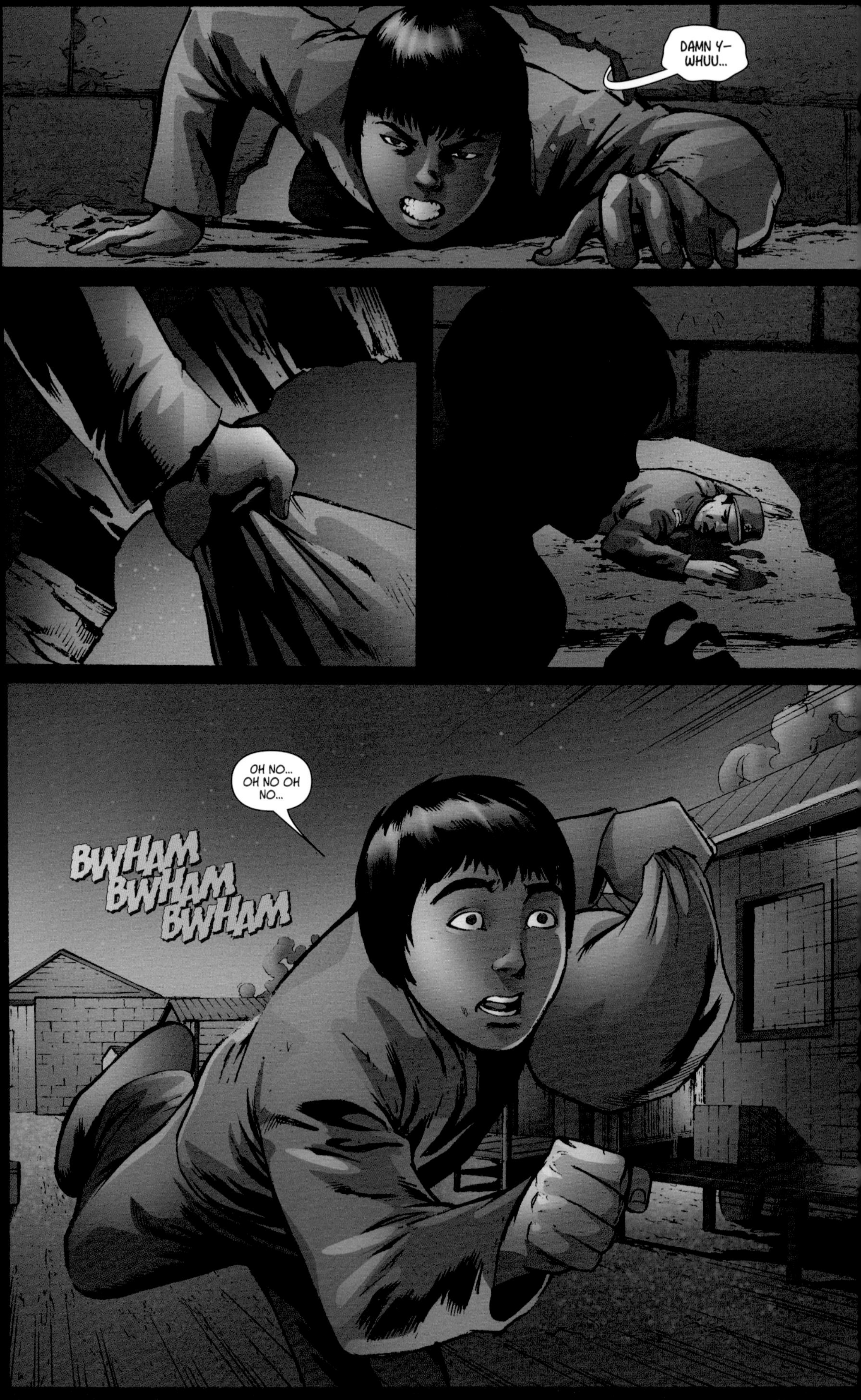
DAMN Y—
WHUU...
OH NO...
OH NO OH
NO...
BWHAM
BWHAM
BWHAM

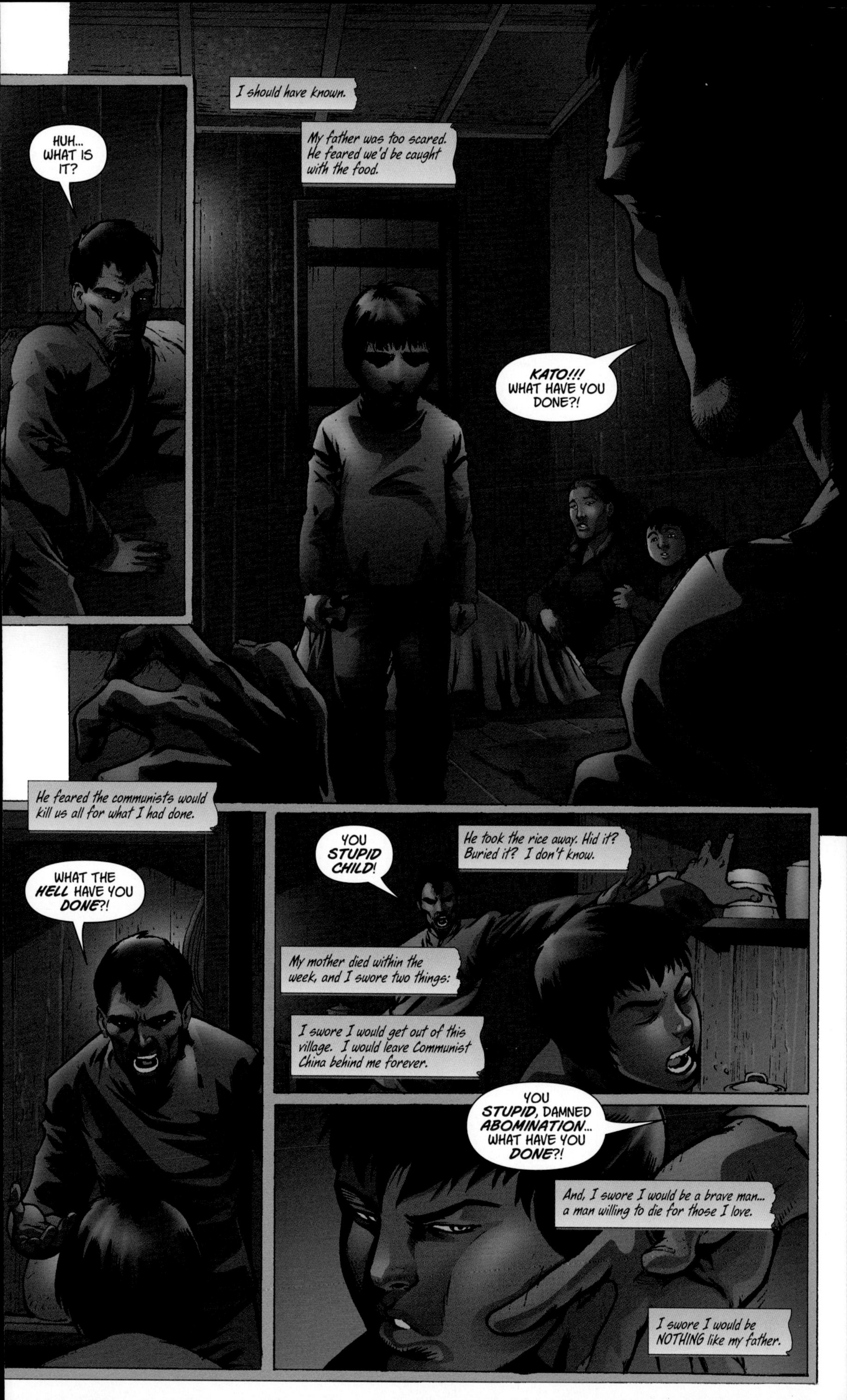
I should have known.
HUH... WHAT IS IT?
My father was too scared. He feared we'd be caught with the food.
KATO!!! WHAT HAVE YOU DONE?!
He feared the communists would kill us all for what I had done.
WHAT THE HELL HAVE YOU DONE?!
YOU STUPID CHILD!
He took the rice away. Hid it? Buried it? I don't know.
My mother died within the week, and I swore two things:
I swore I would get out of this village. I would leave Communist China behind me forever.
YOU STUPID, DAMNED ABOMINATION... WHAT HAVE YOU DONE?!
And, I swore I would be a brave man... a man willing to die for those I love.
I swore I would be NOTHING like my father.

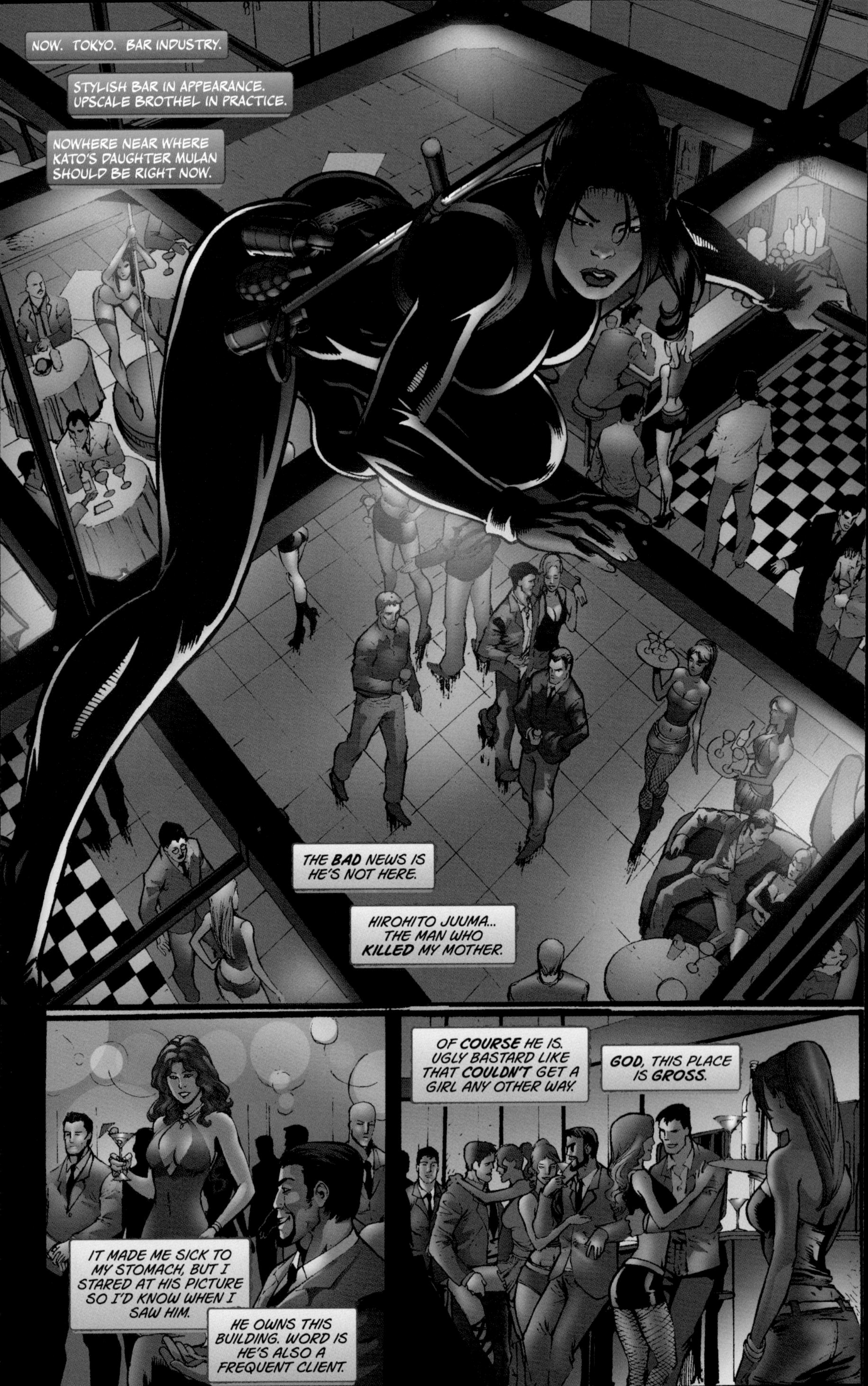
NOW. TOKYO. BAR INDUSTRY.
STYLISH BAR IN APPEARANCE. UPSCALE BROTHEL IN PRACTICE.
NOWHERE NEAR WHERE KATO'S DAUGHTER MULAN SHOULD BE RIGHT NOW.
THE BAD NEWS IS HE'S NOT HERE.
HIROHITO JUUMA... THE MAN WHO KILLED MY MOTHER.
IT MADE ME SICK TO MY STOMACH, BUT I STARED AT HIS PICTURE SO I'D KNOW WHEN I SAW HIM.
HE OWNS THIS BUILDING. WORD IS HE'S ALSO A FREQUENT CLIENT.
OF COURSE HE IS. UGLY BASTARD LIKE THAT COULDN'T GET A GIRL ANY OTHER WAY.
GOD, THIS PLACE IS GROSS.

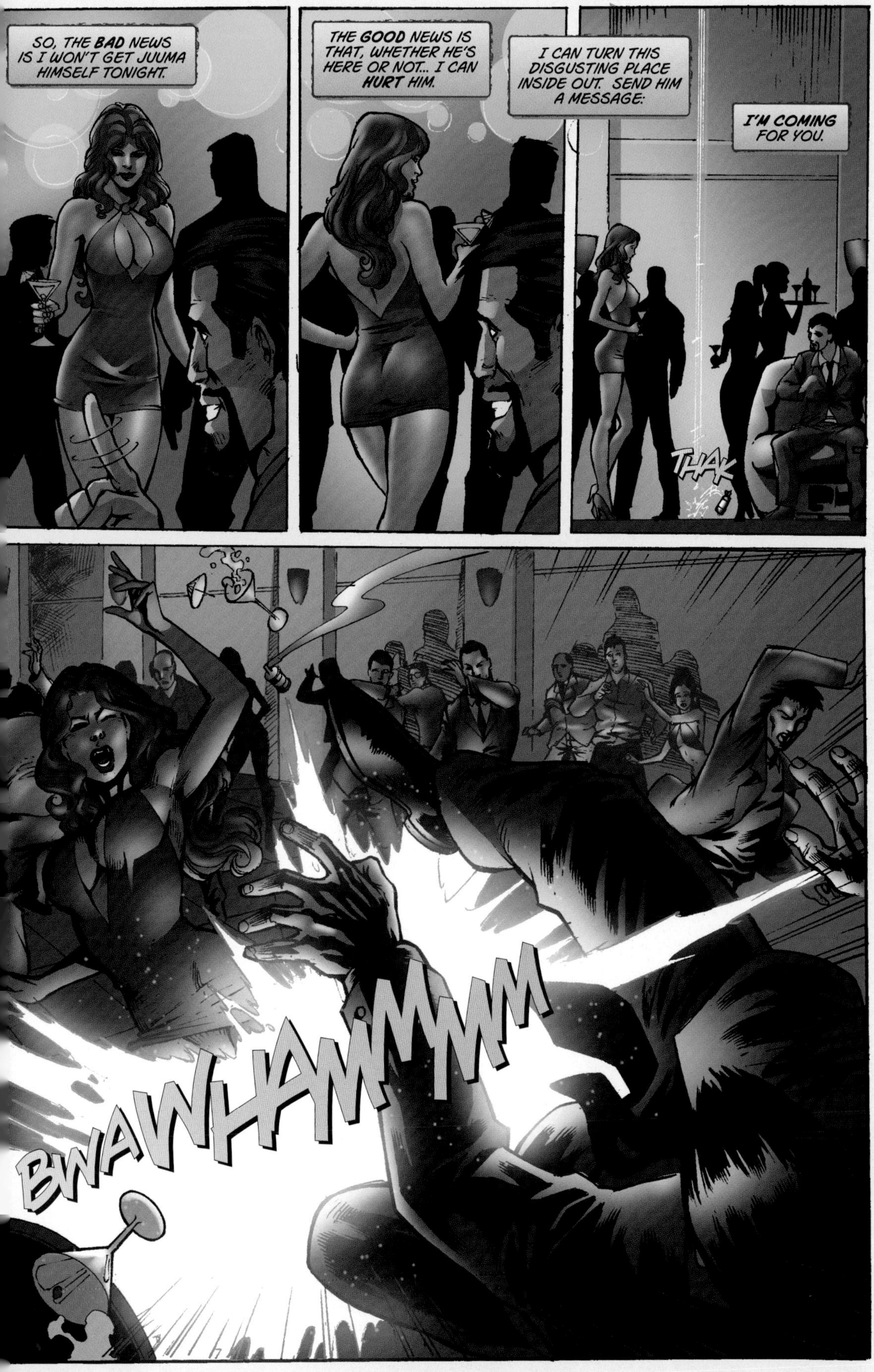
SO, THE BAD NEWS IS I WON'T GET JUUMA HIMSELF TONIGHT.
THE GOOD NEWS IS THAT, WHETHER HE'S HERE OR NOT... I CAN HURT HIM.
I CAN TURN THIS DISGUSTING PLACE INSIDE OUT. SEND HIM A MESSAGE:
I'M COMING FOR YOU.
THAK
BWAWHAMMMM

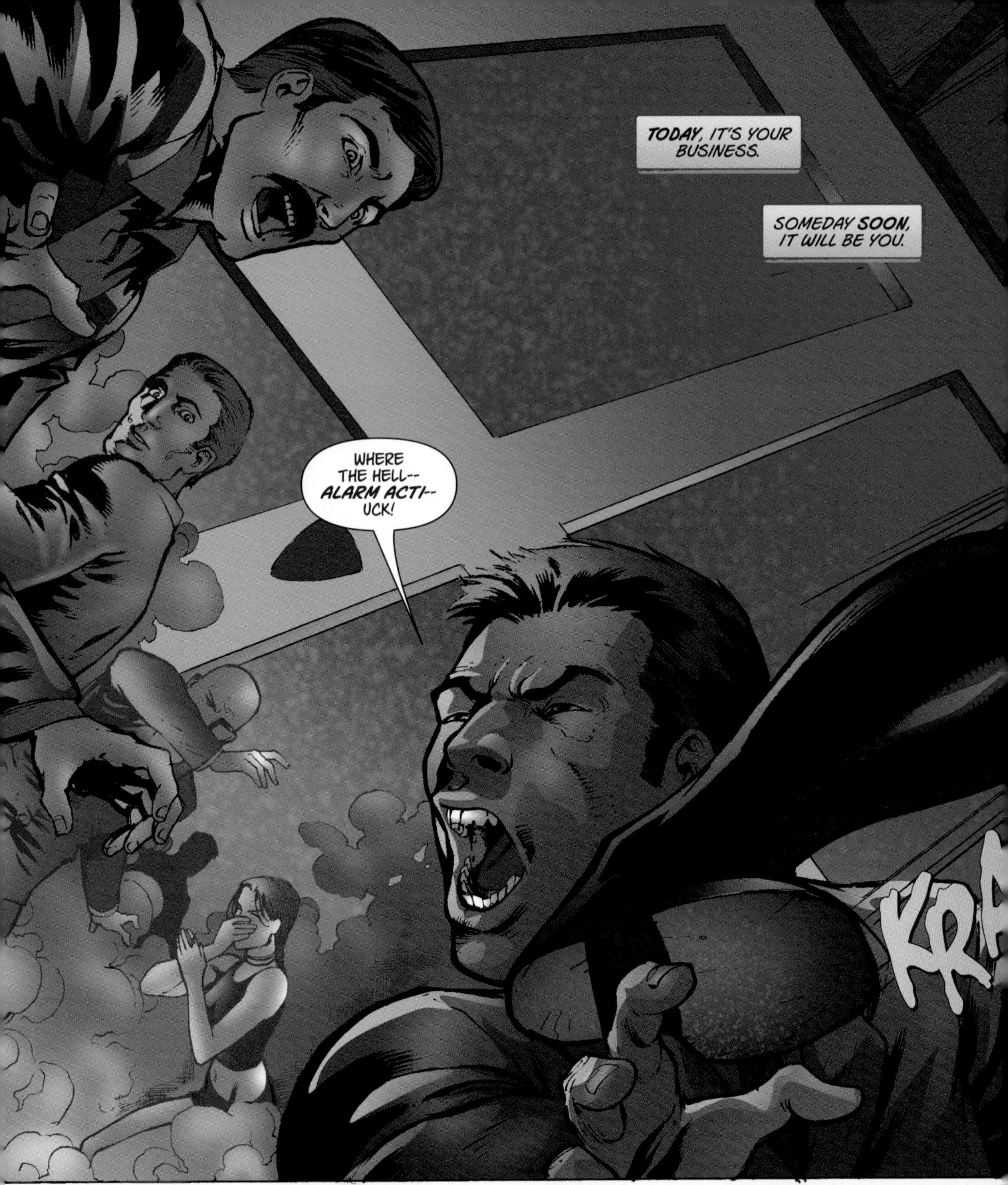
TODAY, IT'S YOUR BUSINESS.
SOMEDAY SOON, IT WILL BE YOU.
WHERE THE HELL-- ALARM ACTI-- UCK!
KRA

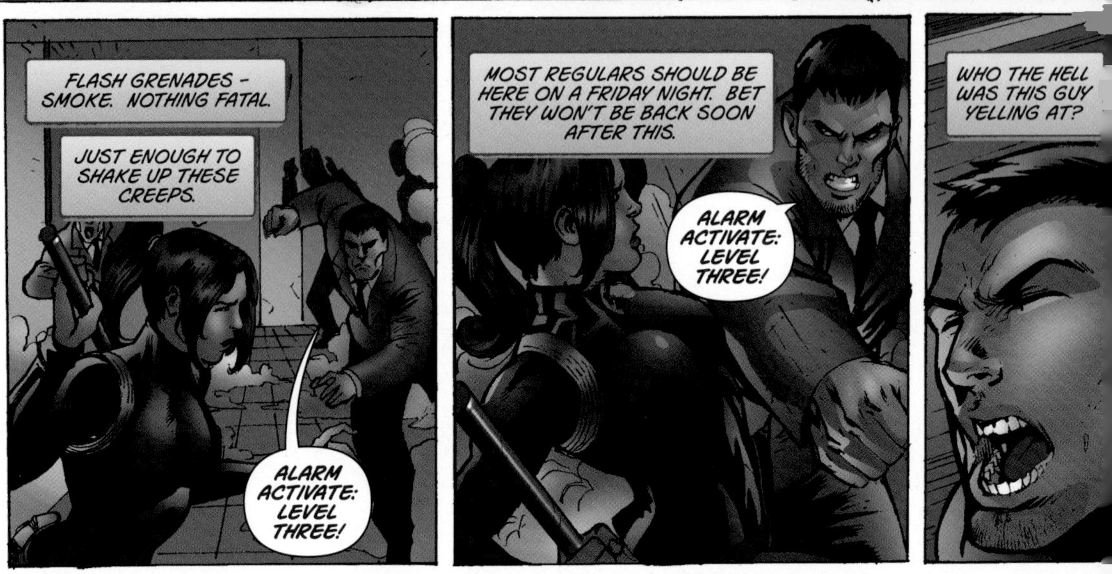
FLASH GRENADES - SMOKE. NOTHING FATAL.
JUST ENOUGH TO SHAKE UP THESE CREEPS.
ALARM ACTIVATE: LEVEL THREE!
MOST REGULARS SHOULD BE HERE ON A FRIDAY NIGHT. BET THEY WON'T BE BACK SOON AFTER THIS.
ALARM ACTIVATE: LEVEL THREE!
WHO THE HELL WAS THIS GUY YELLING AT?

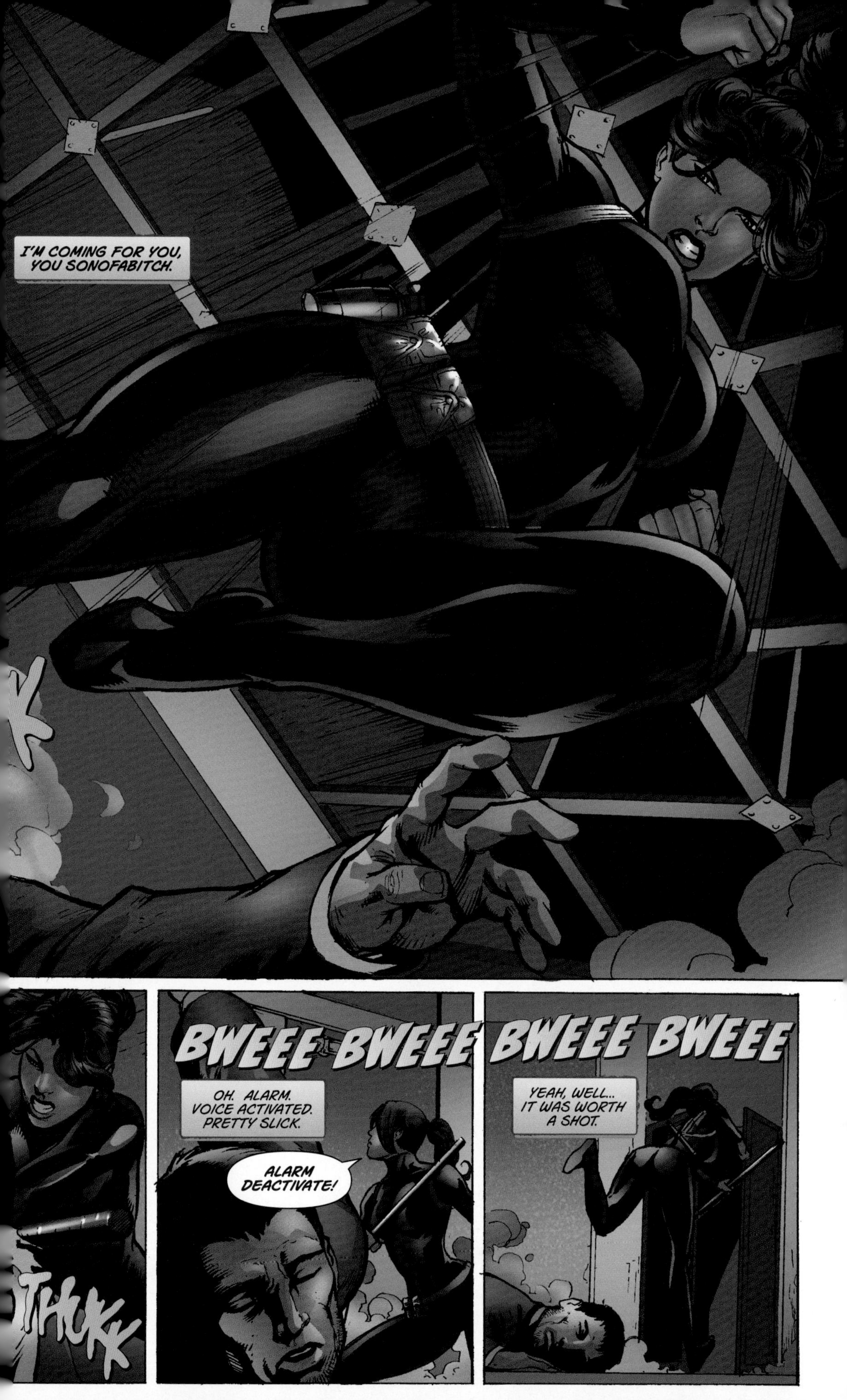
I'M COMING FOR YOU,
YOU SONOFABITCH.
THUKK
BWEEE BWEEE BWEEE BWEEE
OH. ALARM.
VOICE ACTIVATED.
PRETTY SLICK.
ALARM
DEACTIVATE!
YEAH, WELL...
IT WAS WORTH
A SHOT.

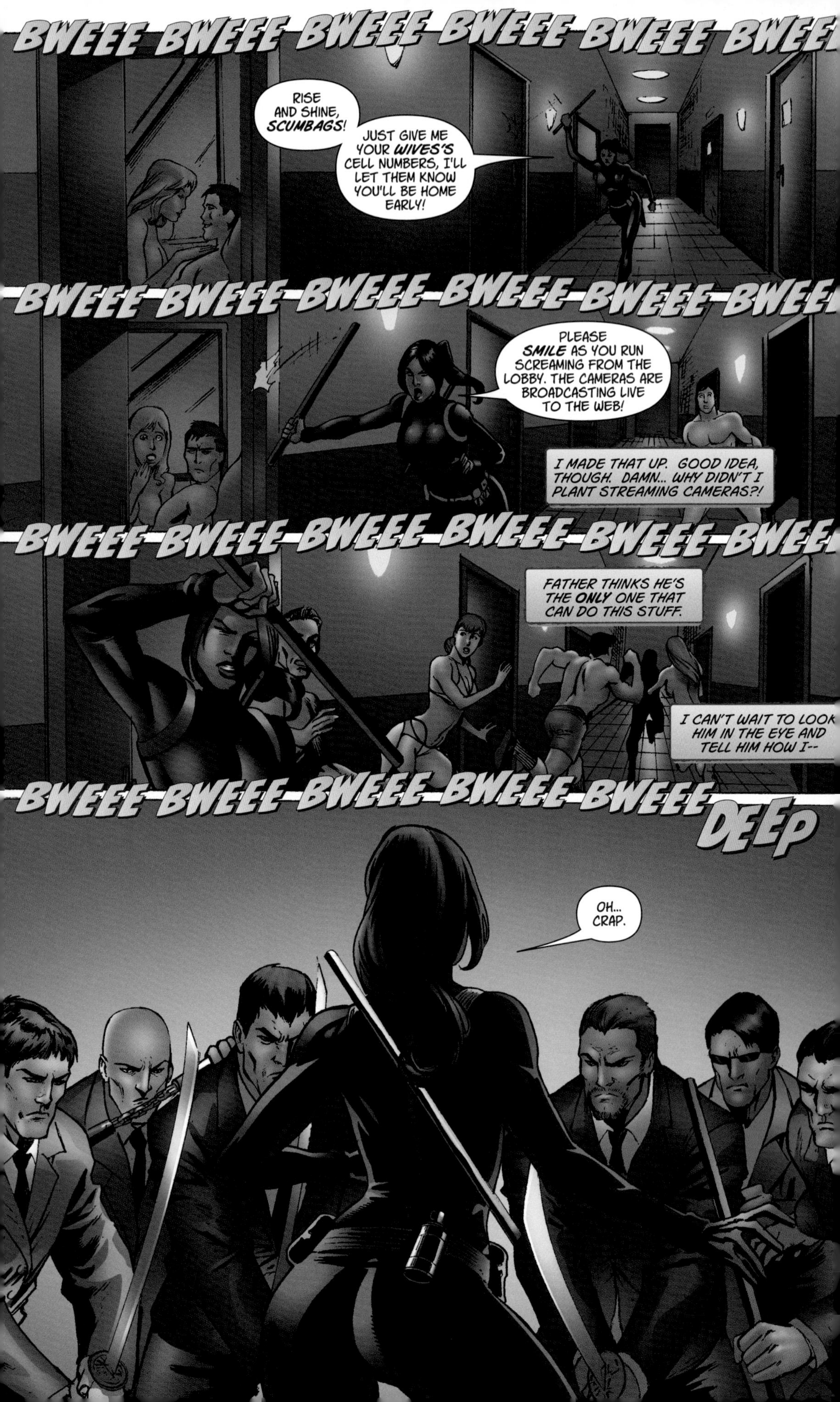
BWEEE BWEEE BWEEE BWEEE BWEEE BWEE
RISE AND SHINE, SCUMBAGS!
JUST GIVE ME YOUR WIVES'S CELL NUMBERS, I'LL LET THEM KNOW YOU'LL BE HOME EARLY!
BWEEE BWEEE BWEEE BWEEE BWEEE BWEE
PLEASE SMILE AS YOU RUN SCREAMING FROM THE LOBBY. THE CAMERAS ARE BROADCASTING LIVE TO THE WEB!
I MADE THAT UP. GOOD IDEA, THOUGH. DAMN... WHY DIDN'T I PLANT STREAMING CAMERAS?!
BWEEE BWEEE BWEEE BWEEE BWEEE BWEE
FATHER THINKS HE'S THE ONLY ONE THAT CAN DO THIS STUFF.
I CAN'T WAIT TO LOOK HIM IN THE EYE AND TELL HIM HOW I--
BWEEE BWEEE BWEEE BWEEE BWEEE DEEP
OH... CRAP.

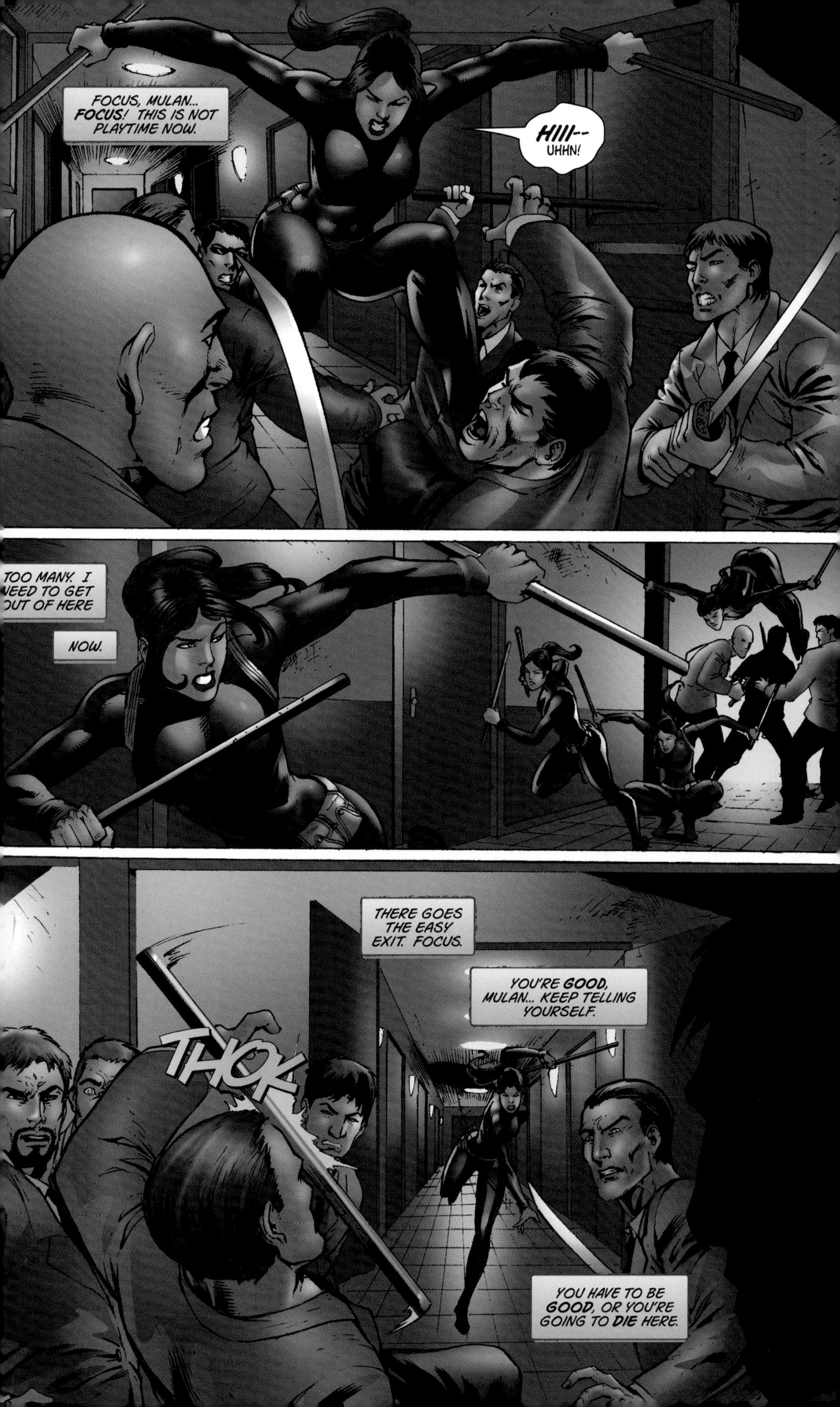
FOCUS, MULAN... FOCUS! THIS IS NOT PLAYTIME NOW.
HIII-- UHHN!
TOO MANY. I NEED TO GET OUT OF HERE
NOW.
THERE GOES THE EASY EXIT. FOCUS.
YOU'RE GOOD, MULAN... KEEP TELLING YOURSELF.
THOK
YOU HAVE TO BE GOOD, OR YOU'RE GOING TO DIE HERE.

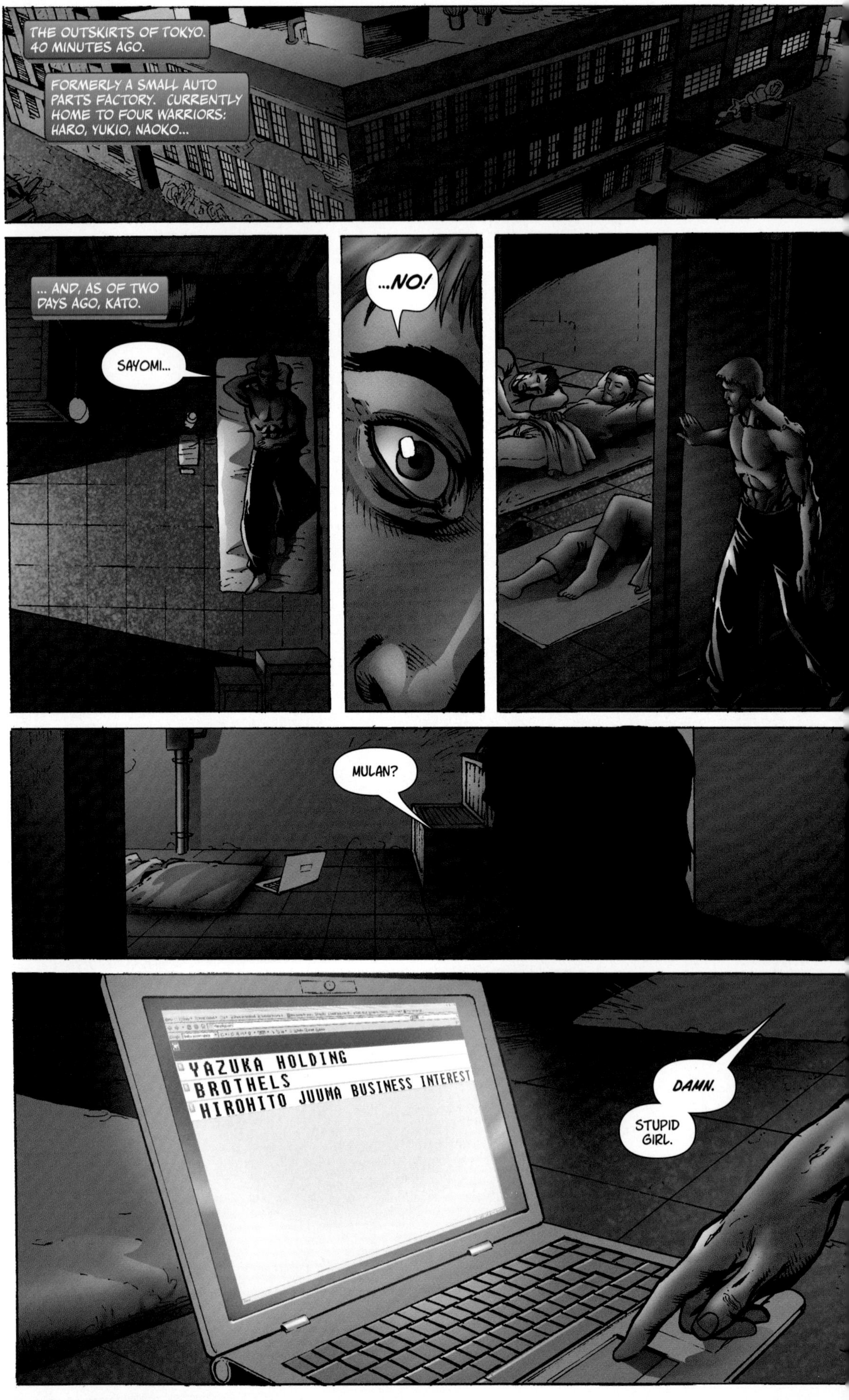
THE OUTSKIRTS OF TOKYO. 40 MINUTES AGO.
FORMERLY A SMALL AUTO PARTS FACTORY. CURRENTLY HOME TO FOUR WARRIORS: HARO, YUKIO, NAOKO...
... AND, AS OF TWO DAYS AGO, KATO.
SAYOMI...
...NO!
MULAN?
YAZUKA HOLDING
BROTHELS
HIROHITO JUUMA BUSINESS INTEREST
DAMN.
STUPID GIRL.

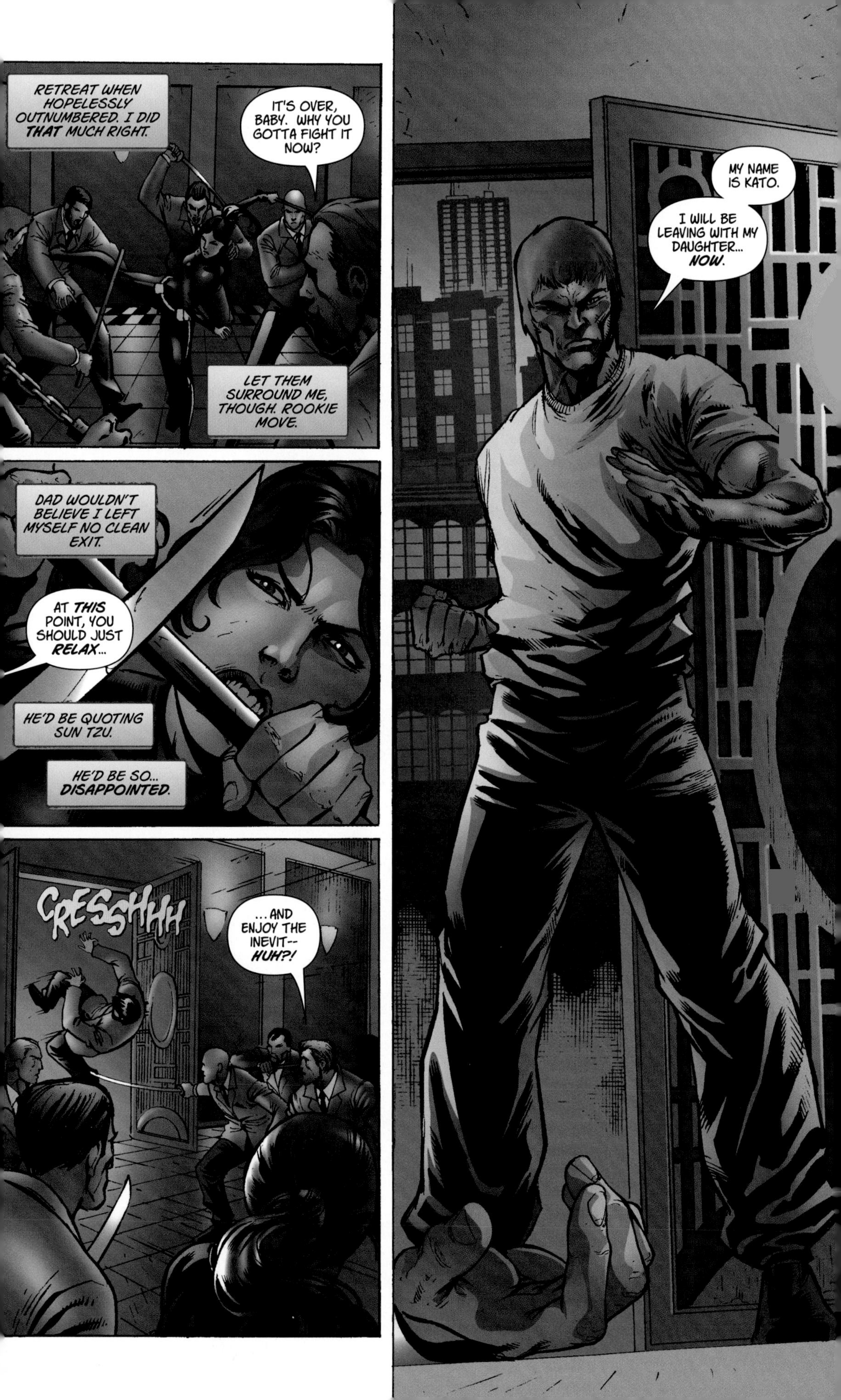
RETREAT WHEN HOPELESSLY OUTNUMBERED. I DID THAT MUCH RIGHT.
IT'S OVER, BABY. WHY YOU GOTTA FIGHT IT NOW?
LET THEM SURROUND ME, THOUGH. ROOKIE MOVE.
DAD WOULDN'T BELIEVE I LEFT MYSELF NO CLEAN EXIT.
AT THIS POINT, YOU SHOULD JUST RELAX...
HE'D BE QUOTING SUN TZU.
HE'D BE SO... DISAPPOINTED.
CRESSHHH
...AND ENJOY THE INEVIT-- HUH?!
MY NAME IS KATO.
I WILL BE LEAVING WITH MY DAUGHTER... NOW.

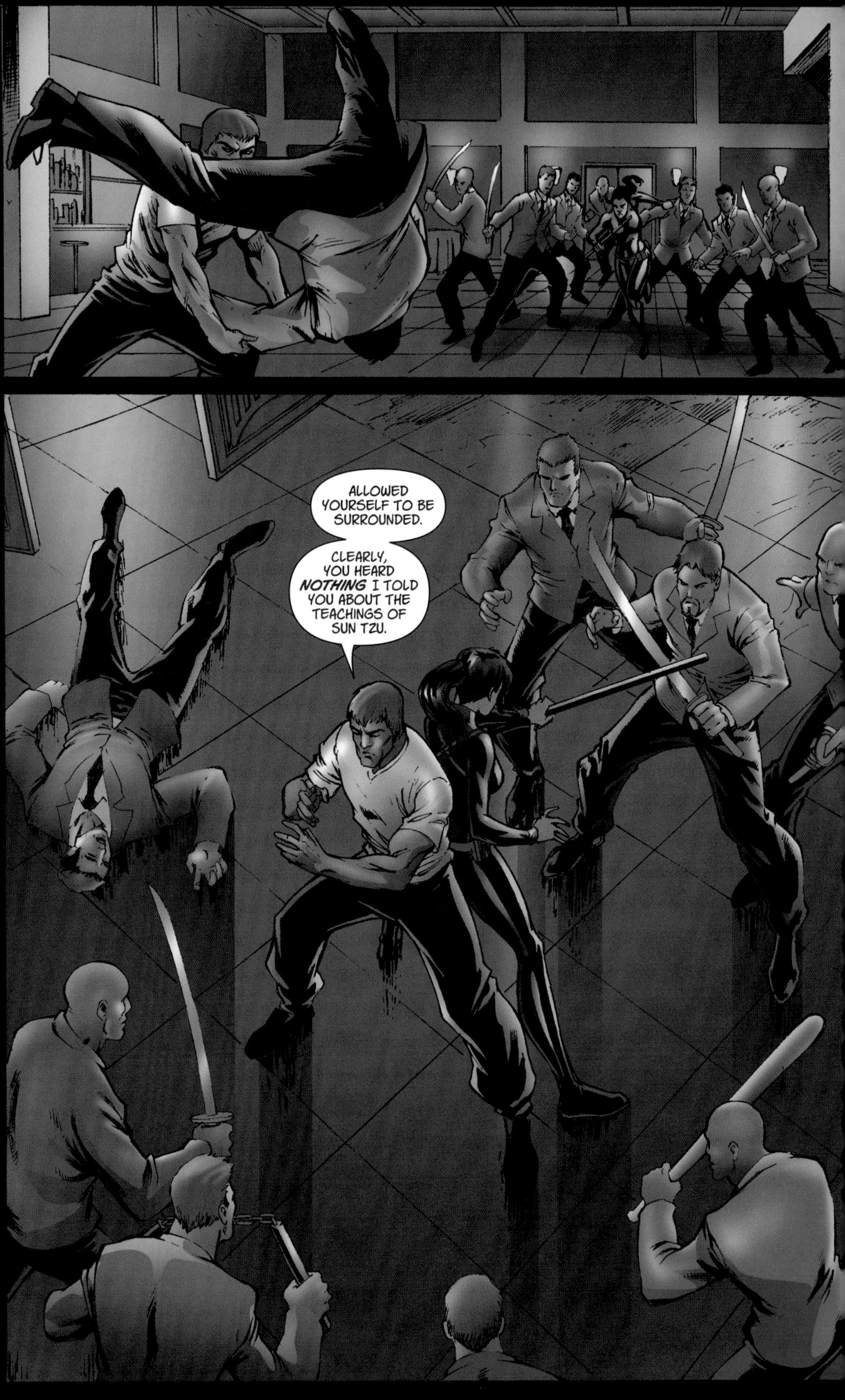
ALLOWED YOURSELF TO BE SURROUNDED.
CLEARLY, YOU HEARD NOTHING I TOLD YOU ABOUT THE TEACHINGS OF SUN TZU.

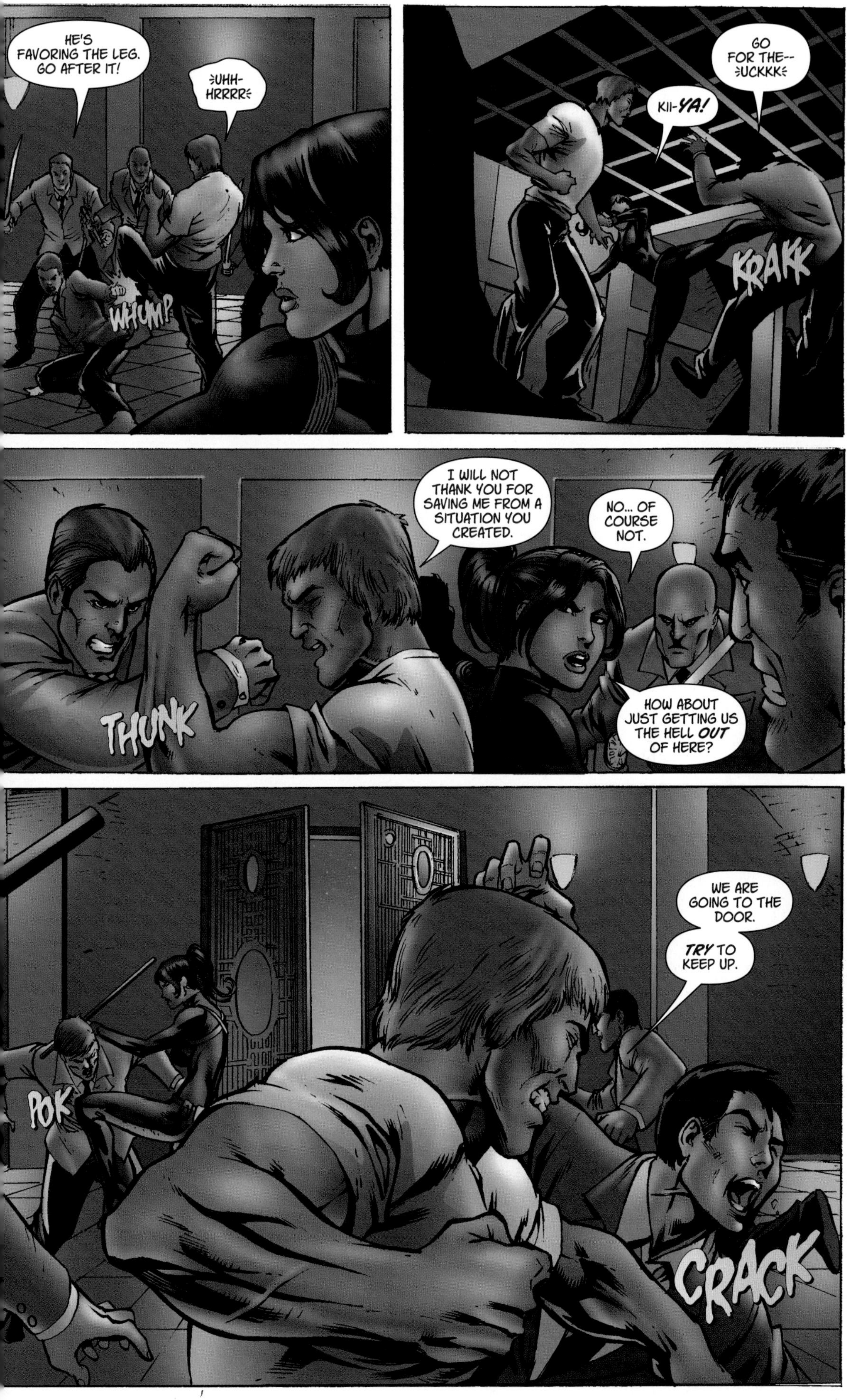
HE'S FAVORING THE LEG. GO AFTER IT!
UHH-HRRRR
WHUMP
GO FOR THE-- UCKKK
KII-YA!
KRAKK
I WILL NOT THANK YOU FOR SAVING ME FROM A SITUATION YOU CREATED.
NO... OF COURSE NOT.
THUNK
HOW ABOUT JUST GETTING US THE HELL OUT OF HERE?
WE ARE GOING TO THE DOOR.
TRY TO KEEP UP.
POK
CRACK

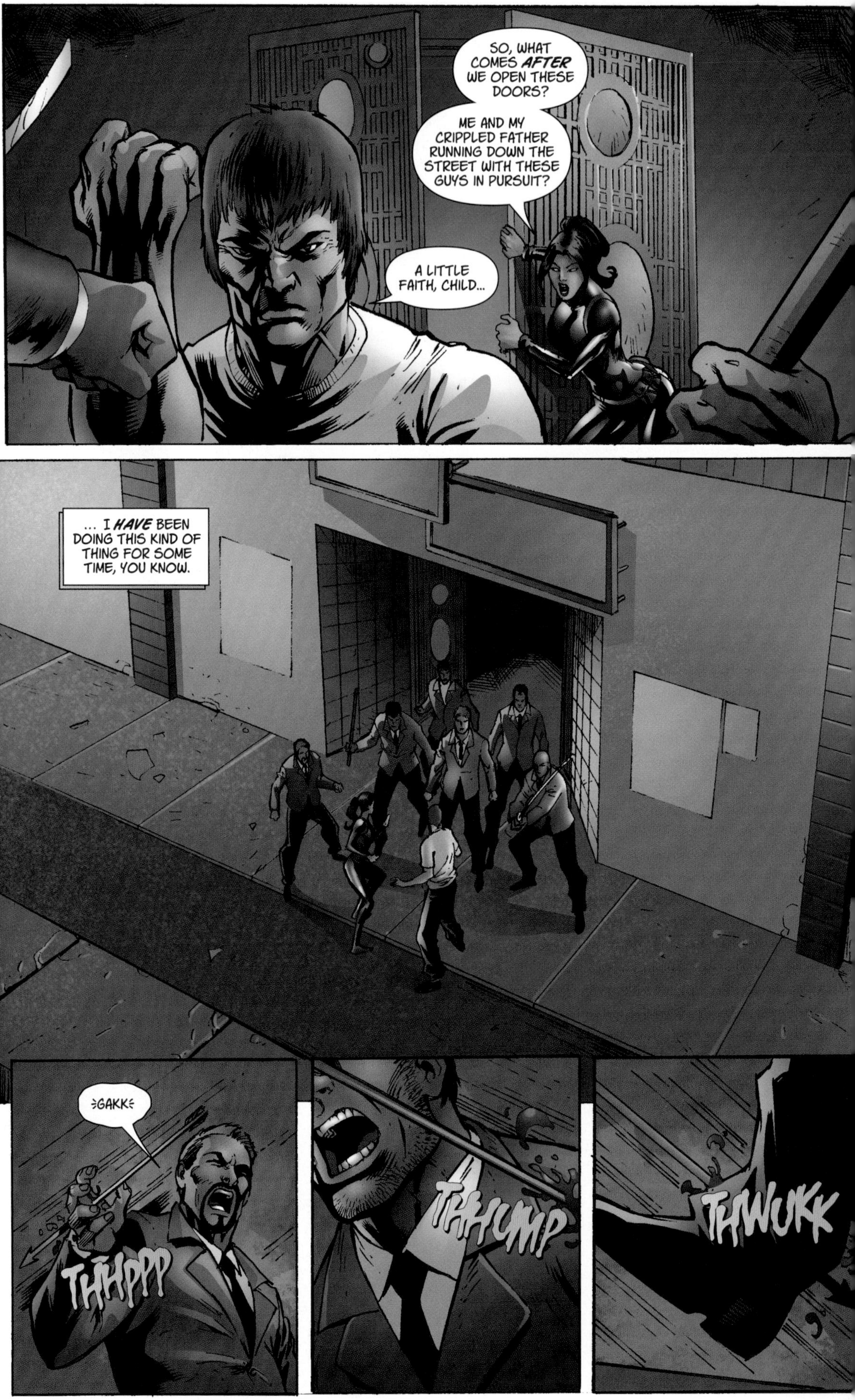
SO, WHAT COMES AFTER WE OPEN THESE DOORS?
ME AND MY CRIPPLED FATHER RUNNING DOWN THE STREET WITH THESE GUYS IN PURSUIT?
A LITTLE FAITH, CHILD...
... I HAVE BEEN DOING THIS KIND OF THING FOR SOME TIME, YOU KNOW.
GAKK
THHPPP
THHUMP
THWUKK

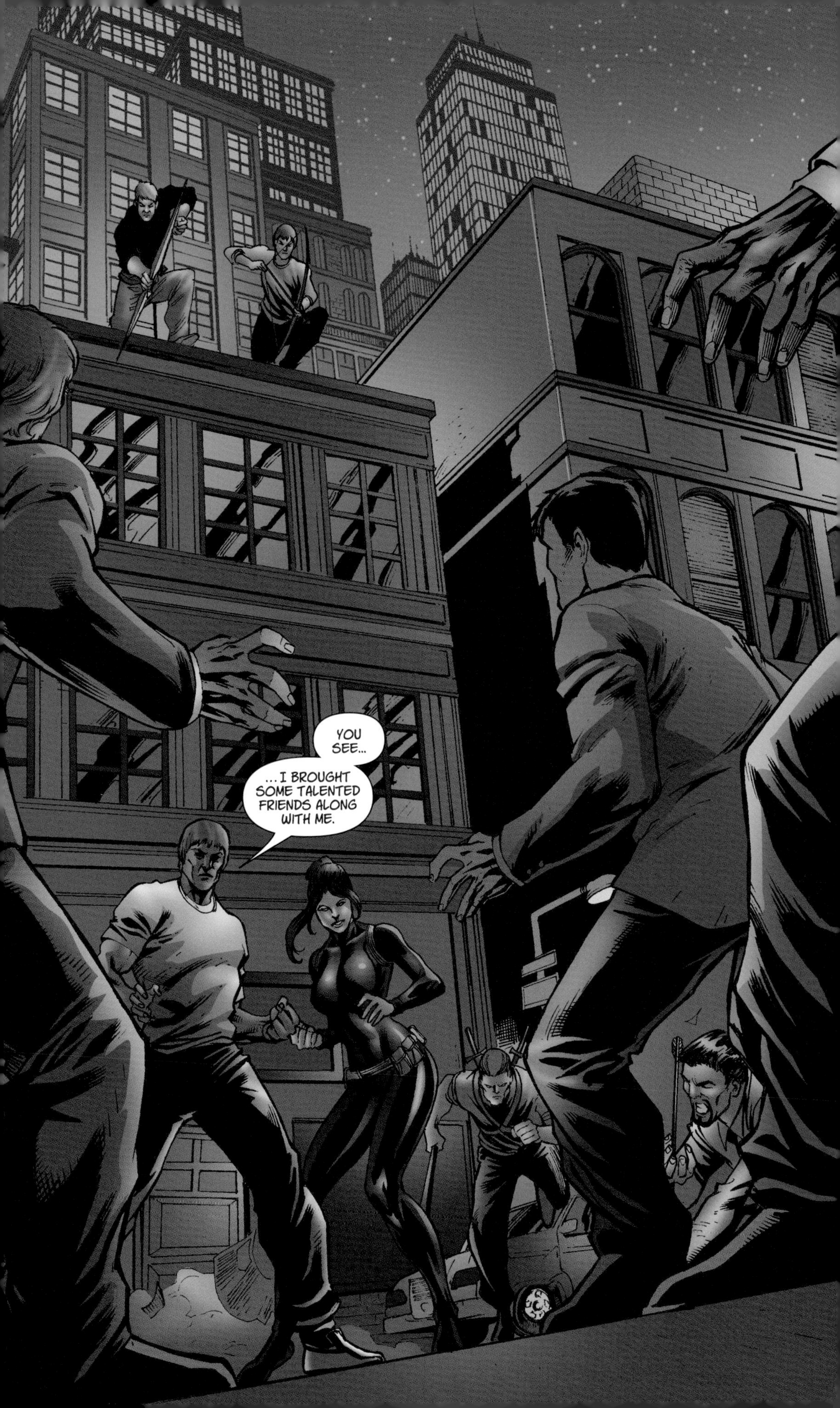
YOU SEE...
...I BROUGHT SOME TALENTED FRIENDS ALONG WITH ME.

FORTY MINUTES LATER.

IT DIDN'T GO AS I HOPED.

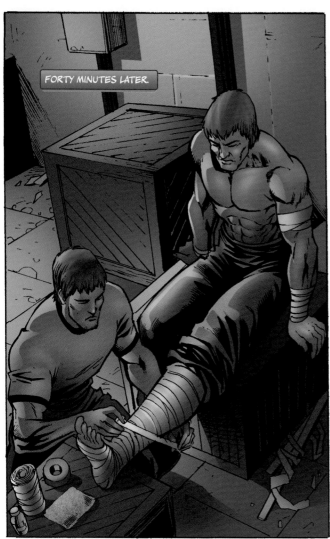

I'M SORRY YOU ALL HAD TO GET INVOLVED.

AS YOU *HOPED*?!

YOU RUN OFF ON YOUR OWN, TO A WHOREHOUSE FULL OF JUUMA'S MEN.

KATO, PLEASE...

HOW, *EXACTLY*, DID YOU HOPE IT WOULD GO?!

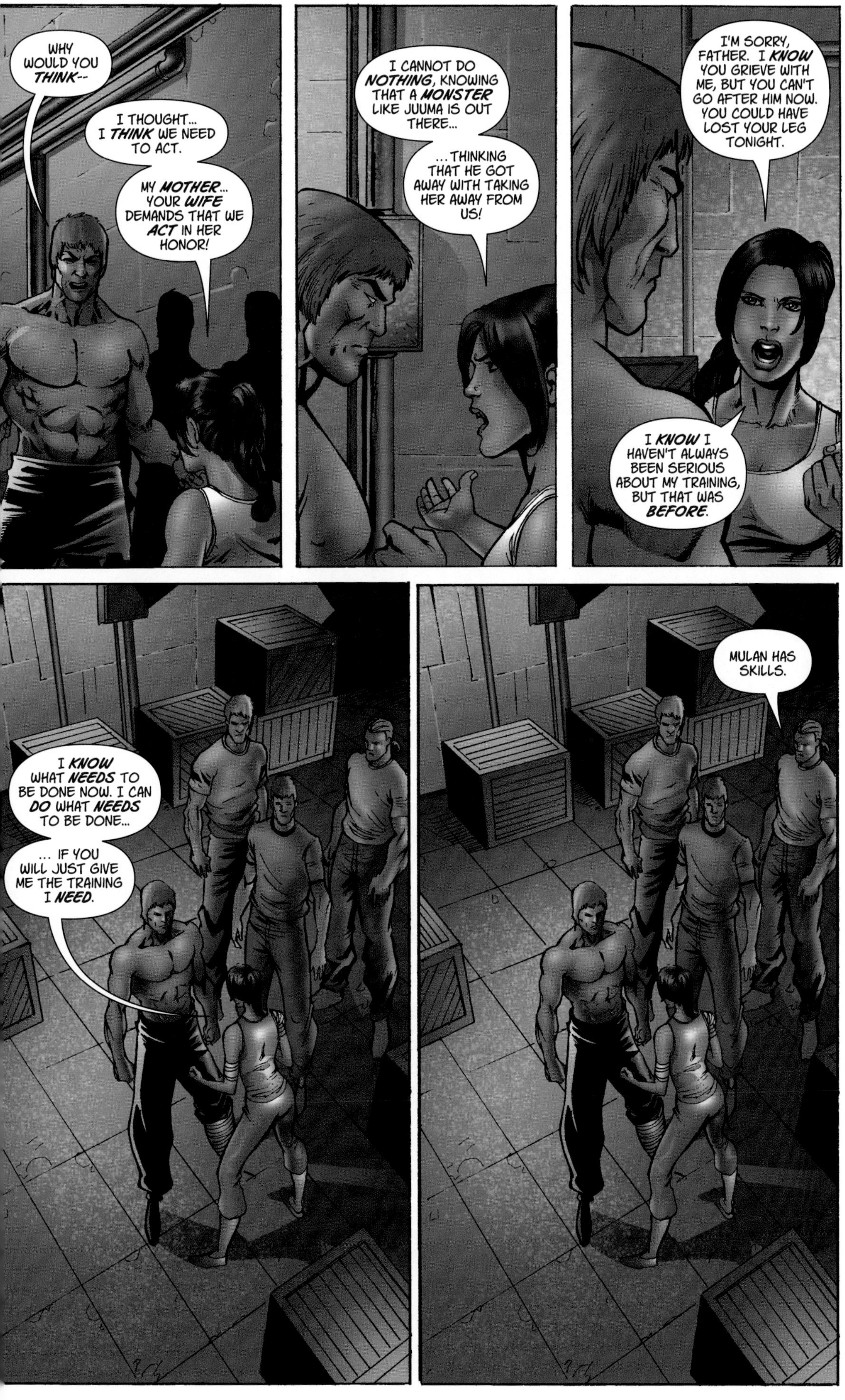
WHY WOULD YOU THINK--
I THOUGHT... I THINK WE NEED TO ACT.
MY MOTHER... YOUR WIFE DEMANDS THAT WE ACT IN HER HONOR!
I CANNOT DO NOTHING, KNOWING THAT A MONSTER LIKE JUUMA IS OUT THERE...
...THINKING THAT HE GOT AWAY WITH TAKING HER AWAY FROM US!
I'M SORRY, FATHER. I KNOW YOU GRIEVE WITH ME, BUT YOU CAN'T GO AFTER HIM NOW. YOU COULD HAVE LOST YOUR LEG TONIGHT.
I KNOW I HAVEN'T ALWAYS BEEN SERIOUS ABOUT MY TRAINING, BUT THAT WAS BEFORE.
I KNOW WHAT NEEDS TO BE DONE NOW. I CAN DO WHAT NEEDS TO BE DONE...
... IF YOU WILL JUST GIVE ME THE TRAINING I NEED.
MULAN HAS SKILLS.

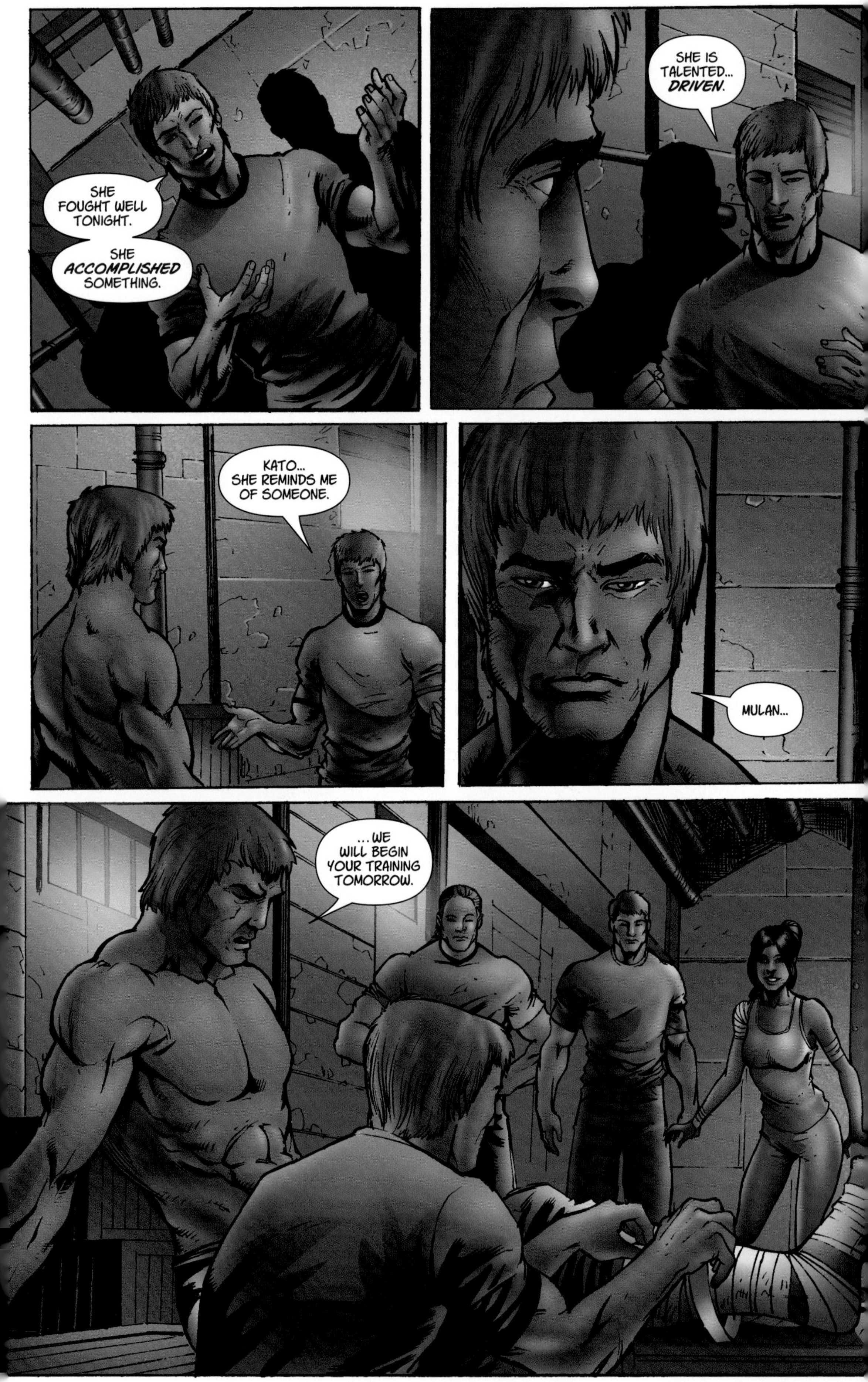
SHE FOUGHT WELL TONIGHT.
SHE ACCOMPLISHED SOMETHING.
SHE IS TALENTED... DRIVEN.
KATO... SHE REMINDS ME OF SOMEONE.
MULAN...
...WE WILL BEGIN YOUR TRAINING TOMORROW.

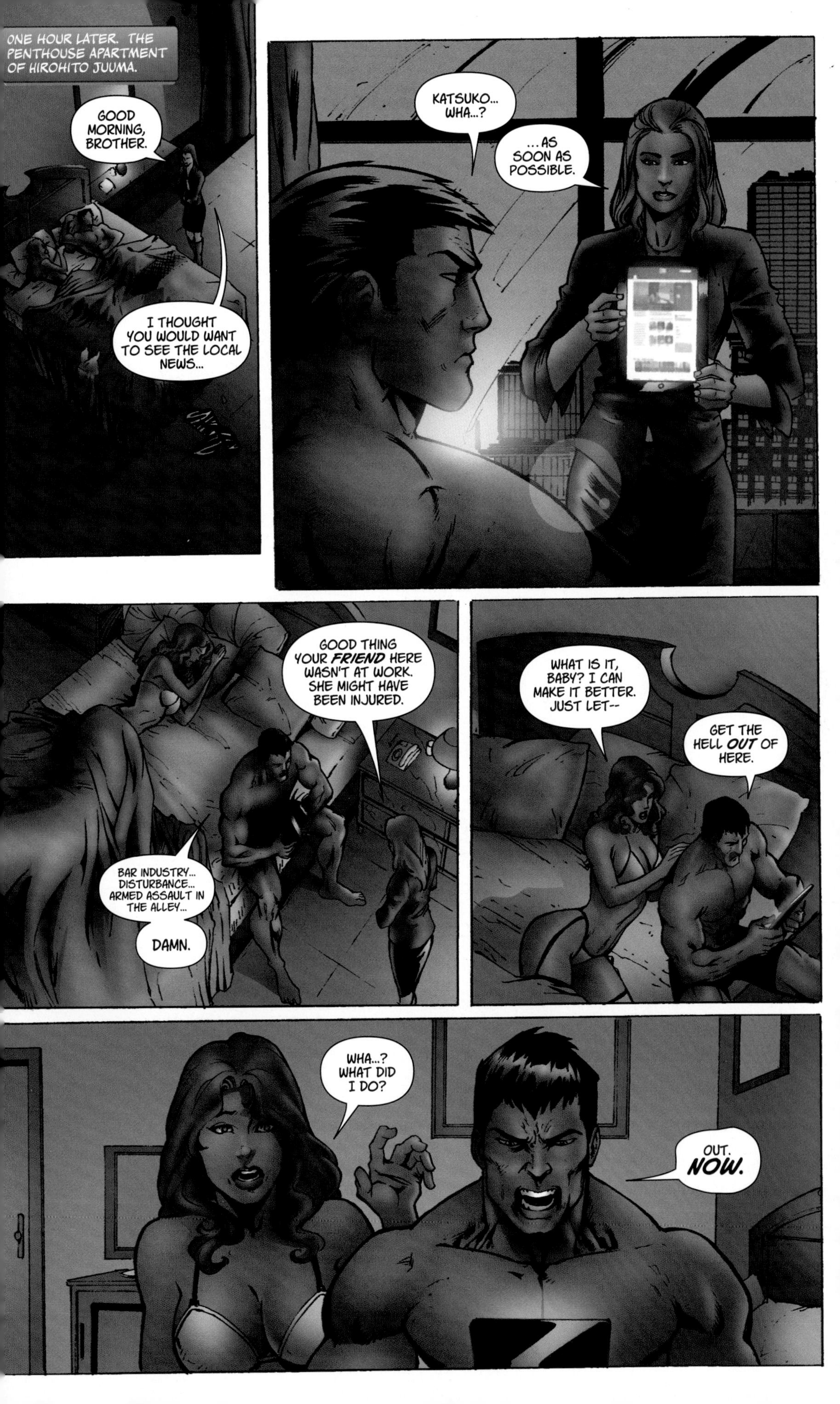

ONE HOUR LATER. THE PENTHOUSE APARTMENT OF HIROHITO JUUMA.
GOOD MORNING, BROTHER.
I THOUGHT YOU WOULD WANT TO SEE THE LOCAL NEWS...
KATSUKO... WHA...?
...AS SOON AS POSSIBLE.
GOOD THING YOUR FRIEND HERE WASN'T AT WORK. SHE MIGHT HAVE BEEN INJURED.
BAR INDUSTRY... DISTURBANCE... ARMED ASSAULT IN THE ALLEY...
DAMN.
WHAT IS IT, BABY? I CAN MAKE IT BETTER. JUST LET--
GET THE HELL OUT OF HERE.
WHA...? WHAT DID I DO?
OUT. NOW.

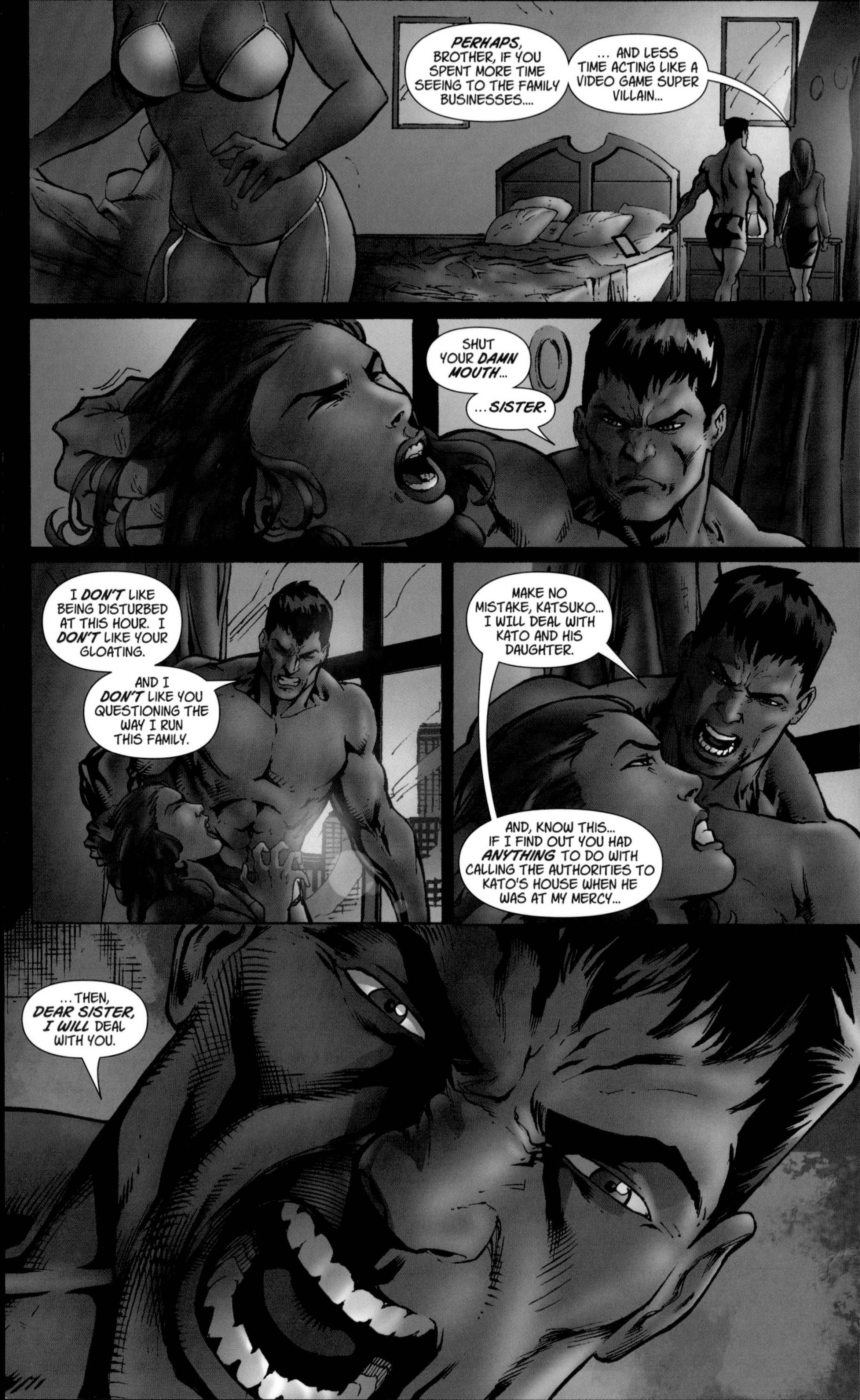
PERHAPS, BROTHER, IF YOU SPENT MORE TIME SEEING TO THE FAMILY BUSINESSES....
... AND LESS TIME ACTING LIKE A VIDEO GAME SUPER VILLAIN...
SHUT YOUR DAMN MOUTH...
...SISTER.
I DON'T LIKE BEING DISTURBED AT THIS HOUR. I DON'T LIKE YOUR GLOATING.
AND I DON'T LIKE YOU QUESTIONING THE WAY I RUN THIS FAMILY.
MAKE NO MISTAKE, KATSUKO... I WILL DEAL WITH KATO AND HIS DAUGHTER.
AND, KNOW THIS... IF I FIND OUT YOU HAD ANYTHING TO DO WITH CALLING THE AUTHORITIES TO KATO'S HOUSE WHEN HE WAS AT MY MERCY...
...THEN, DEAR SISTER, I WILL DEAL WITH YOU.

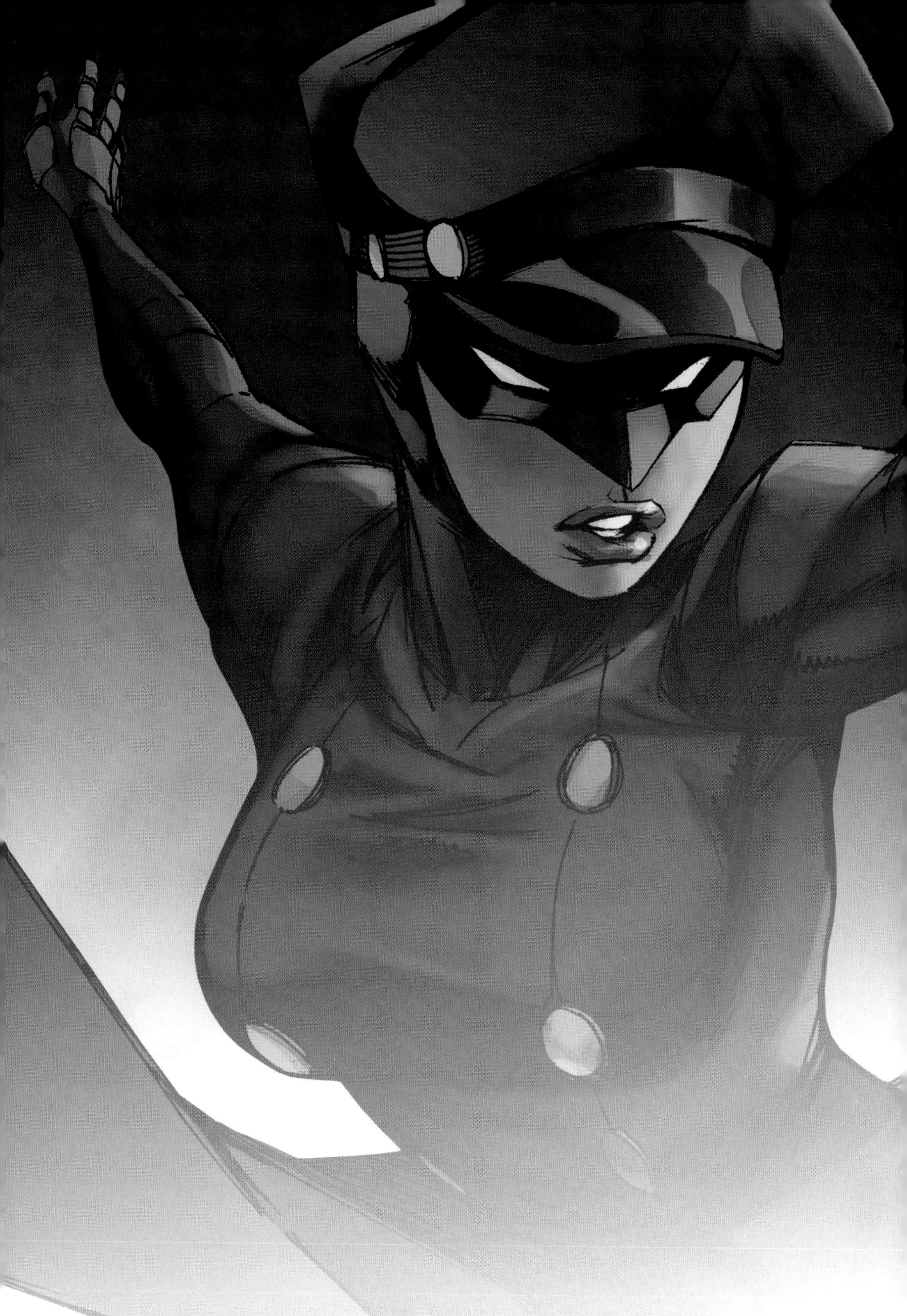

Issue FOUR

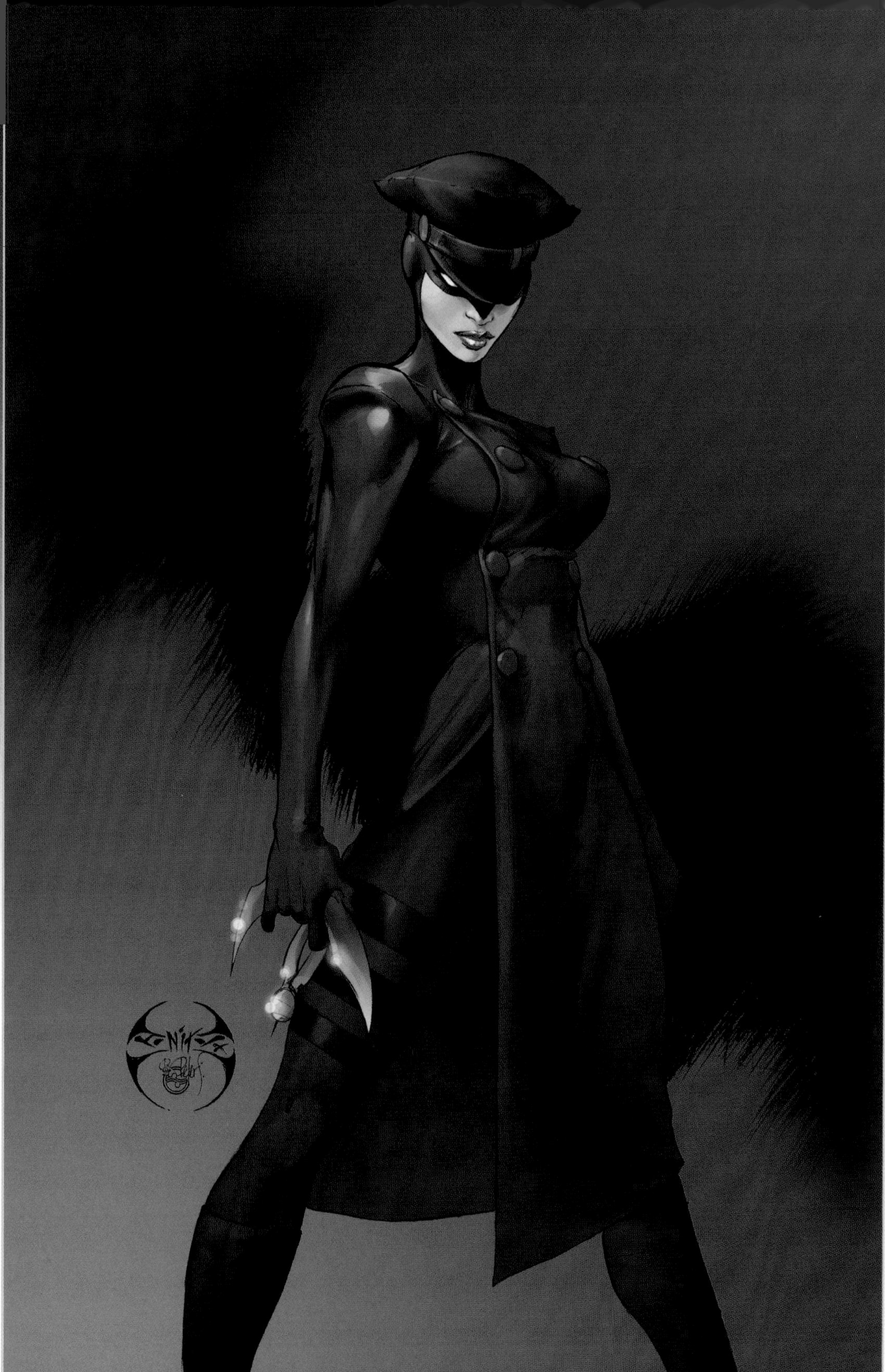

Issue four cover by **JOE BENITEZ**

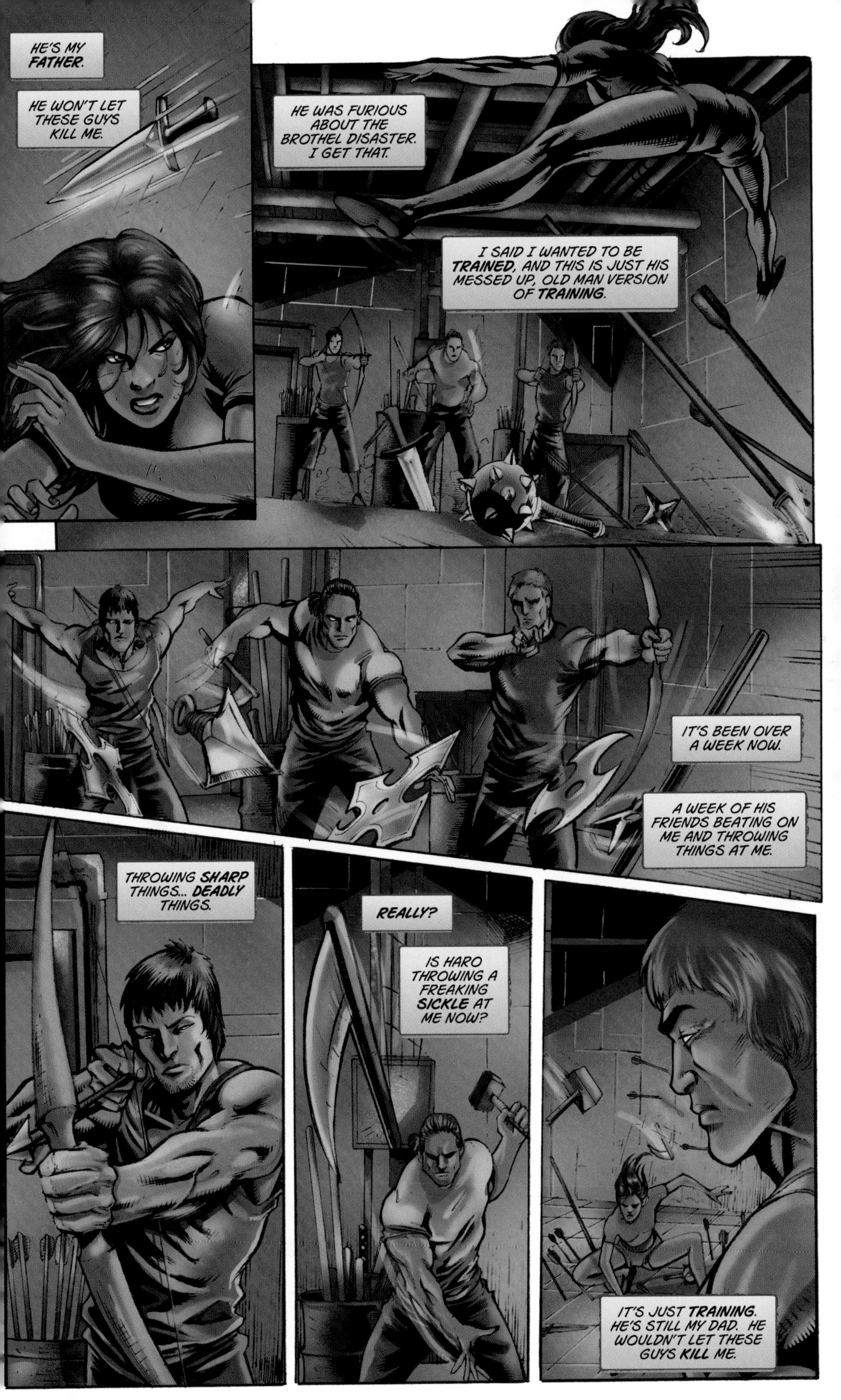

HE'S MY FATHER.
HE WON'T LET THESE GUYS KILL ME.
HE WAS FURIOUS ABOUT THE BROTHEL DISASTER. I GET THAT.
I SAID I WANTED TO BE TRAINED, AND THIS IS JUST HIS MESSED UP, OLD MAN VERSION OF TRAINING.
IT'S BEEN OVER A WEEK NOW.
A WEEK OF HIS FRIENDS BEATING ON ME AND THROWING THINGS AT ME.
THROWING SHARP THINGS... DEADLY THINGS.
REALLY?
IS HARO THROWING A FREAKING SICKLE AT ME NOW?
IT'S JUST TRAINING. HE'S STILL MY DAD. HE WOULDN'T LET THESE GUYS KILL ME.

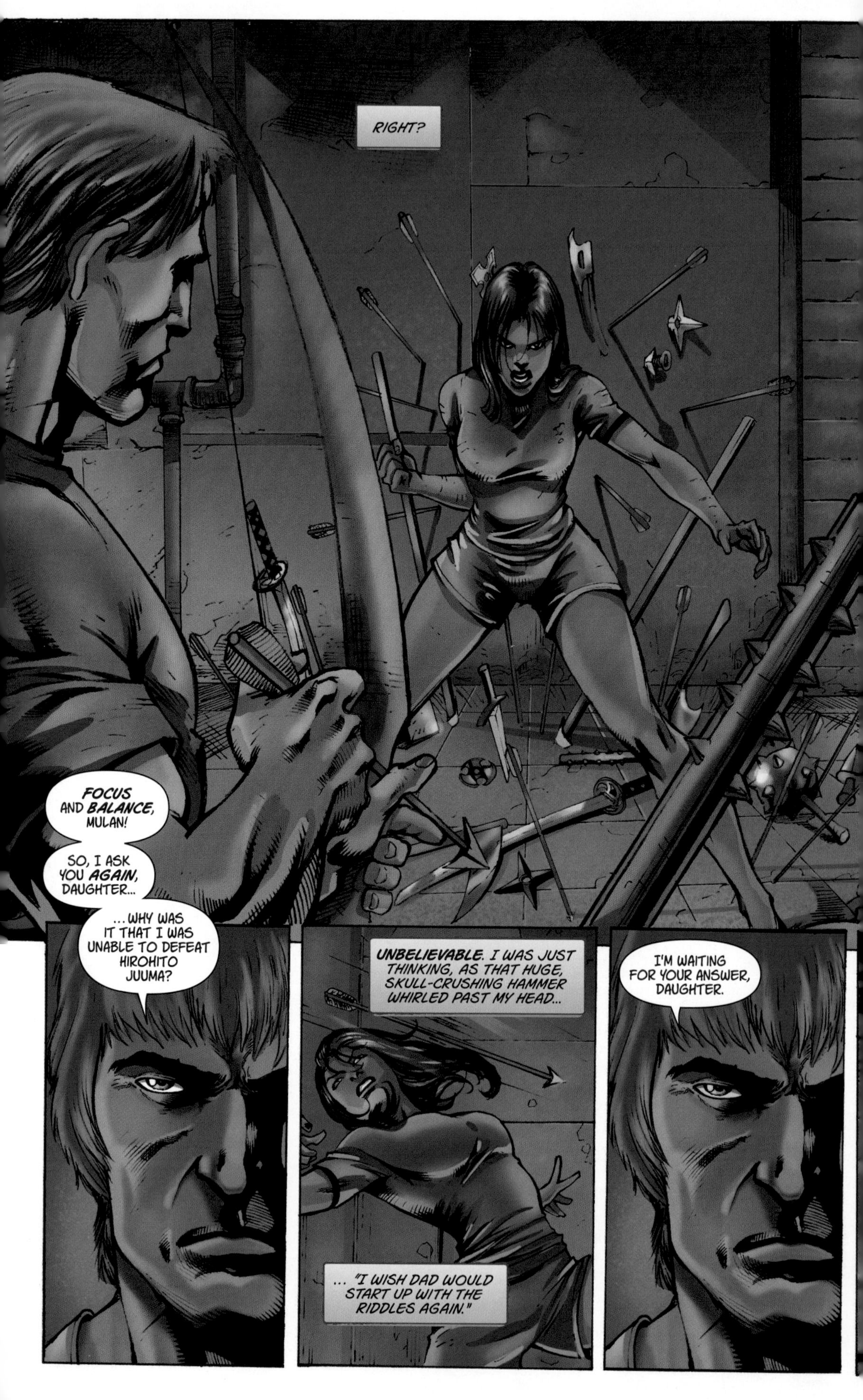
RIGHT?
FOCUS AND BALANCE, MULAN!
SO, I ASK YOU AGAIN, DAUGHTER...
...WHY WAS IT THAT I WAS UNABLE TO DEFEAT HIROHITO JUUMA?
UNBELIEVABLE. I WAS JUST THINKING, AS THAT HUGE, SKULL-CRUSHING HAMMER WHIRLED PAST MY HEAD...
... "I WISH DAD WOULD START UP WITH THE RIDDLES AGAIN."
I'M WAITING FOR YOUR ANSWER, DAUGHTER.

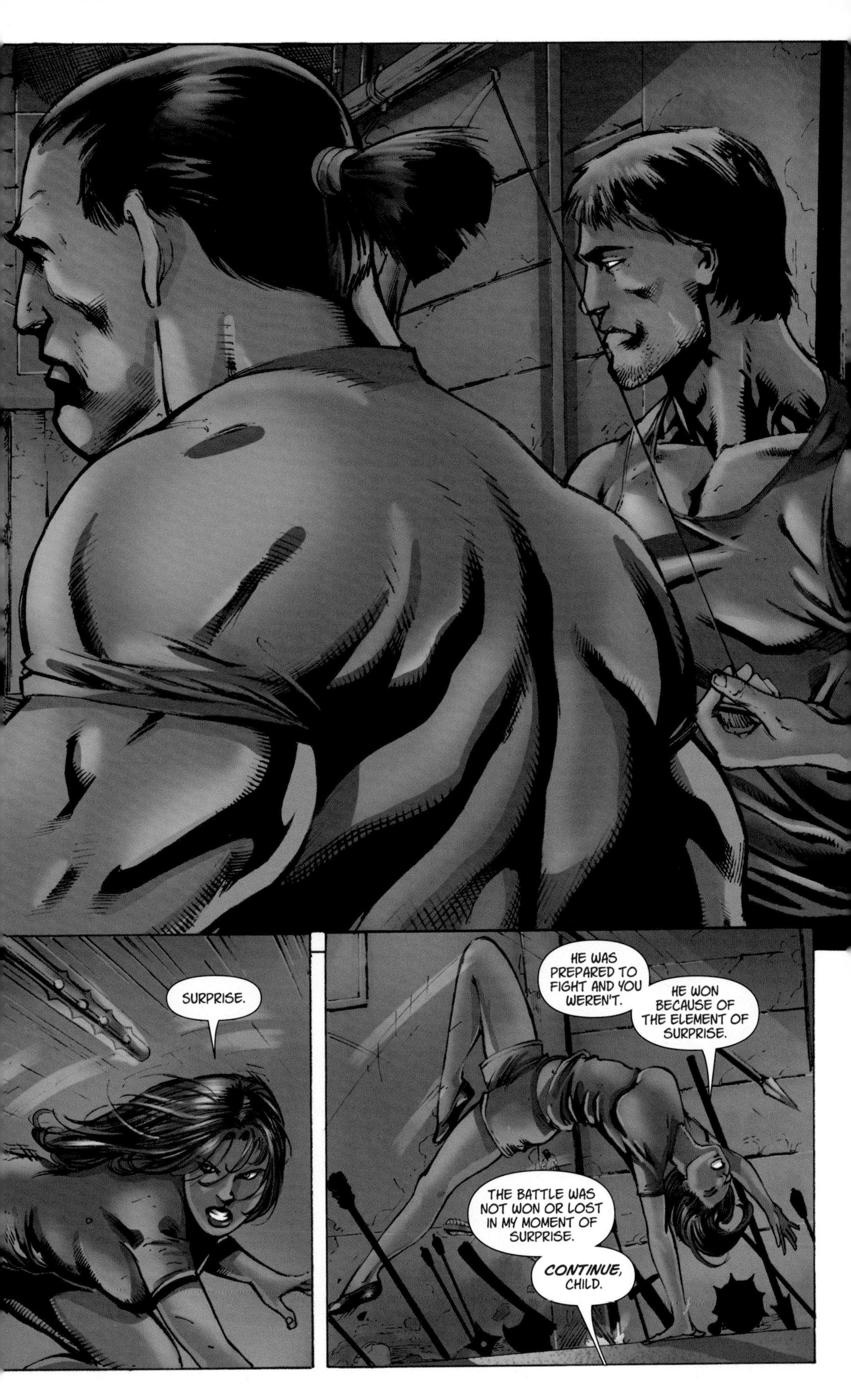
SURPRISE.
HE WAS PREPARED TO FIGHT AND YOU WEREN'T.
HE WON BECAUSE OF THE ELEMENT OF SURPRISE.
THE BATTLE WAS NOT WON OR LOST IN MY MOMENT OF SURPRISE.
CONTINUE, CHILD.

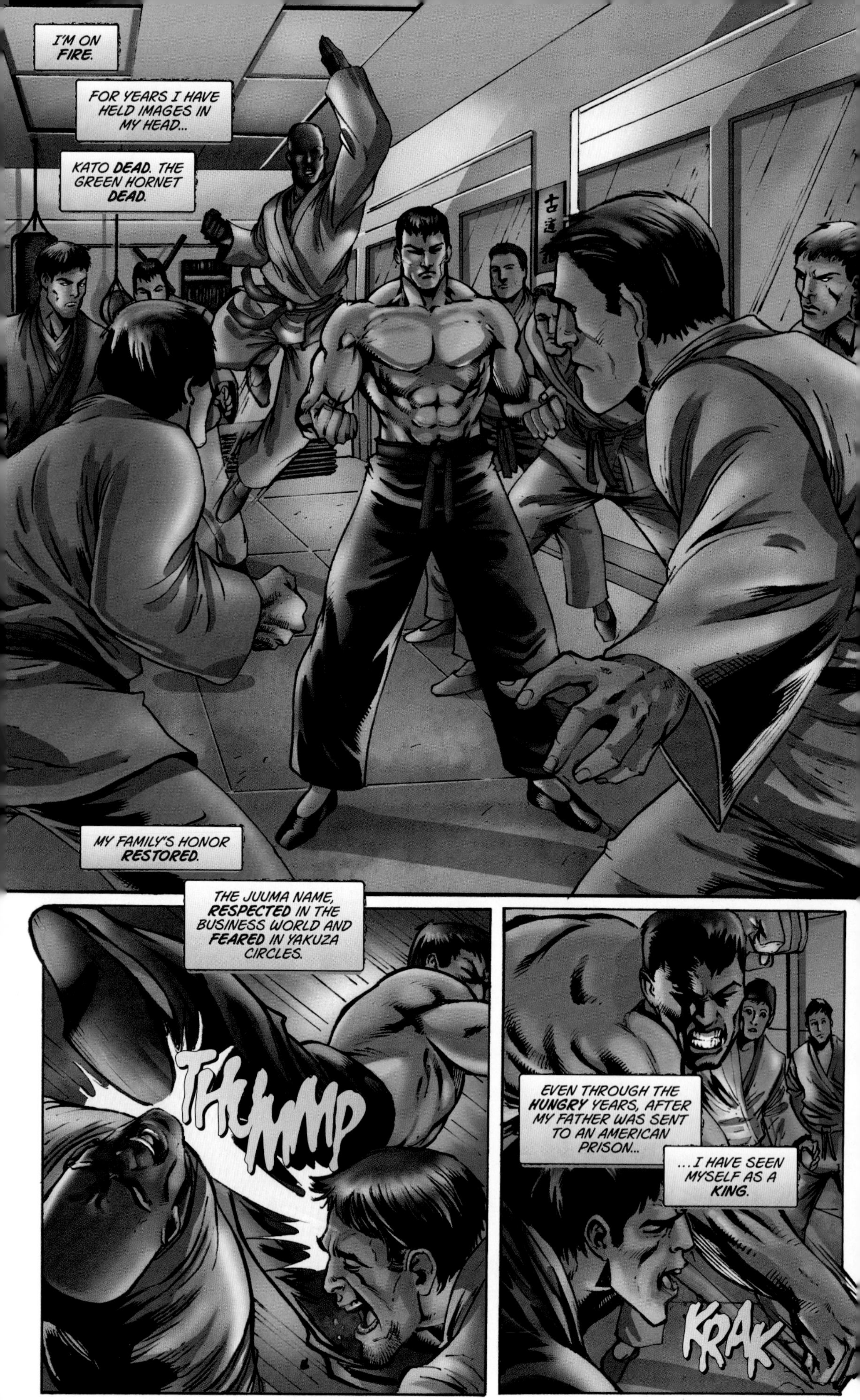
I'M ON FIRE.
FOR YEARS I HAVE HELD IMAGES IN MY HEAD...
KATO DEAD. THE GREEN HORNET DEAD.
MY FAMILY'S HONOR RESTORED.
THE JUUMA NAME, RESPECTED IN THE BUSINESS WORLD AND FEARED IN YAKUZA CIRCLES.
THUMMP
EVEN THROUGH THE HUNGRY YEARS, AFTER MY FATHER WAS SENT TO AN AMERICAN PRISON...
...I HAVE SEEN MYSELF AS A KING.
KRAK

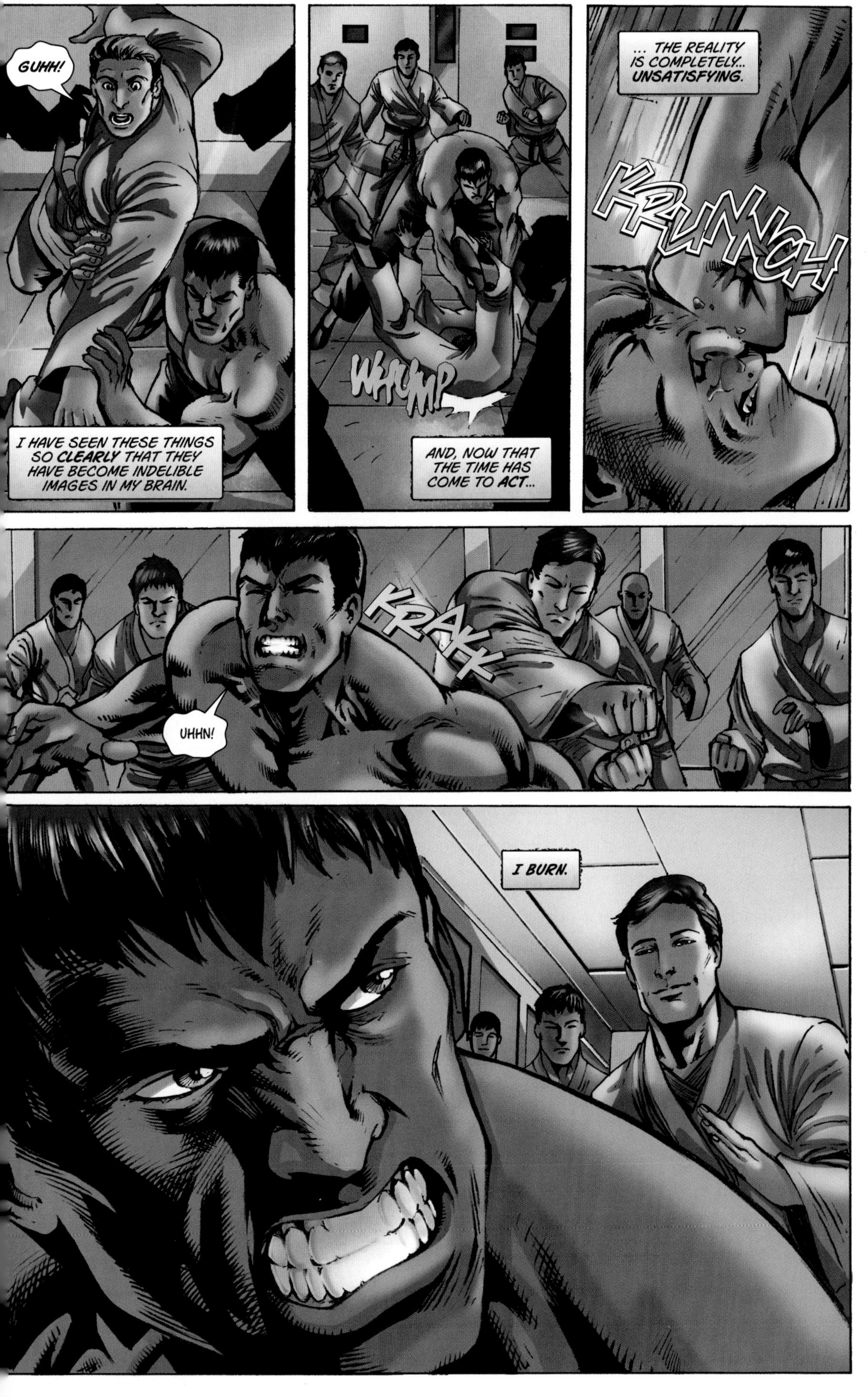
GUHH!
I HAVE SEEN THESE THINGS SO CLEARLY THAT THEY HAVE BECOME INDELIBLE IMAGES IN MY BRAIN.
WHUMP
AND, NOW THAT THE TIME HAS COME TO ACT...
... THE REALITY IS COMPLETELY... UNSATISFYING.
KRUNNCH
KRAKK
UHHN!
I BURN.

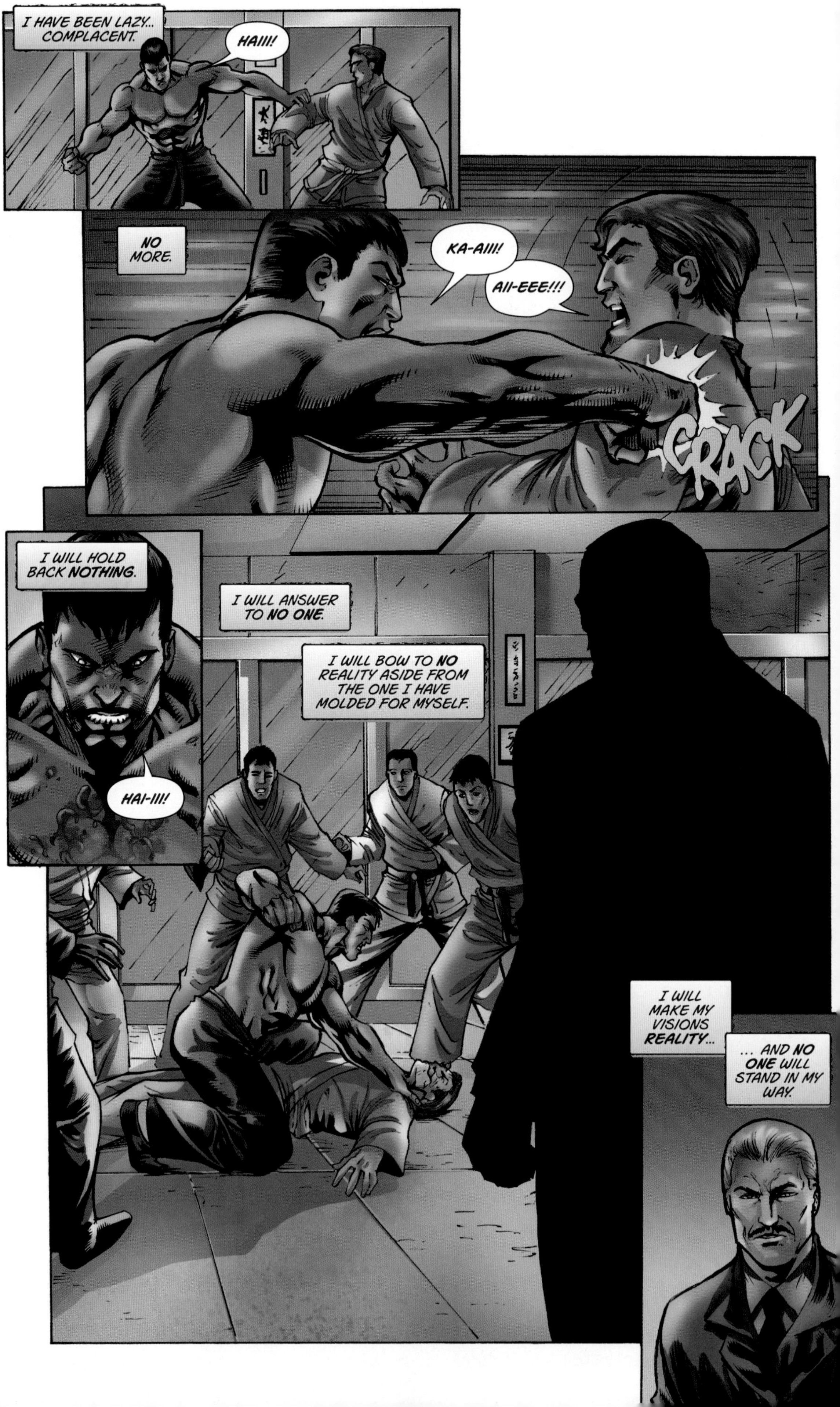
I HAVE BEEN LAZY... COMPLACENT.
HAIII!
NO MORE.
KA-AIII!
AII-EEE!!!
CRACK
I WILL HOLD BACK NOTHING.
HAI-III!
I WILL ANSWER TO NO ONE.
I WILL BOW TO NO REALITY ASIDE FROM THE ONE I HAVE MOLDED FOR MYSELF.
I WILL MAKE MY VISIONS REALITY...
... AND NO ONE WILL STAND IN MY WAY.

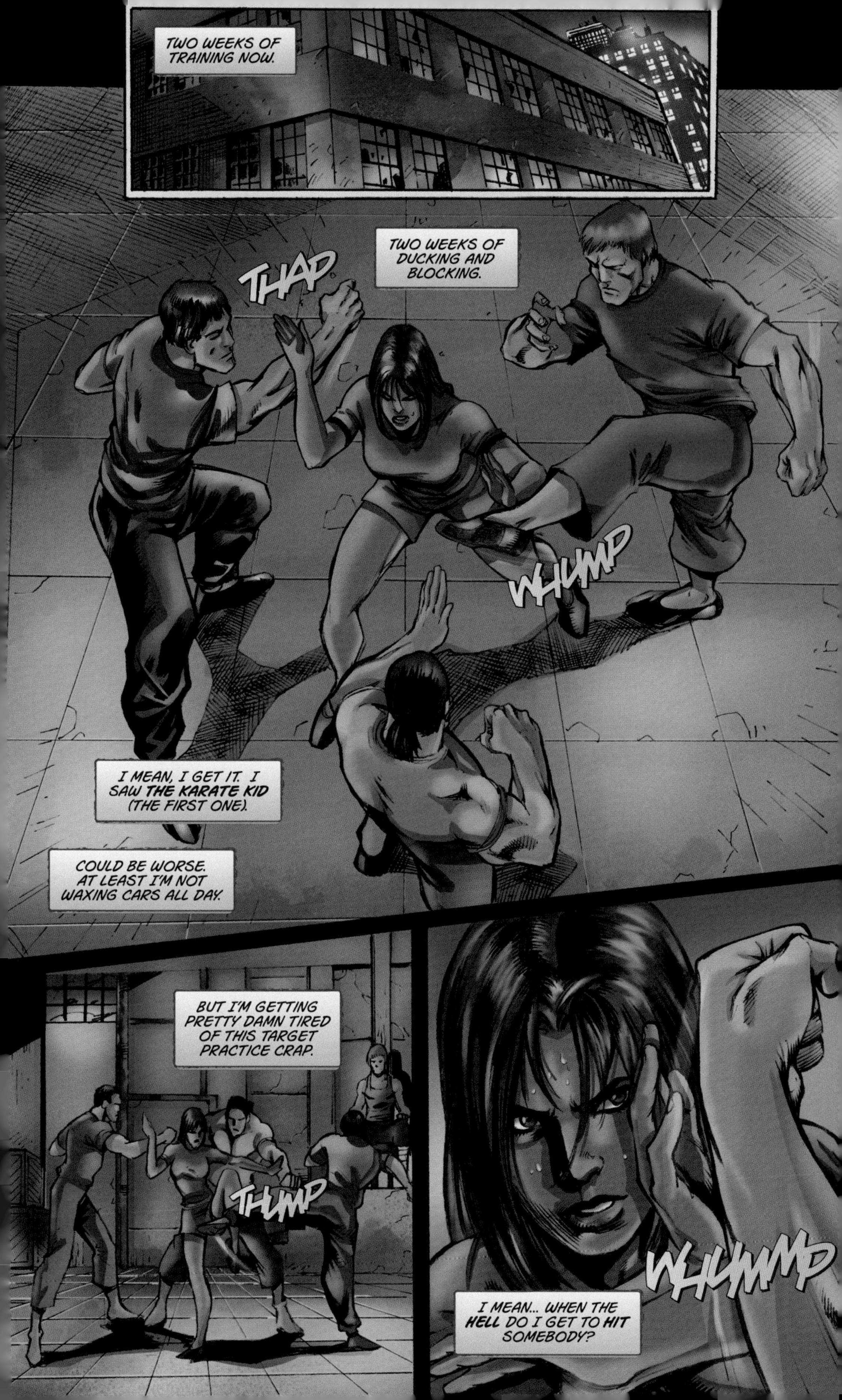
TWO WEEKS OF TRAINING NOW.
TWO WEEKS OF DUCKING AND BLOCKING.
THAP
WHUMP
I MEAN, I GET IT. I SAW THE KARATE KID (THE FIRST ONE).
COULD BE WORSE. AT LEAST I'M NOT WAXING CARS ALL DAY.
BUT I'M GETTING PRETTY DAMN TIRED OF THIS TARGET PRACTICE CRAP.
THUMP
WHUMMP
I MEAN... WHEN THE HELL DO I GET TO HIT SOMEBODY?

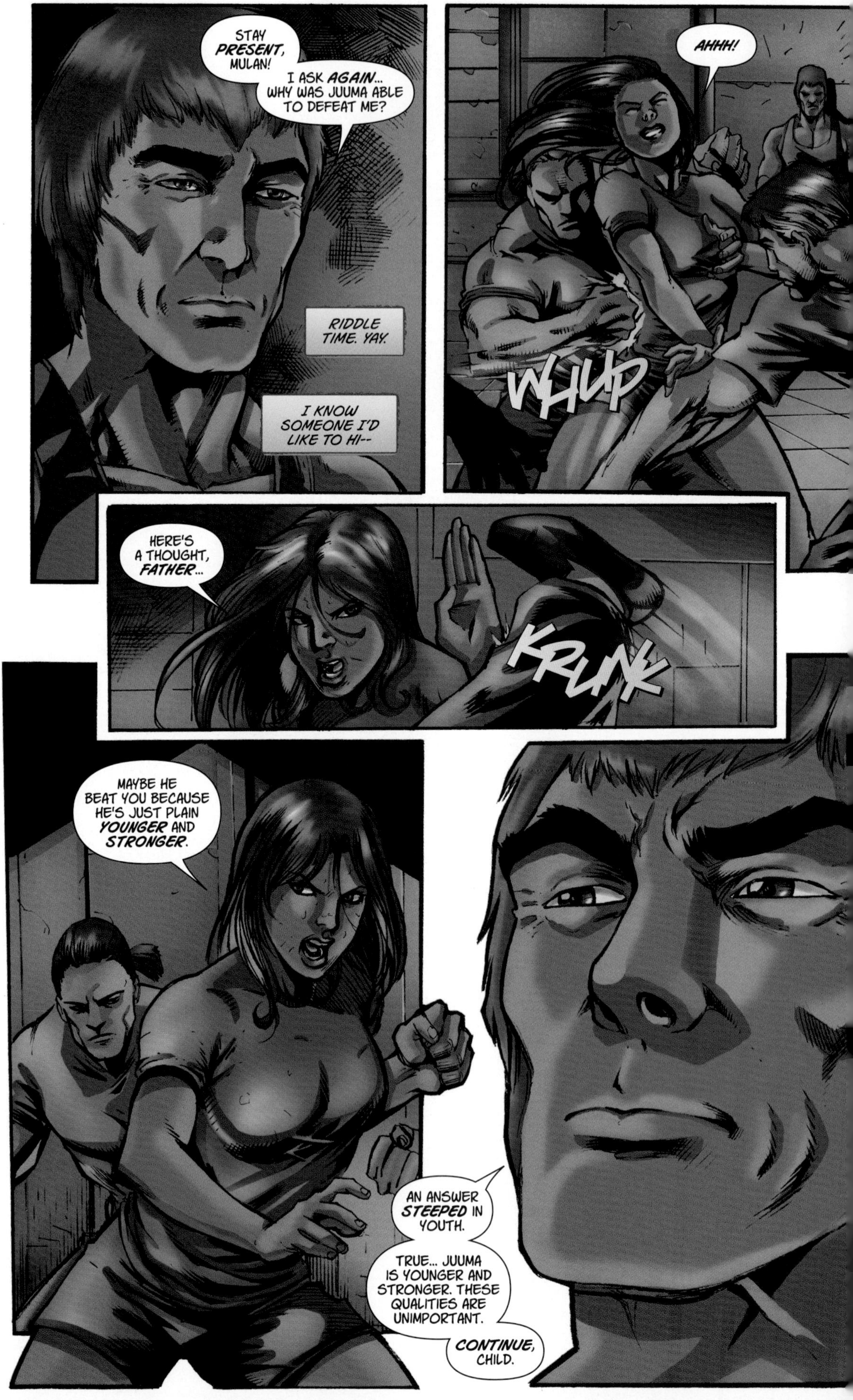

STAY PRESENT, MULAN!
I ASK AGAIN... WHY WAS JUUMA ABLE TO DEFEAT ME?
RIDDLE TIME. YAY.
I KNOW SOMEONE I'D LIKE TO HI--
AHHH!
WHUP
HERE'S A THOUGHT, FATHER...
KRUNK
MAYBE HE BEAT YOU BECAUSE HE'S JUST PLAIN YOUNGER AND STRONGER.
AN ANSWER STEEPED IN YOUTH.
TRUE... JUUMA IS YOUNGER AND STRONGER. THESE QUALITIES ARE UNIMPORTANT.
CONTINUE, CHILD.

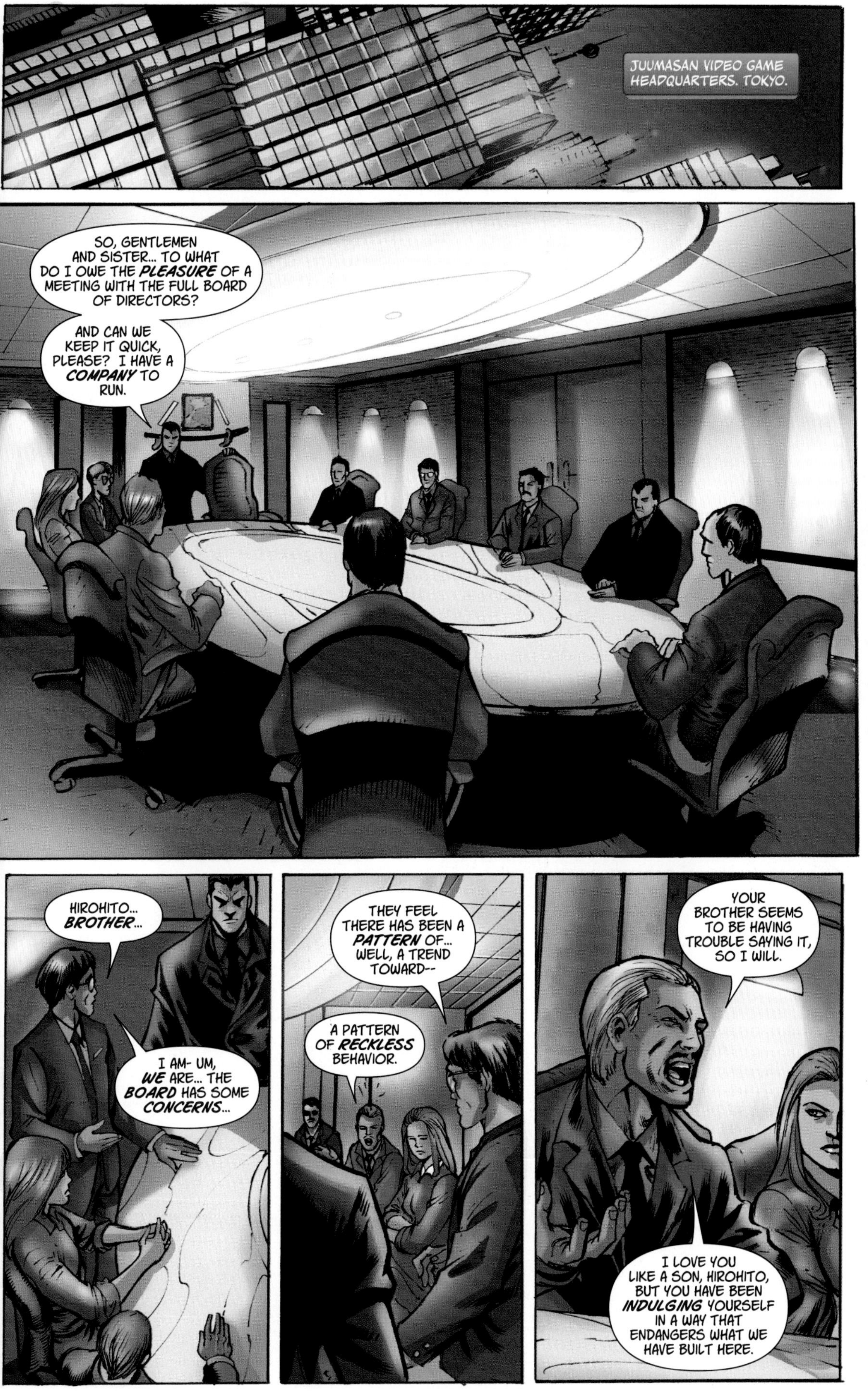

JUUMASAN VIDEO GAME HEADQUARTERS. TOKYO.
SO, GENTLEMEN AND SISTER... TO WHAT DO I OWE THE PLEASURE OF A MEETING WITH THE FULL BOARD OF DIRECTORS?
AND CAN WE KEEP IT QUICK, PLEASE? I HAVE A COMPANY TO RUN.
HIROHITO... BROTHER...
I AM- UM, WE ARE... THE BOARD HAS SOME CONCERNS...
THEY FEEL THERE HAS BEEN A PATTERN OF... WELL, A TREND TOWARD--
A PATTERN OF RECKLESS BEHAVIOR.
YOUR BROTHER SEEMS TO BE HAVING TROUBLE SAYING IT, SO I WILL.
I LOVE YOU LIKE A SON, HIROHITO, BUT YOU HAVE BEEN INDULGING YOURSELF IN A WAY THAT ENDANGERS WHAT WE HAVE BUILT HERE.

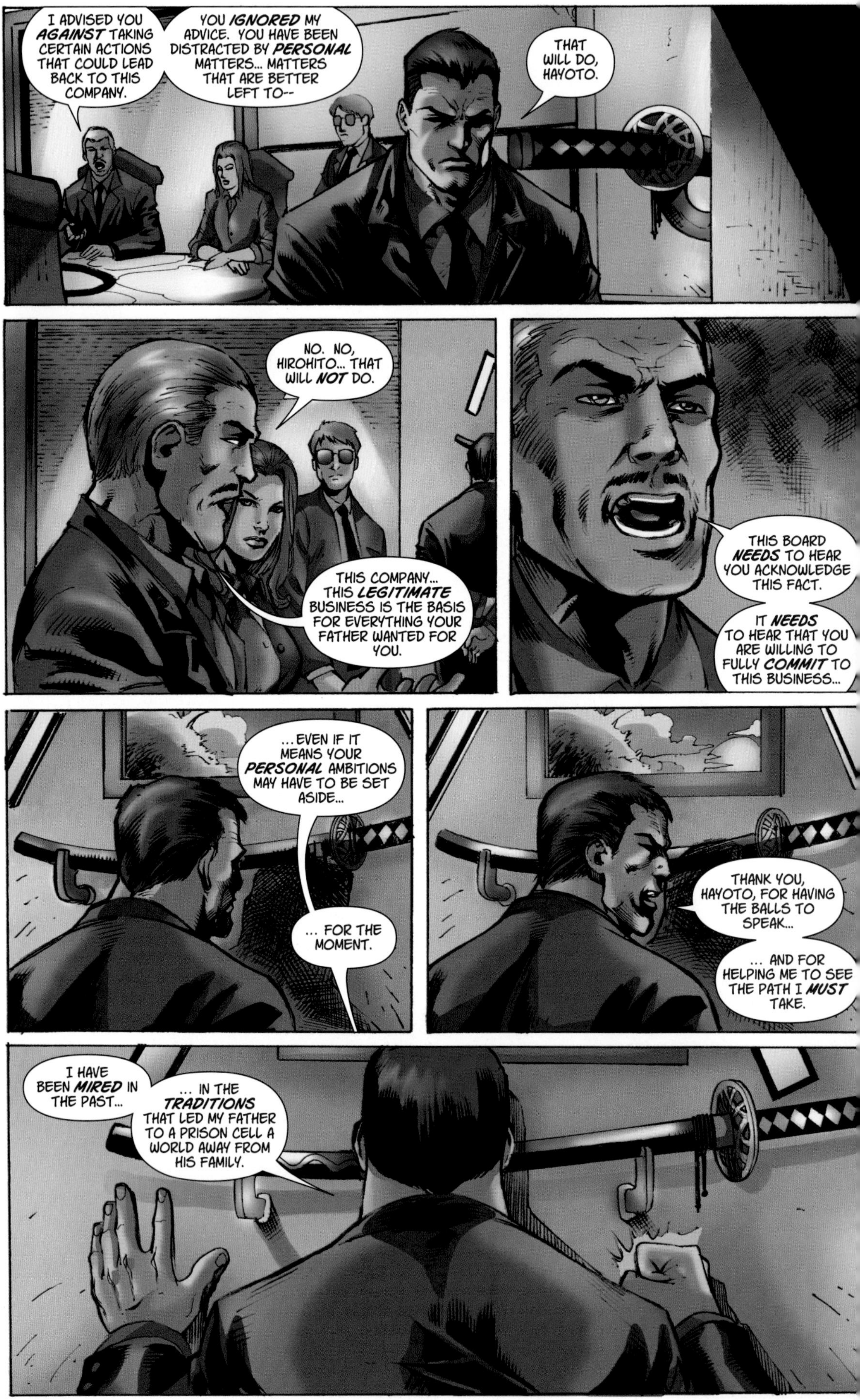

I ADVISED YOU AGAINST TAKING CERTAIN ACTIONS THAT COULD LEAD BACK TO THIS COMPANY.
YOU IGNORED MY ADVICE. YOU HAVE BEEN DISTRACTED BY PERSONAL MATTERS... MATTERS THAT ARE BETTER LEFT TO--
THAT WILL DO, HAYOTO.
NO. NO, HIROHITO... THAT WILL NOT DO.
THIS COMPANY... THIS LEGITIMATE BUSINESS IS THE BASIS FOR EVERYTHING YOUR FATHER WANTED FOR YOU.
THIS BOARD NEEDS TO HEAR YOU ACKNOWLEDGE THIS FACT.
IT NEEDS TO HEAR THAT YOU ARE WILLING TO FULLY COMMIT TO THIS BUSINESS...
...EVEN IF IT MEANS YOUR PERSONAL AMBITIONS MAY HAVE TO BE SET ASIDE...
... FOR THE MOMENT.
THANK YOU, HAYOTO, FOR HAVING THE BALLS TO SPEAK...
... AND FOR HELPING ME TO SEE THE PATH I MUST TAKE.
I HAVE BEEN MIRED IN THE PAST...
... IN THE TRADITIONS THAT LED MY FATHER TO A PRISON CELL A WORLD AWAY FROM HIS FAMILY.

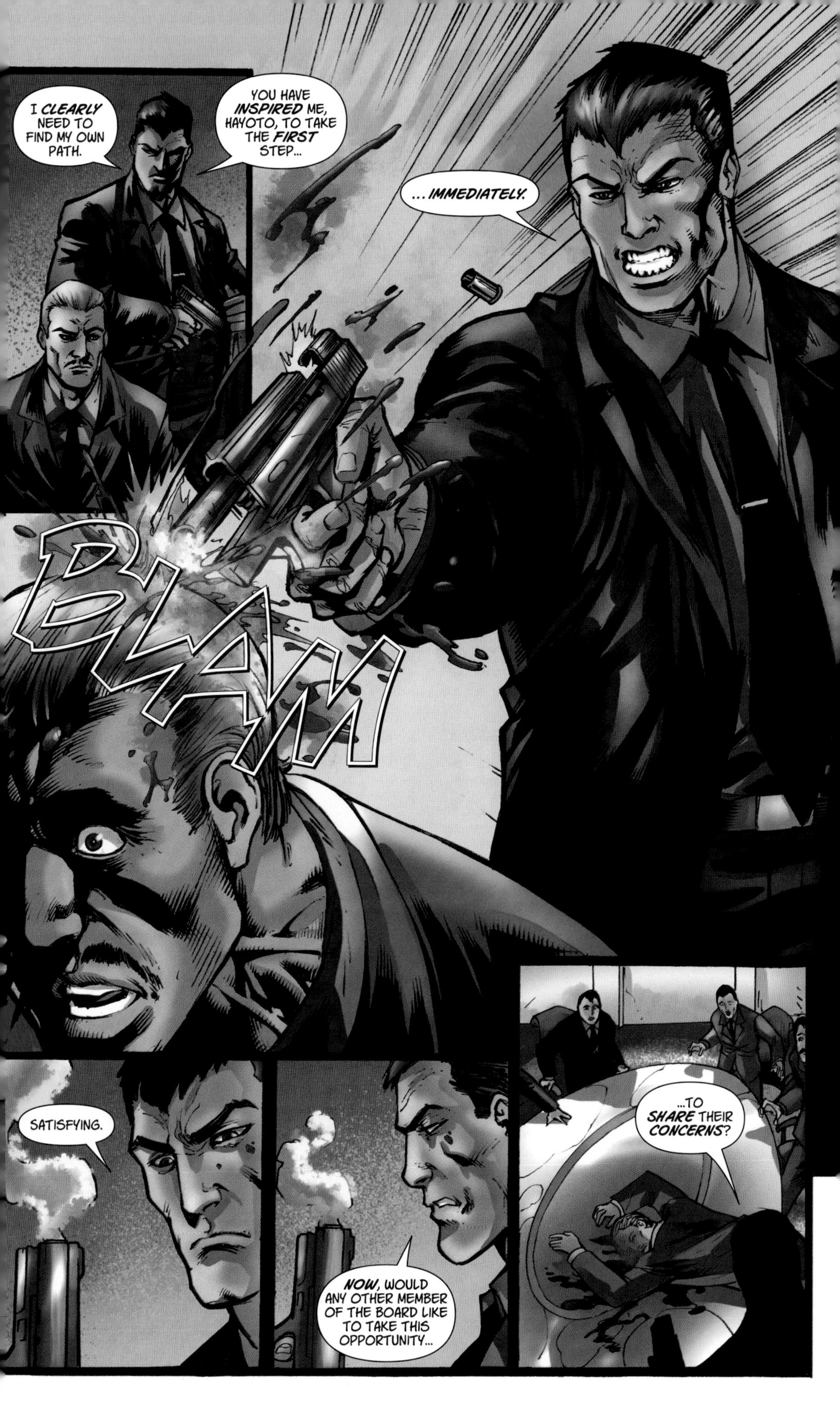
I CLEARLY NEED TO FIND MY OWN PATH.
YOU HAVE INSPIRED ME, HAYOTO, TO TAKE THE FIRST STEP...
... IMMEDIATELY.
BLAM
SATISFYING.
NOW, WOULD ANY OTHER MEMBER OF THE BOARD LIKE TO TAKE THIS OPPORTUNITY...
...TO SHARE THEIR CONCERNS?

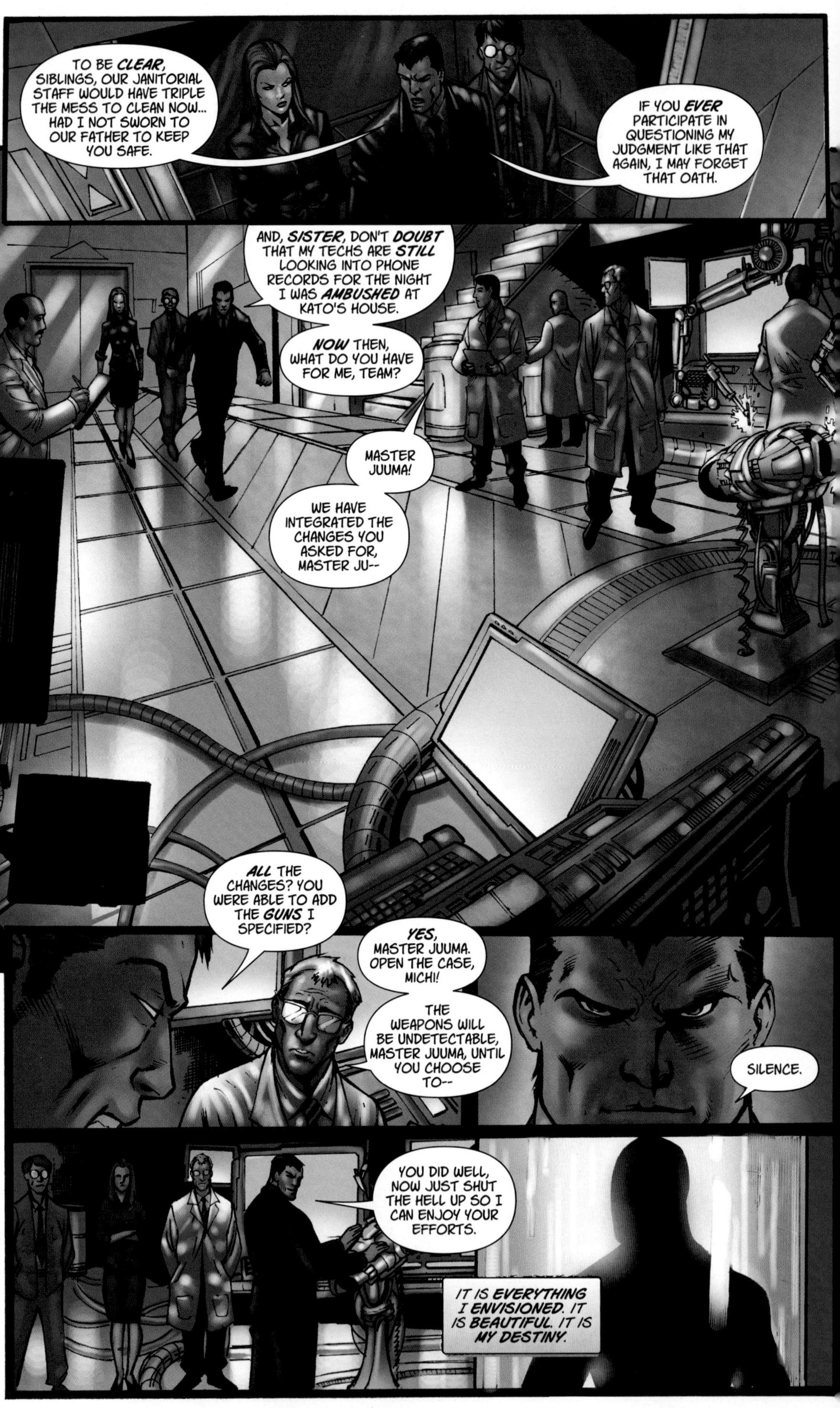
TO BE CLEAR, SIBLINGS, OUR JANITORIAL STAFF WOULD HAVE TRIPLE THE MESS TO CLEAN NOW... HAD I NOT SWORN TO OUR FATHER TO KEEP YOU SAFE.
IF YOU EVER PARTICIPATE IN QUESTIONING MY JUDGMENT LIKE THAT AGAIN, I MAY FORGET THAT OATH.
AND, SISTER, DON'T DOUBT THAT MY TECHS ARE STILL LOOKING INTO PHONE RECORDS FOR THE NIGHT I WAS AMBUSHED AT KATO'S HOUSE.
NOW THEN, WHAT DO YOU HAVE FOR ME, TEAM?
MASTER JUUMA!
WE HAVE INTEGRATED THE CHANGES YOU ASKED FOR, MASTER JU--
ALL THE CHANGES? YOU WERE ABLE TO ADD THE GUNS I SPECIFIED?
YES, MASTER JUUMA. OPEN THE CASE, MICHI!
THE WEAPONS WILL BE UNDETECTABLE, MASTER JUUMA, UNTIL YOU CHOOSE TO--
SILENCE.
YOU DID WELL, NOW JUST SHUT THE HELL UP SO I CAN ENJOY YOUR EFFORTS.
IT IS EVERYTHING I ENVISIONED. IT IS BEAUTIFUL. IT IS MY DESTINY.

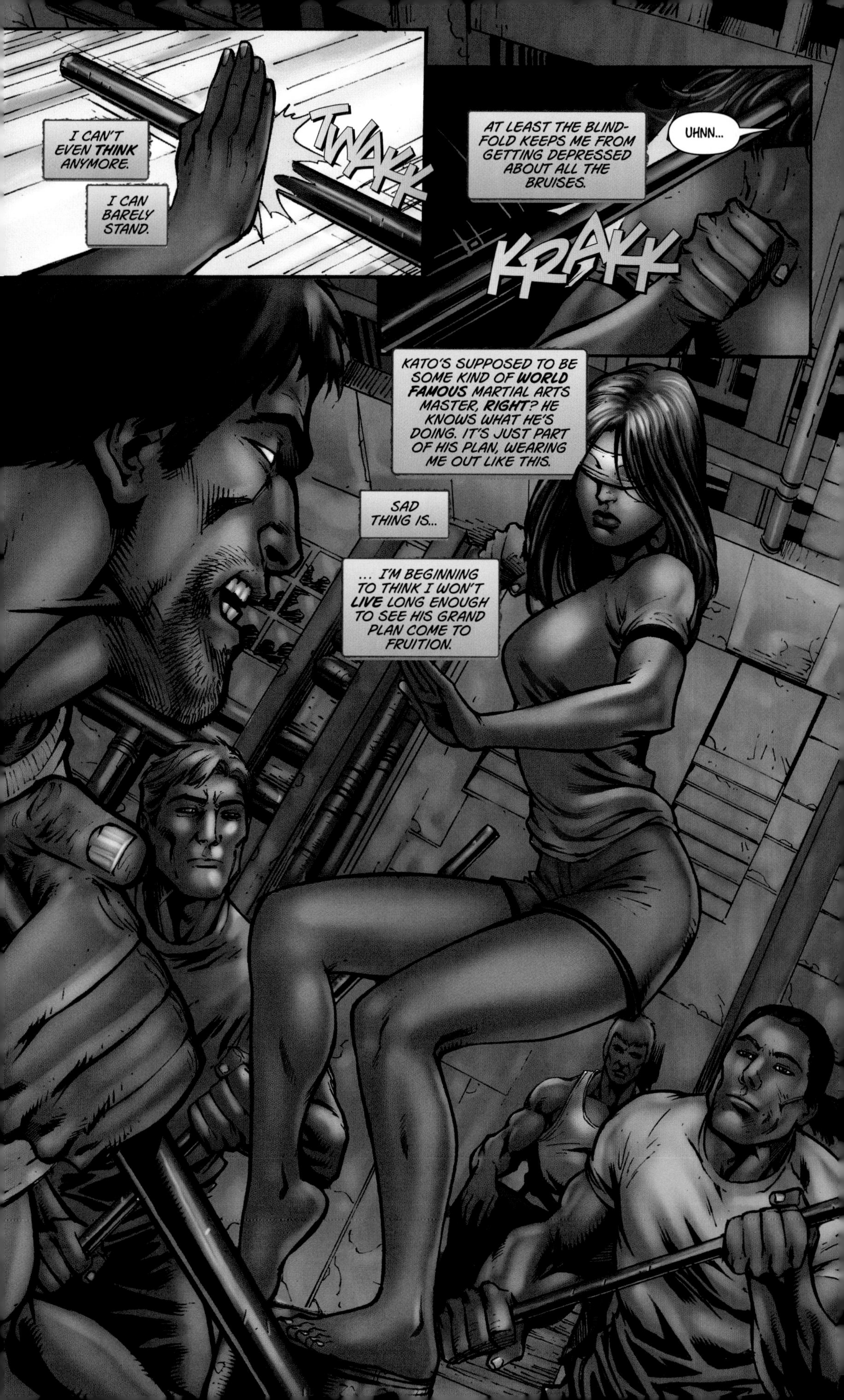
I CAN'T EVEN THINK ANYMORE.
I CAN BARELY STAND.
TWAKK
AT LEAST THE BLIND-FOLD KEEPS ME FROM GETTING DEPRESSED ABOUT ALL THE BRUISES.
UHNN...
KRAKK
KATO'S SUPPOSED TO BE SOME KIND OF WORLD FAMOUS MARTIAL ARTS MASTER, RIGHT? HE KNOWS WHAT HE'S DOING. IT'S JUST PART OF HIS PLAN, WEARING ME OUT LIKE THIS.
SAD THING IS...
... I'M BEGINNING TO THINK I WON'T LIVE LONG ENOUGH TO SEE HIS GRAND PLAN COME TO FRUITION.

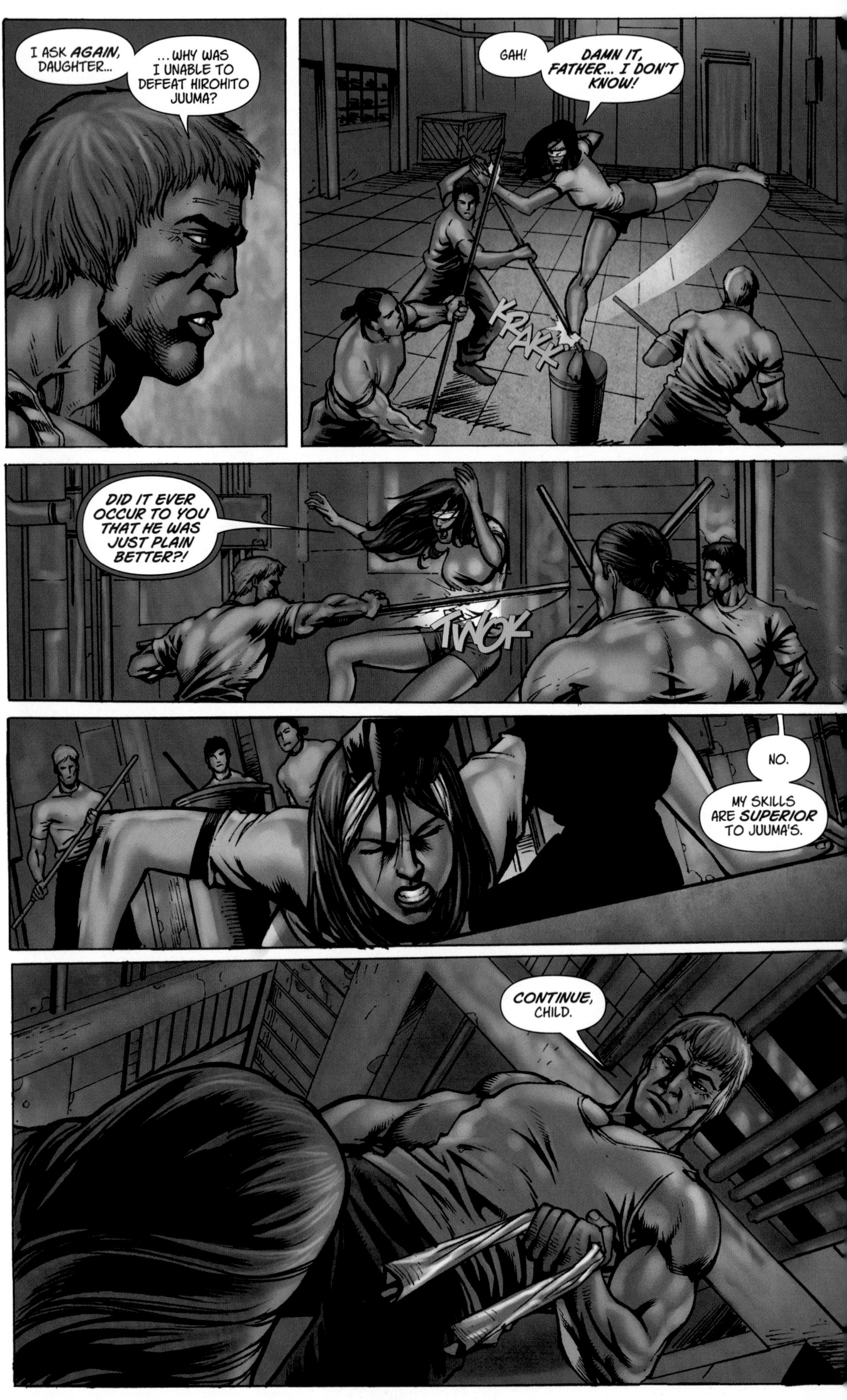

I ASK AGAIN, DAUGHTER...
...WHY WAS I UNABLE TO DEFEAT HIROHITO JUUMA?
GAH!
DAMN IT, FATHER... I DON'T KNOW!
KRAKK
DID IT EVER OCCUR TO YOU THAT HE WAS JUST PLAIN BETTER?!
TWOK
NO.
MY SKILLS ARE SUPERIOR TO JUUMA'S.
CONTINUE, CHILD.

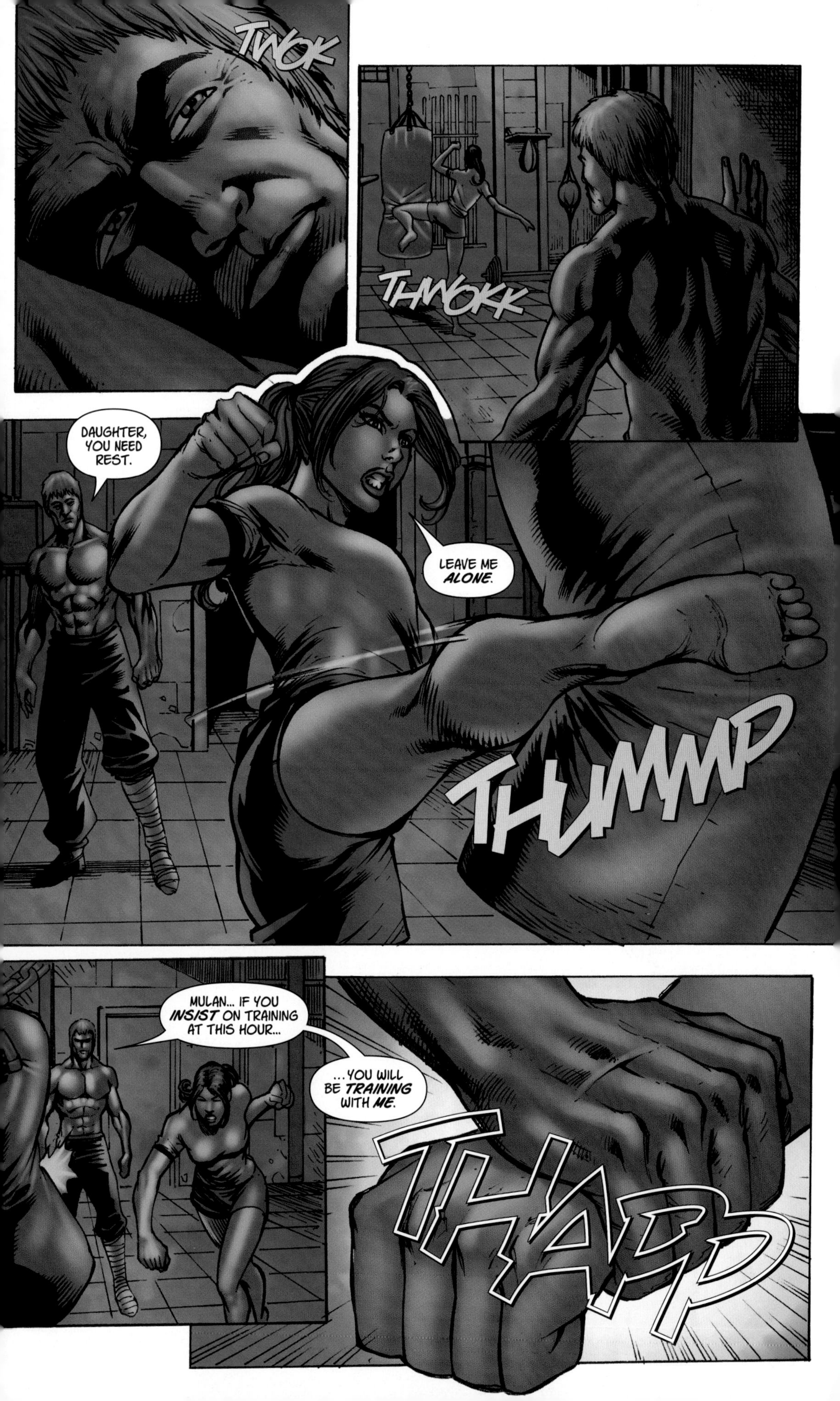
TWOK
THWOKK
DAUGHTER, YOU NEED REST.
LEAVE ME ALONE.
THUMMP
MULAN... IF YOU INSIST ON TRAINING AT THIS HOUR...
...YOU WILL BE TRAINING WITH ME.
THAPP

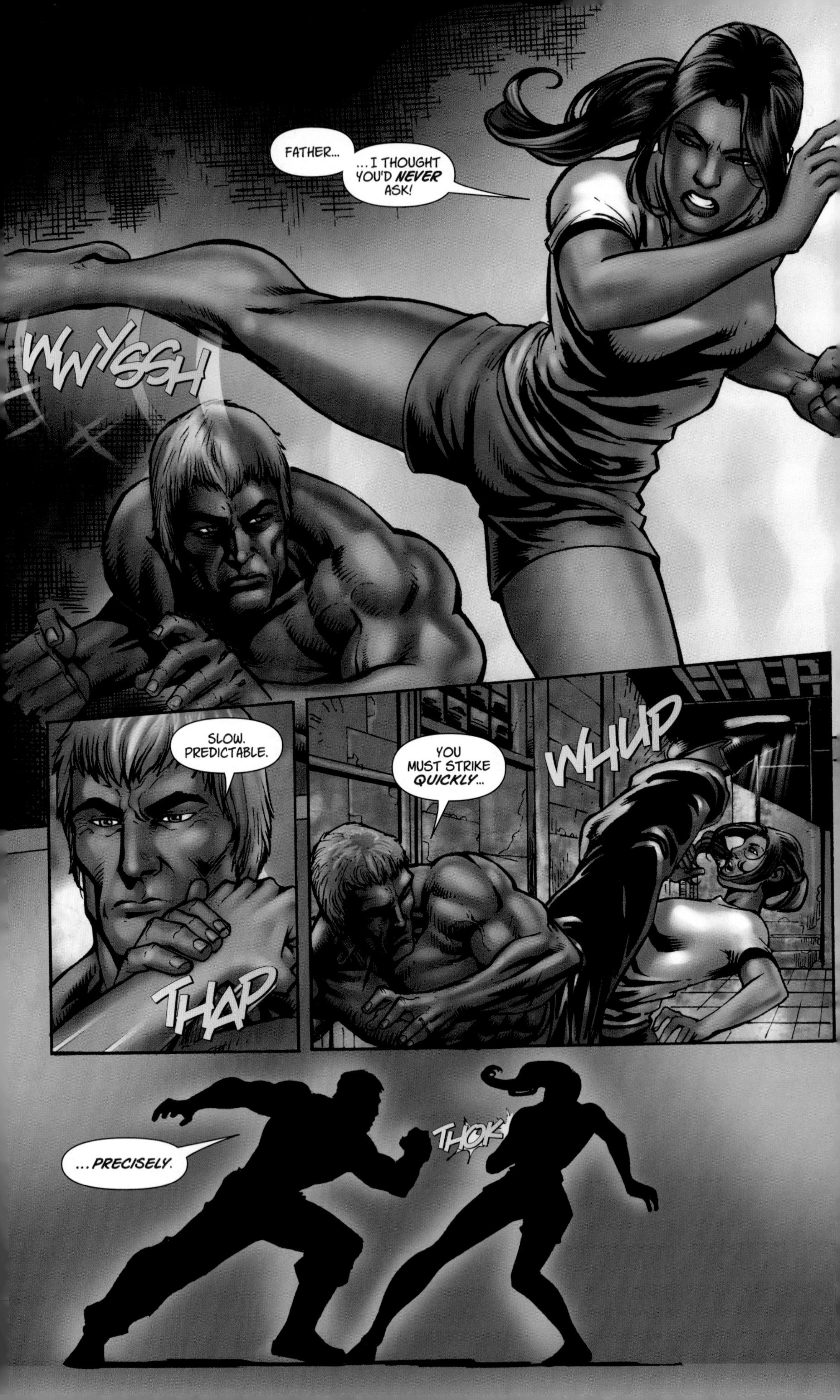
FATHER...
...I THOUGHT YOU'D *NEVER* ASK!
WWYSSH
SLOW. PREDICTABLE.
THAP
YOU MUST STRIKE *QUICKLY*...
WHUP
...*PRECISELY*.
THOK

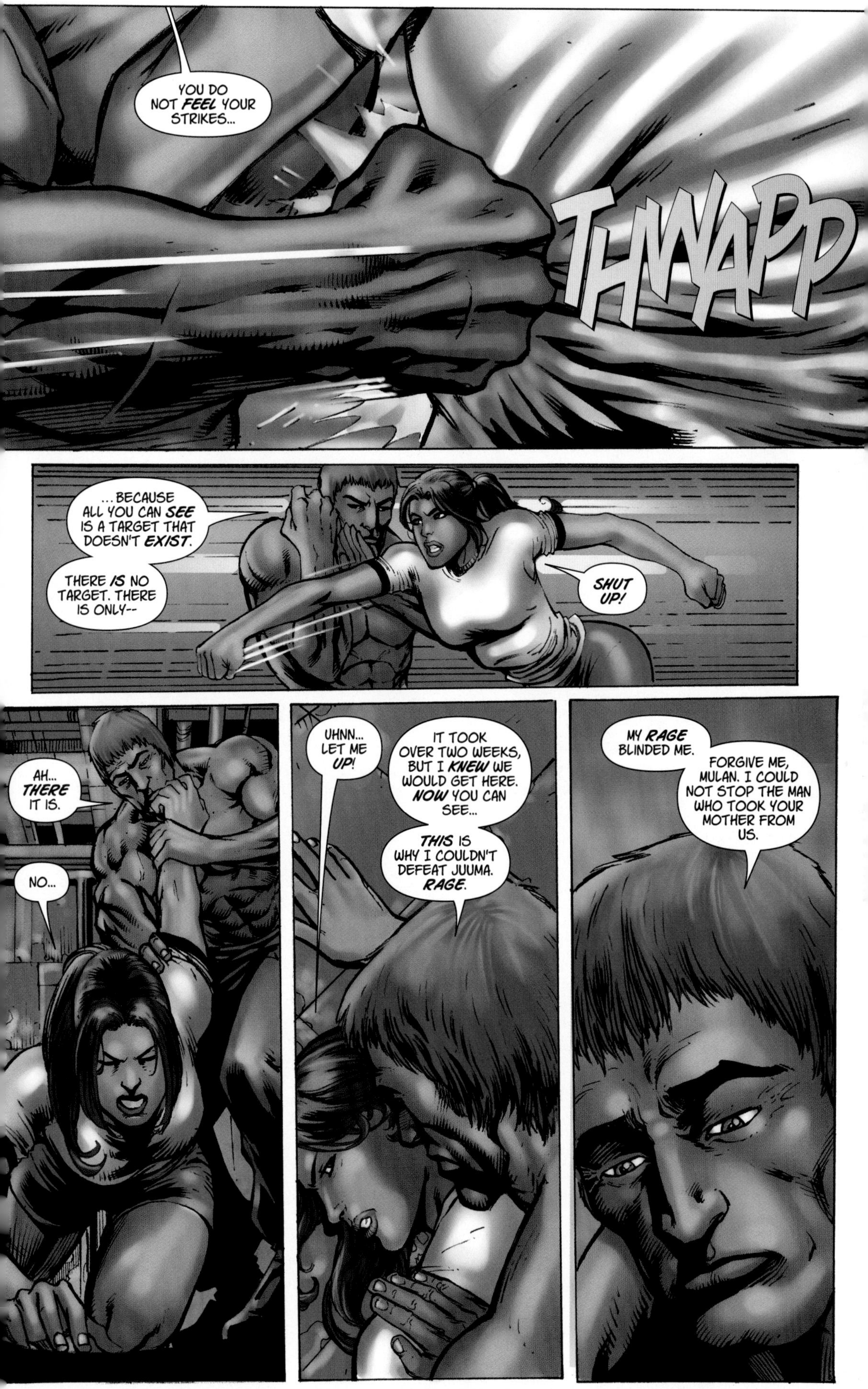
YOU DO NOT FEEL YOUR STRIKES...
THWAPP
...BECAUSE ALL YOU CAN SEE IS A TARGET THAT DOESN'T EXIST.
THERE IS NO TARGET. THERE IS ONLY--
SHUT UP!
AH... THERE IT IS.
NO...
UHNN... LET ME UP!
IT TOOK OVER TWO WEEKS, BUT I KNEW WE WOULD GET HERE. NOW YOU CAN SEE...
THIS IS WHY I COULDN'T DEFEAT JUUMA. RAGE.
MY RAGE BLINDED ME.
FORGIVE ME, MULAN. I COULD NOT STOP THE MAN WHO TOOK YOUR MOTHER FROM US.

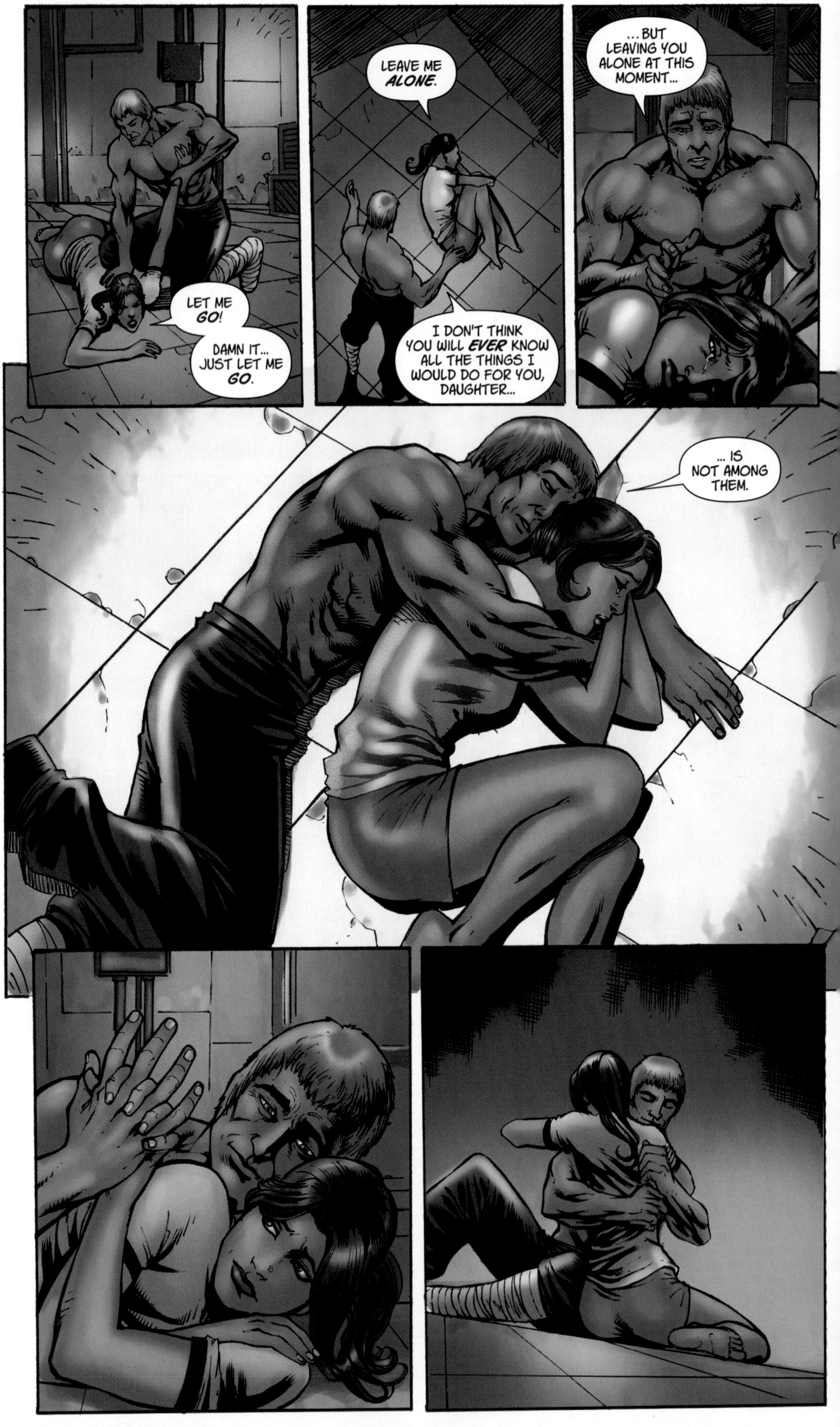

LET ME GO!
DAMN IT... JUST LET ME GO.
LEAVE ME ALONE.
I DON'T THINK YOU WILL EVER KNOW ALL THE THINGS I WOULD DO FOR YOU, DAUGHTER...
... BUT LEAVING YOU ALONE AT THIS MOMENT...
... IS NOT AMONG THEM.

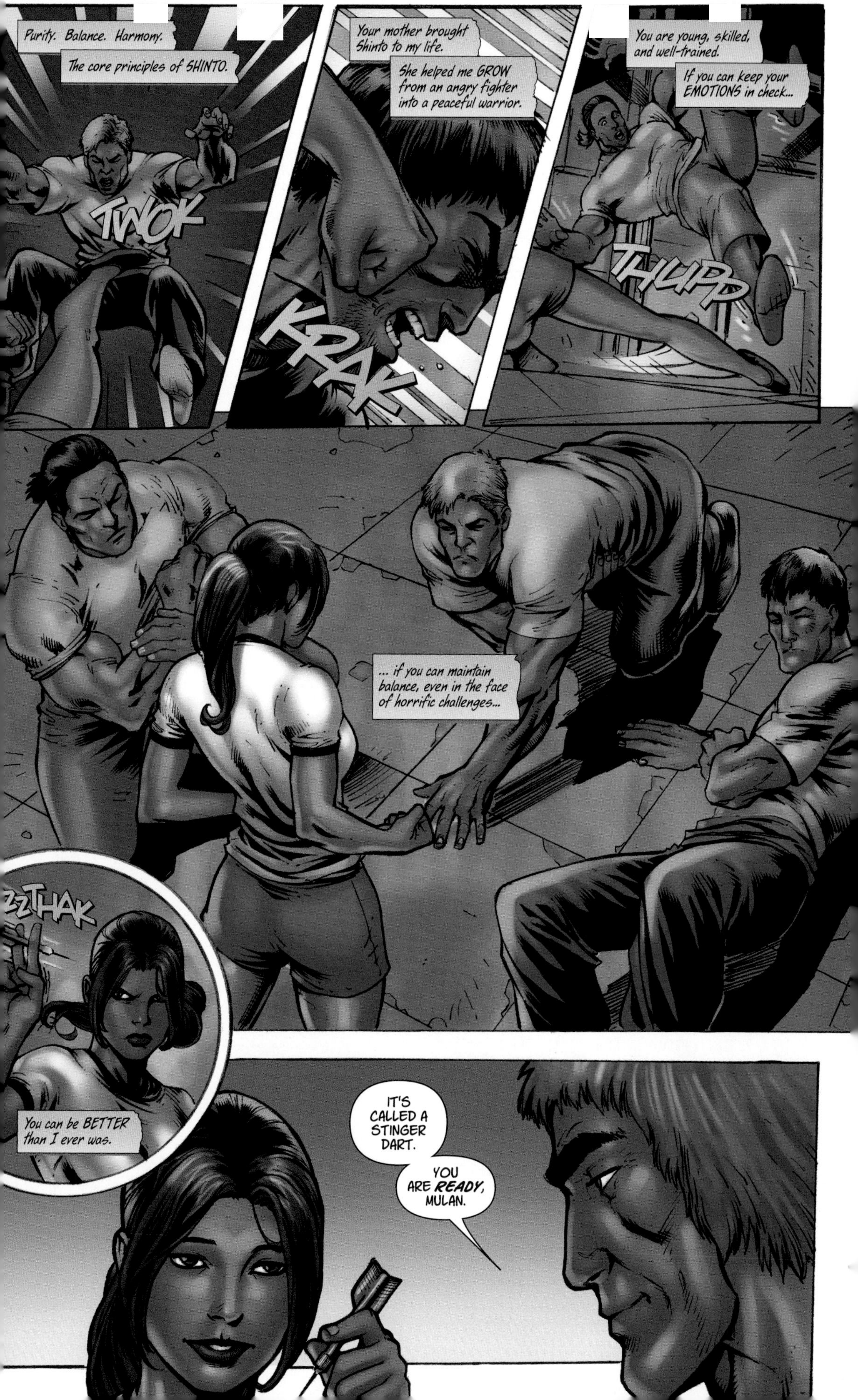

Purity. Balance. Harmony.
The core principles of SHINTO.
TWOK
Your mother brought Shinto to my life.
She helped me GROW from an angry fighter into a peaceful warrior.
KRAK
You are young, skilled, and well-trained.
If you can keep your EMOTIONS in check...
THUPP
... if you can maintain balance, even in the face of horrific challenges...
ZZTHAK
You can be BETTER than I ever was.
IT'S CALLED A STINGER DART.
YOU ARE ***READY***, MULAN.

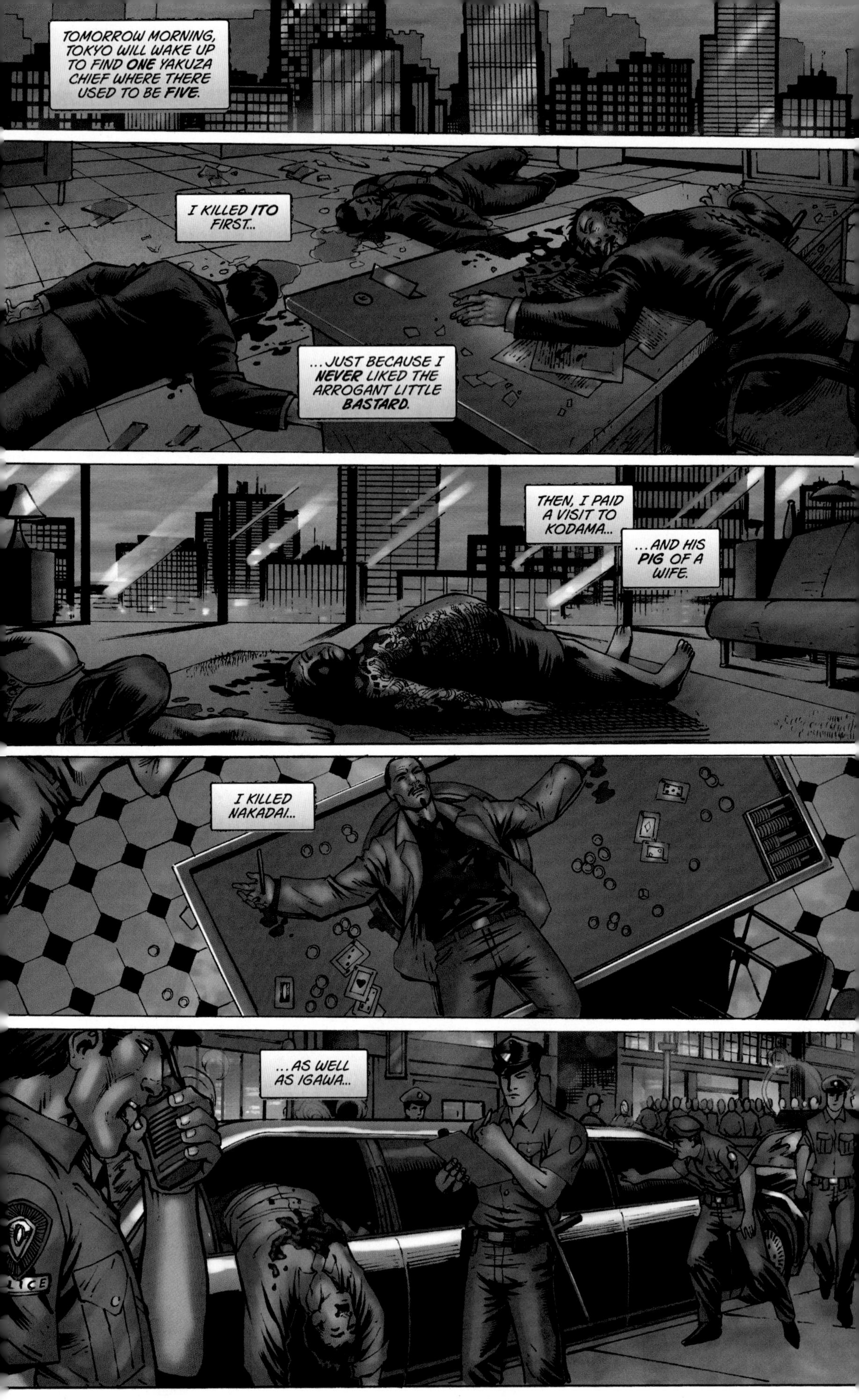
TOMORROW MORNING, TOKYO WILL WAKE UP TO FIND ONE YAKUZA CHIEF WHERE THERE USED TO BE FIVE.
I KILLED ITO FIRST...
...JUST BECAUSE I NEVER LIKED THE ARROGANT LITTLE BASTARD.
THEN, I PAID A VISIT TO KODAMA...
...AND HIS PIG OF A WIFE.
I KILLED NAKADAI...
...AS WELL AS IGAWA...
LICE

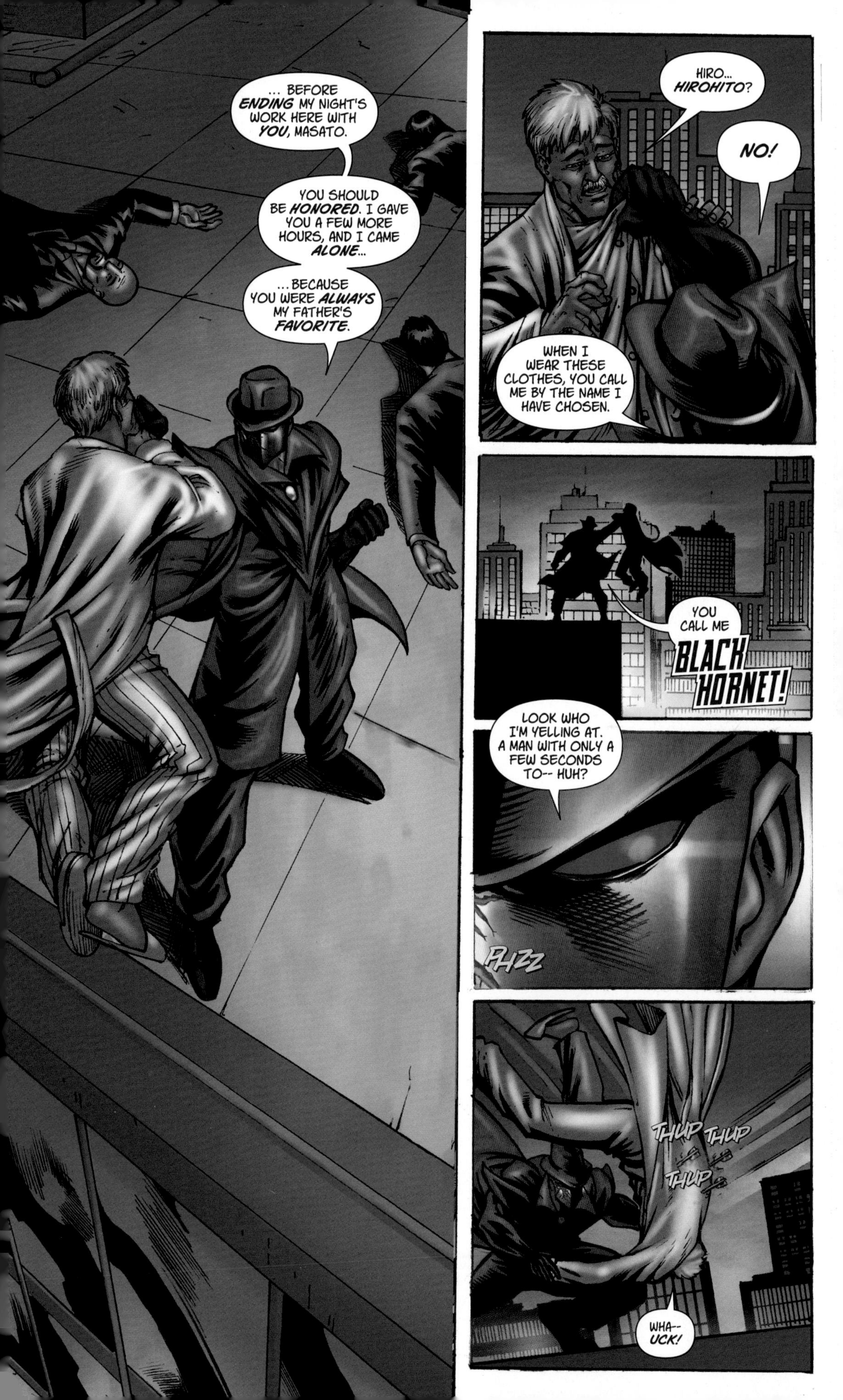
... BEFORE ENDING MY NIGHT'S WORK HERE WITH YOU, MASATO.
YOU SHOULD BE HONORED. I GAVE YOU A FEW MORE HOURS, AND I CAME ALONE...
...BECAUSE YOU WERE ALWAYS MY FATHER'S FAVORITE.
HIRO... HIROHITO?
NO!
WHEN I WEAR THESE CLOTHES, YOU CALL ME BY THE NAME I HAVE CHOSEN.
YOU CALL ME BLACK HORNET!
LOOK WHO I'M YELLING AT. A MAN WITH ONLY A FEW SECONDS TO-- HUH?
PHZZ
THUP THUP
THUP
WHA-- UCK!

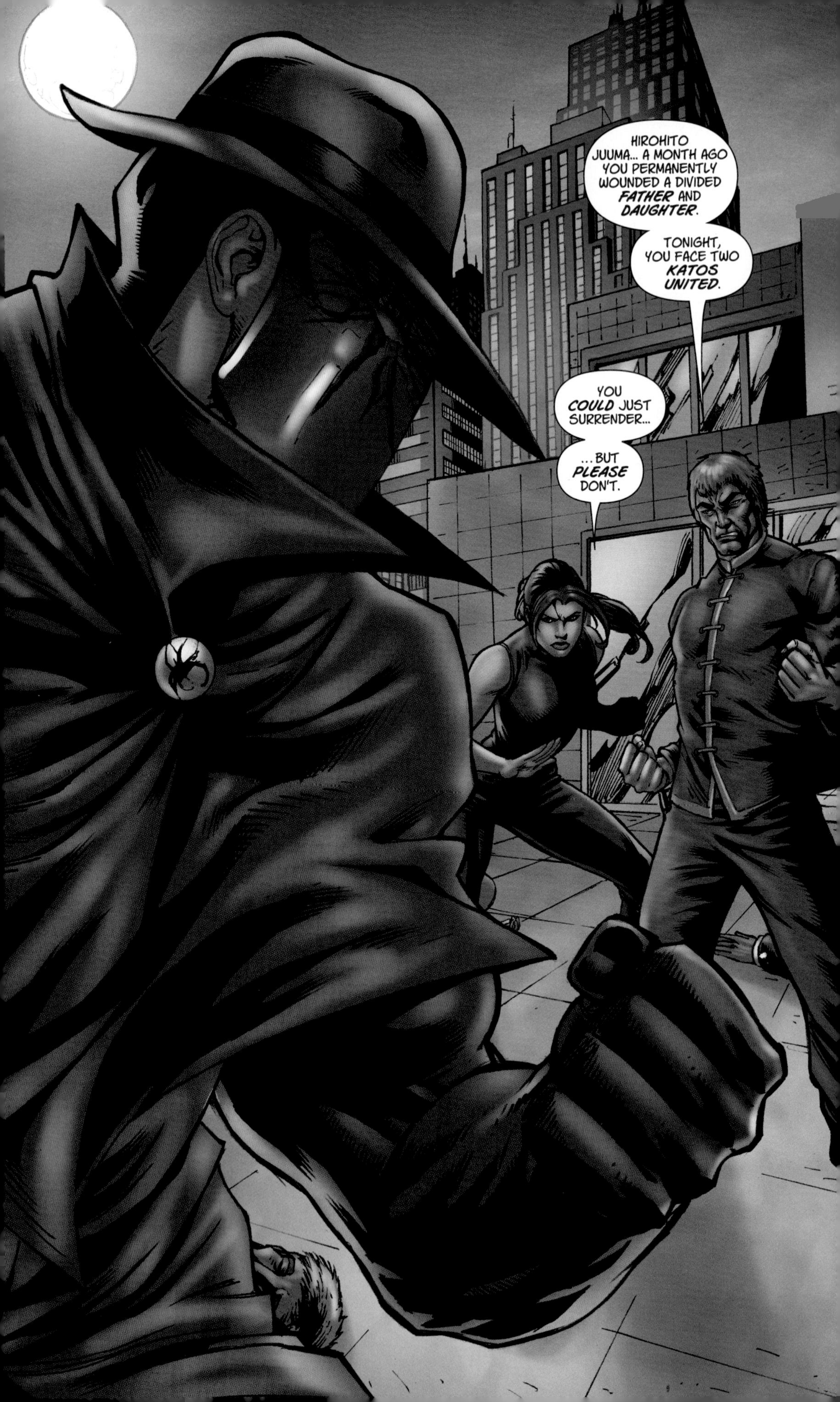

HIROHITO JUUMA... A MONTH AGO YOU PERMANENTLY WOUNDED A DIVIDED FATHER AND DAUGHTER.
TONIGHT, YOU FACE TWO KATOS UNITED.
YOU COULD JUST SURRENDER...
...BUT PLEASE DON'T.

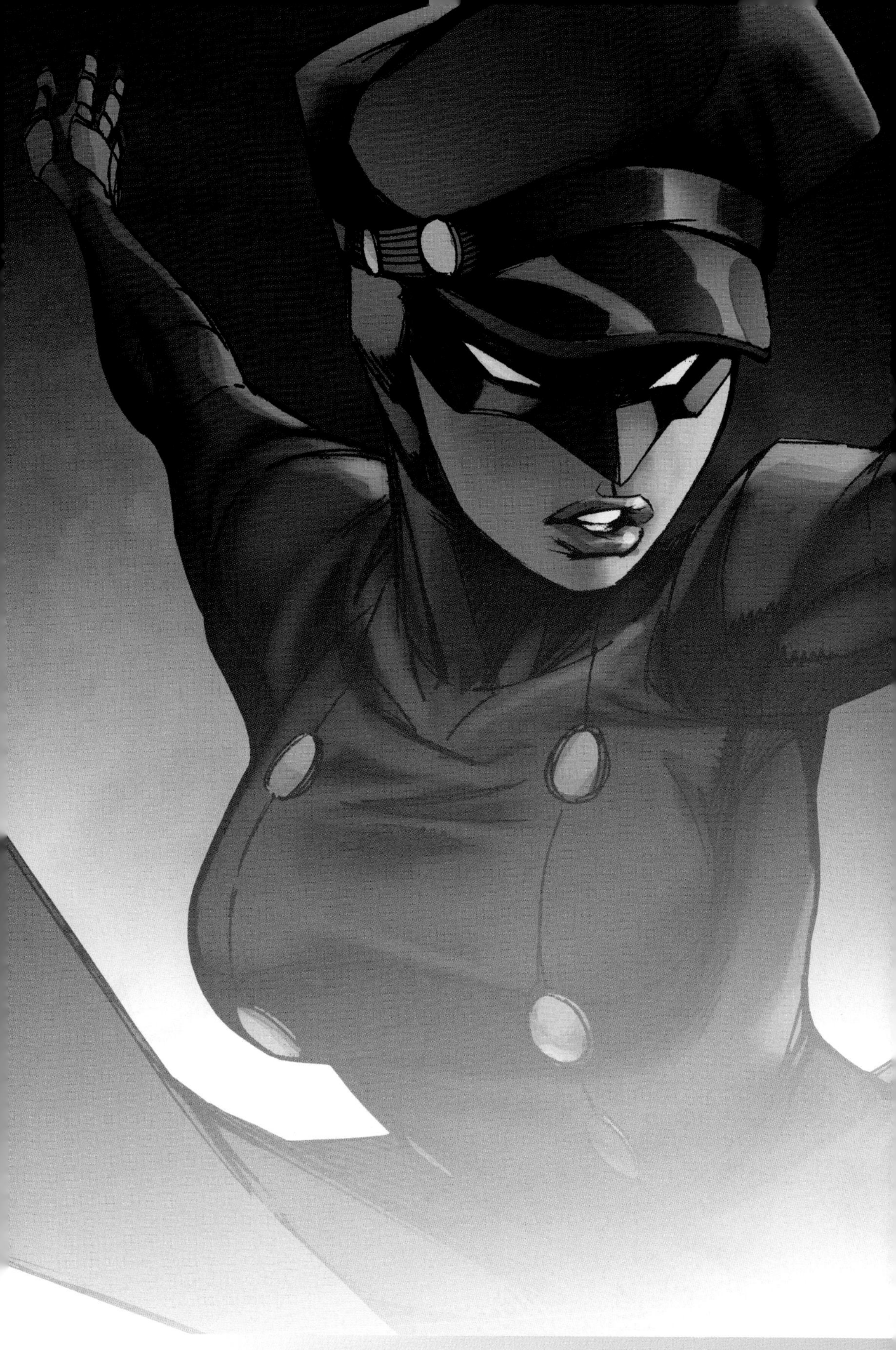

Issue FIVE

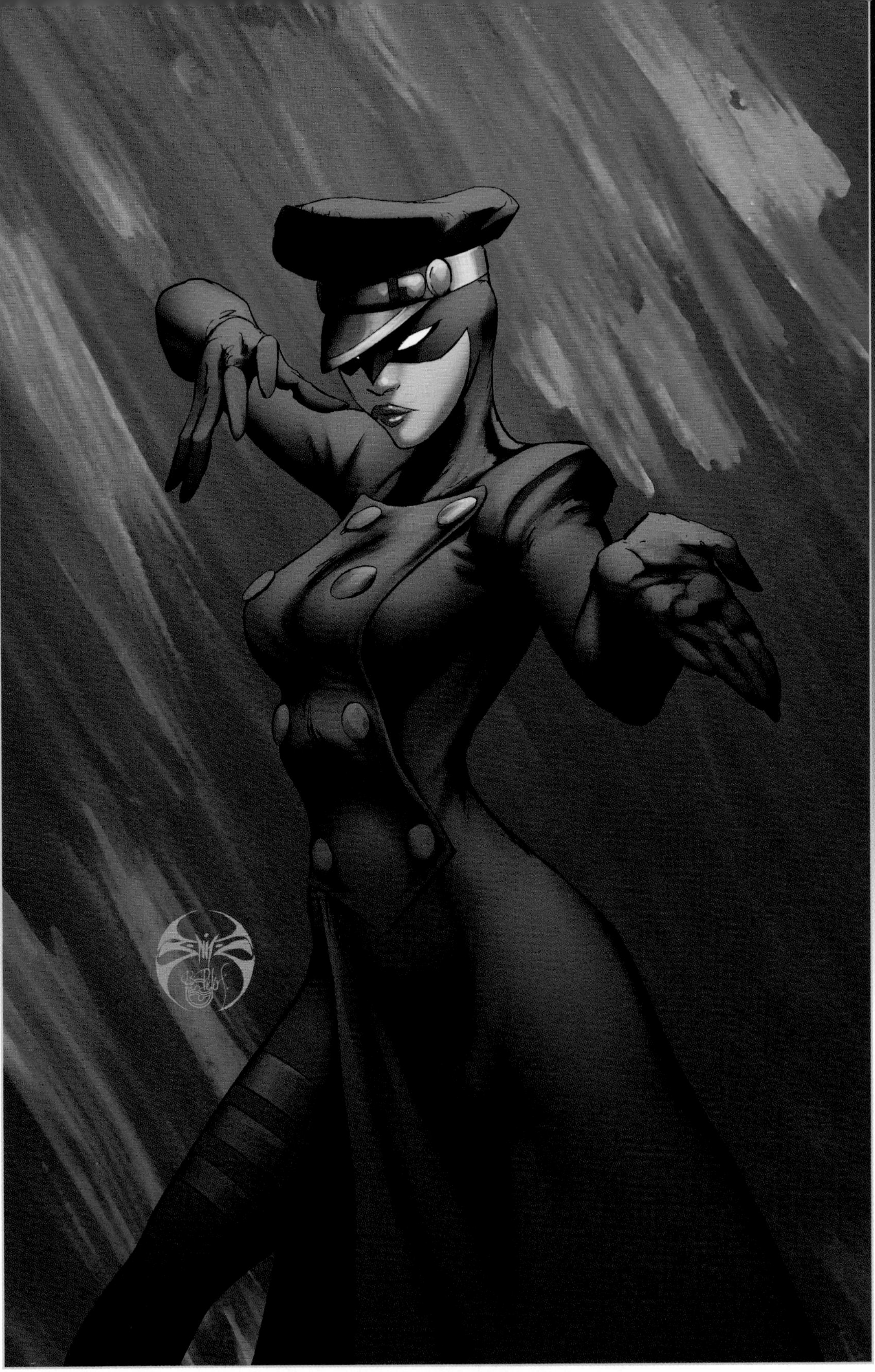

Issue five cover by **JOE BENITEZ**

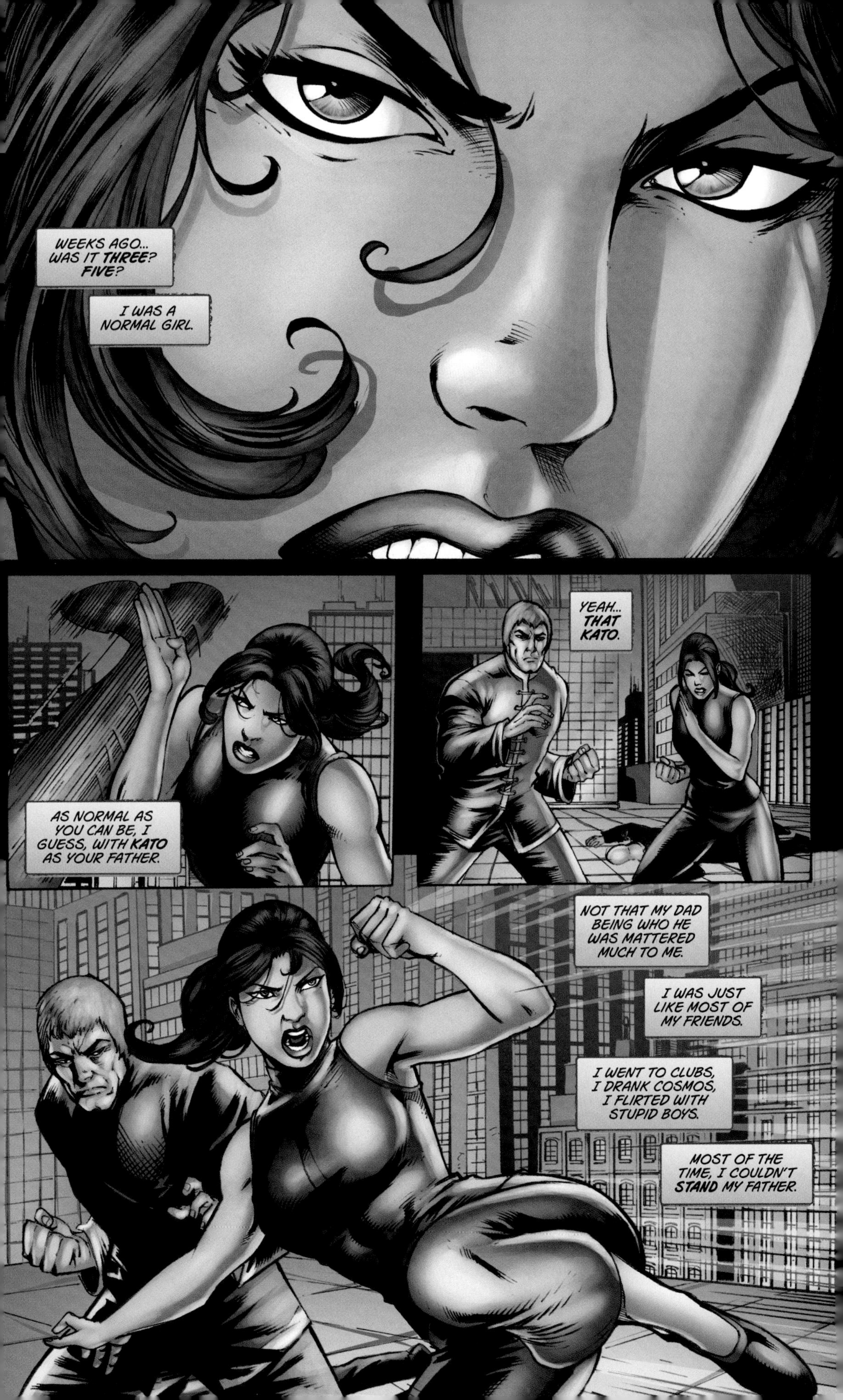
WEEKS AGO... WAS IT **THREE**? **FIVE**?
I WAS A NORMAL GIRL.
AS NORMAL AS YOU CAN BE, I GUESS, WITH **KATO** AS YOUR FATHER.
YEAH... **THAT KATO**.
NOT THAT MY DAD BEING WHO HE WAS MATTERED MUCH TO ME.
I WAS JUST LIKE MOST OF MY FRIENDS.
I WENT TO CLUBS, I DRANK COSMOS, I FLIRTED WITH STUPID BOYS.
MOST OF THE TIME, I COULDN'T **STAND** MY FATHER.

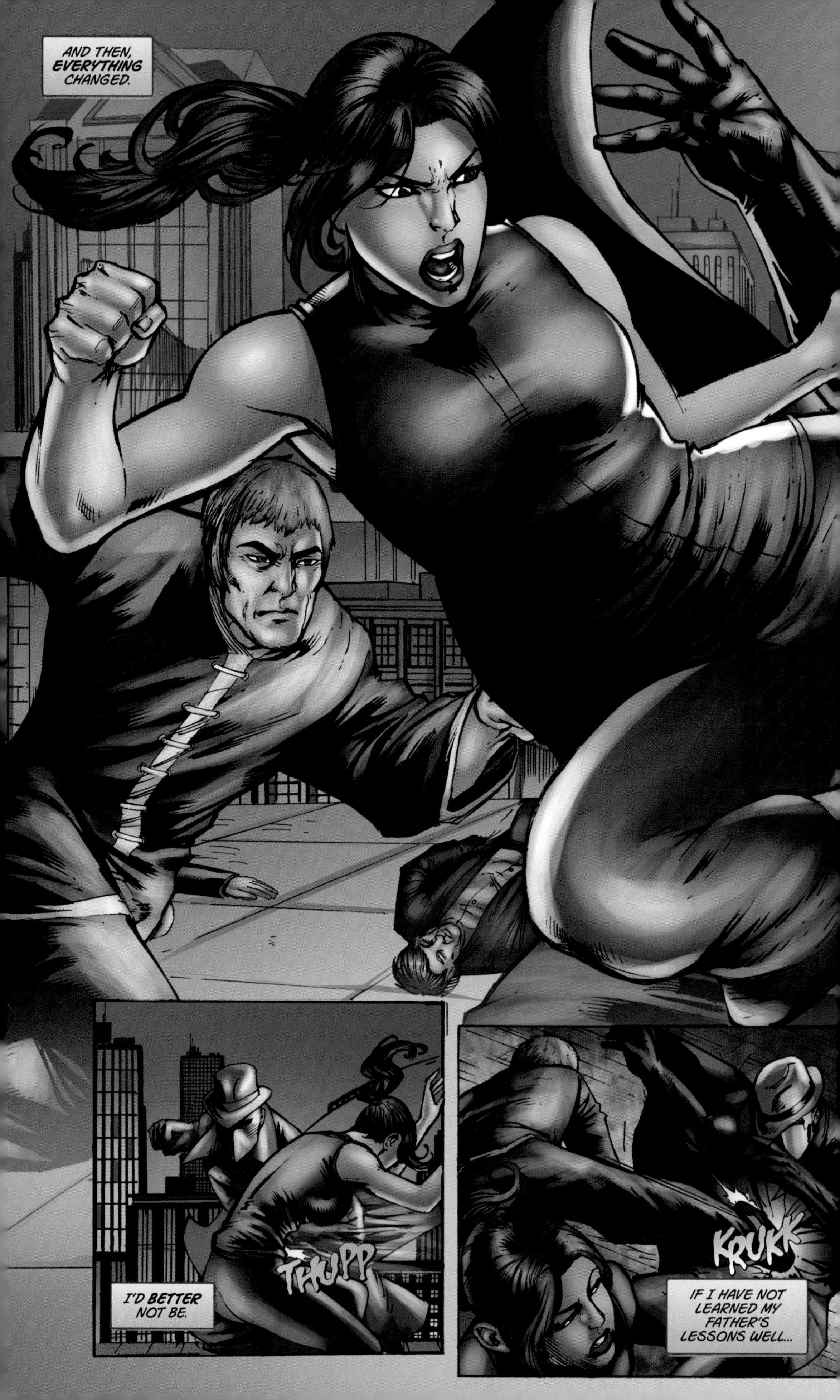
AND THEN, EVERYTHING CHANGED.
THUPP
I'D BETTER NOT BE.
KRUKK
IF I HAVE NOT LEARNED MY FATHER'S LESSONS WELL...

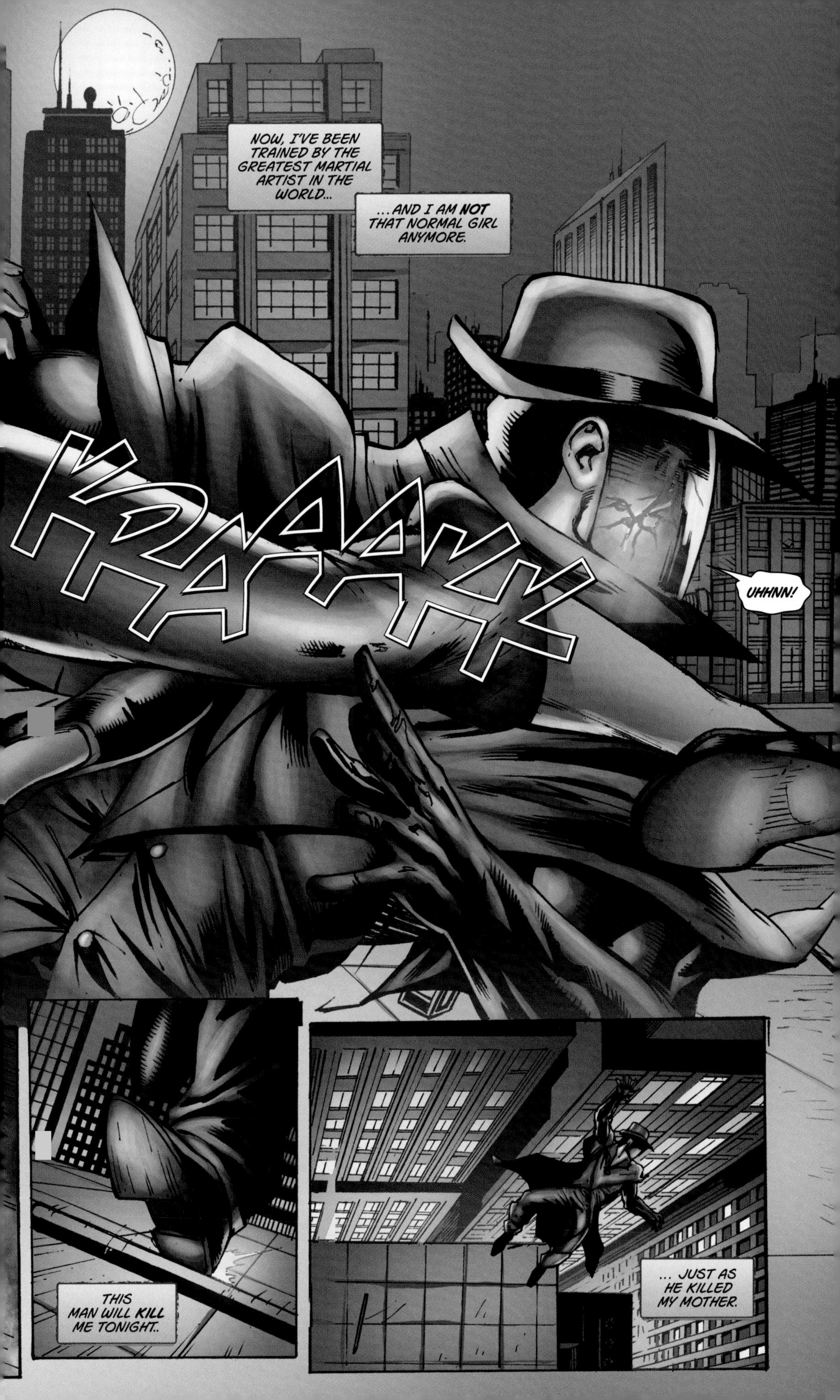
NOW, I'VE BEEN TRAINED BY THE GREATEST MARTIAL ARTIST IN THE WORLD...
...AND I AM NOT THAT NORMAL GIRL ANYMORE.
KRAAAAK
UHHNN!
THIS MAN WILL KILL ME TONIGHT..
... JUST AS HE KILLED MY MOTHER.

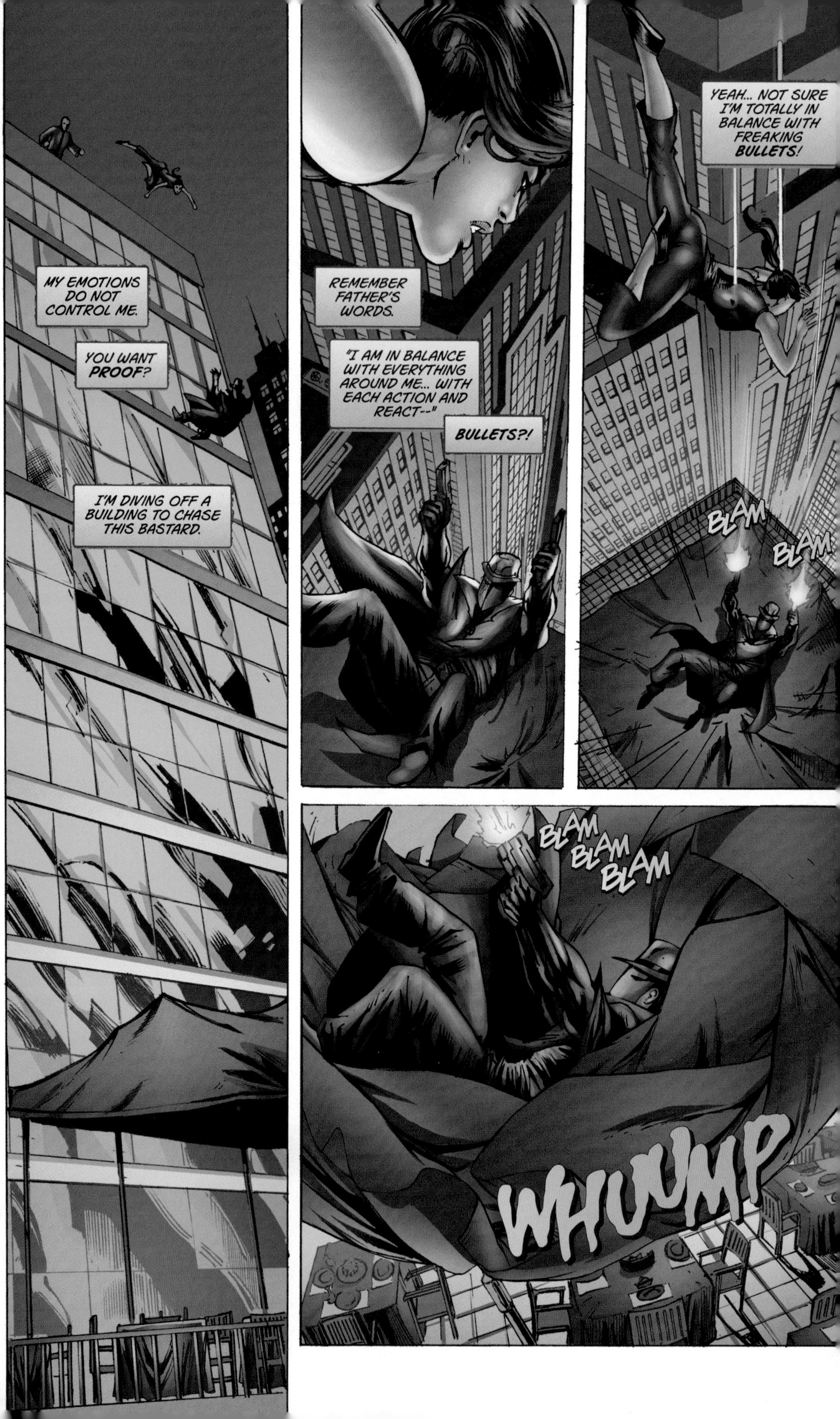
MY EMOTIONS DO NOT CONTROL ME.
YOU WANT PROOF?
I'M DIVING OFF A BUILDING TO CHASE THIS BASTARD.
REMEMBER FATHER'S WORDS.
"I AM IN BALANCE WITH EVERYTHING AROUND ME... WITH EACH ACTION AND REACT--"
BULLETS?!
YEAH... NOT SURE I'M TOTALLY IN BALANCE WITH FREAKING BULLETS!
BLAM
BLAM
BLAM BLAM BLAM
WHUUMP

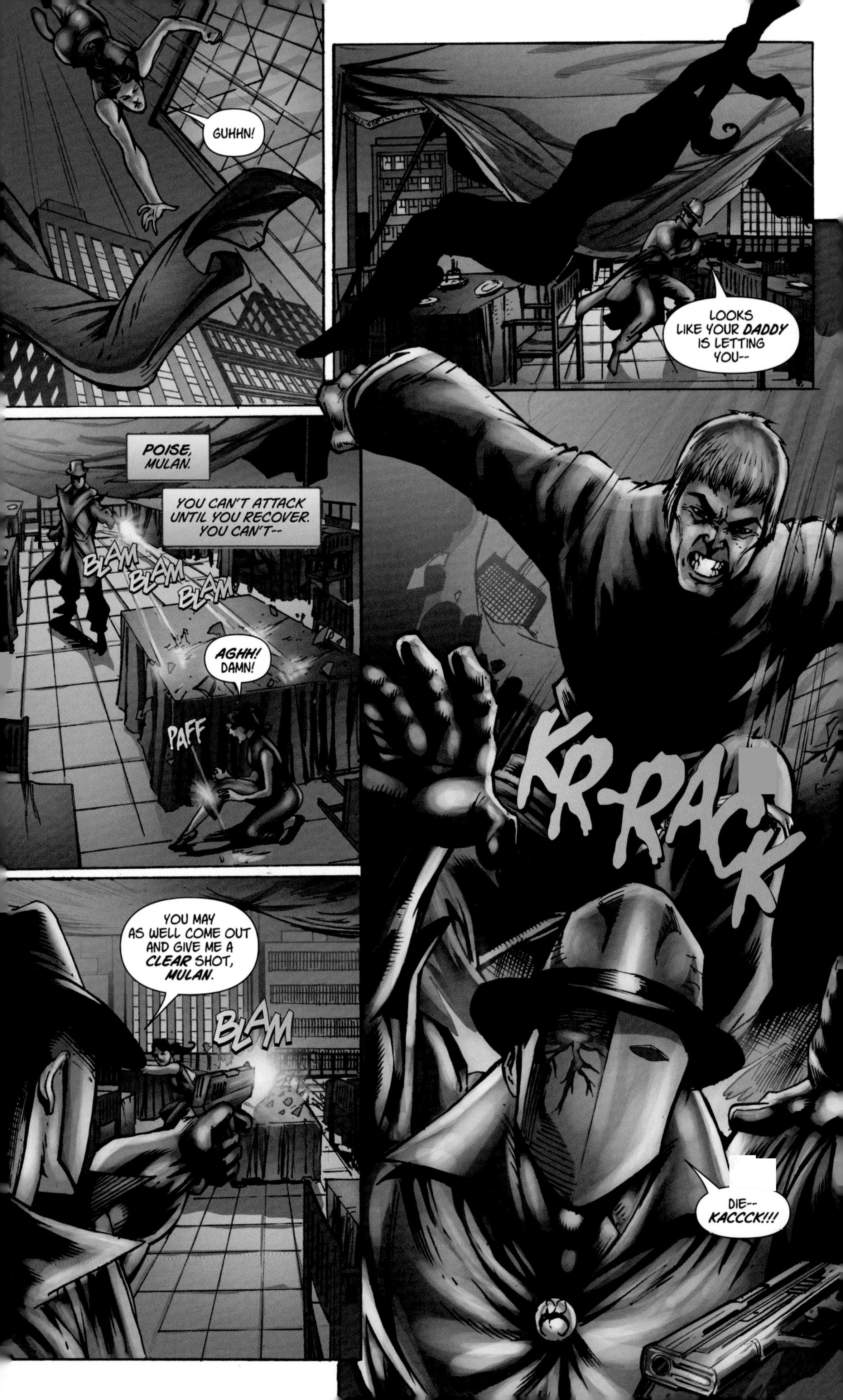
GUHHN!
LOOKS LIKE YOUR DADDY IS LETTING YOU--
POISE, MULAN.
YOU CAN'T ATTACK UNTIL YOU RECOVER. YOU CAN'T--
BLAM BLAM BLAM
AGHH! DAMN!
PAFF
YOU MAY AS WELL COME OUT AND GIVE ME A CLEAR SHOT, MULAN.
BLAM
KR-RACK
DIE-- KACCCK!!!

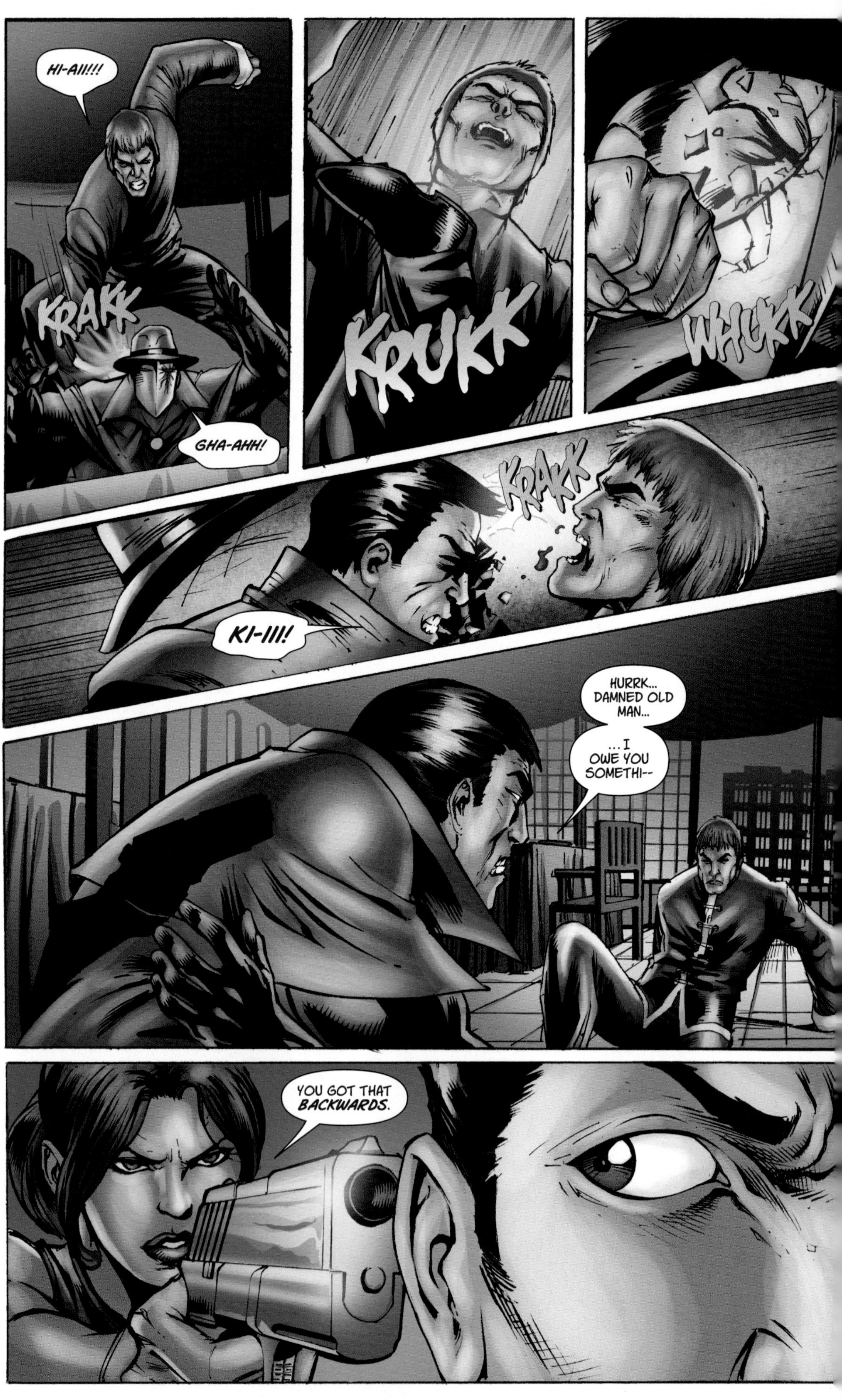

HI-AII!!!
KRAKK
GHA-AHH!
KRUKK
WHUKK
KRAKK
KI-III!
HURRK... DAMNED OLD MAN...
... I OWE YOU SOMETHI--
YOU GOT THAT *BACKWARDS*.

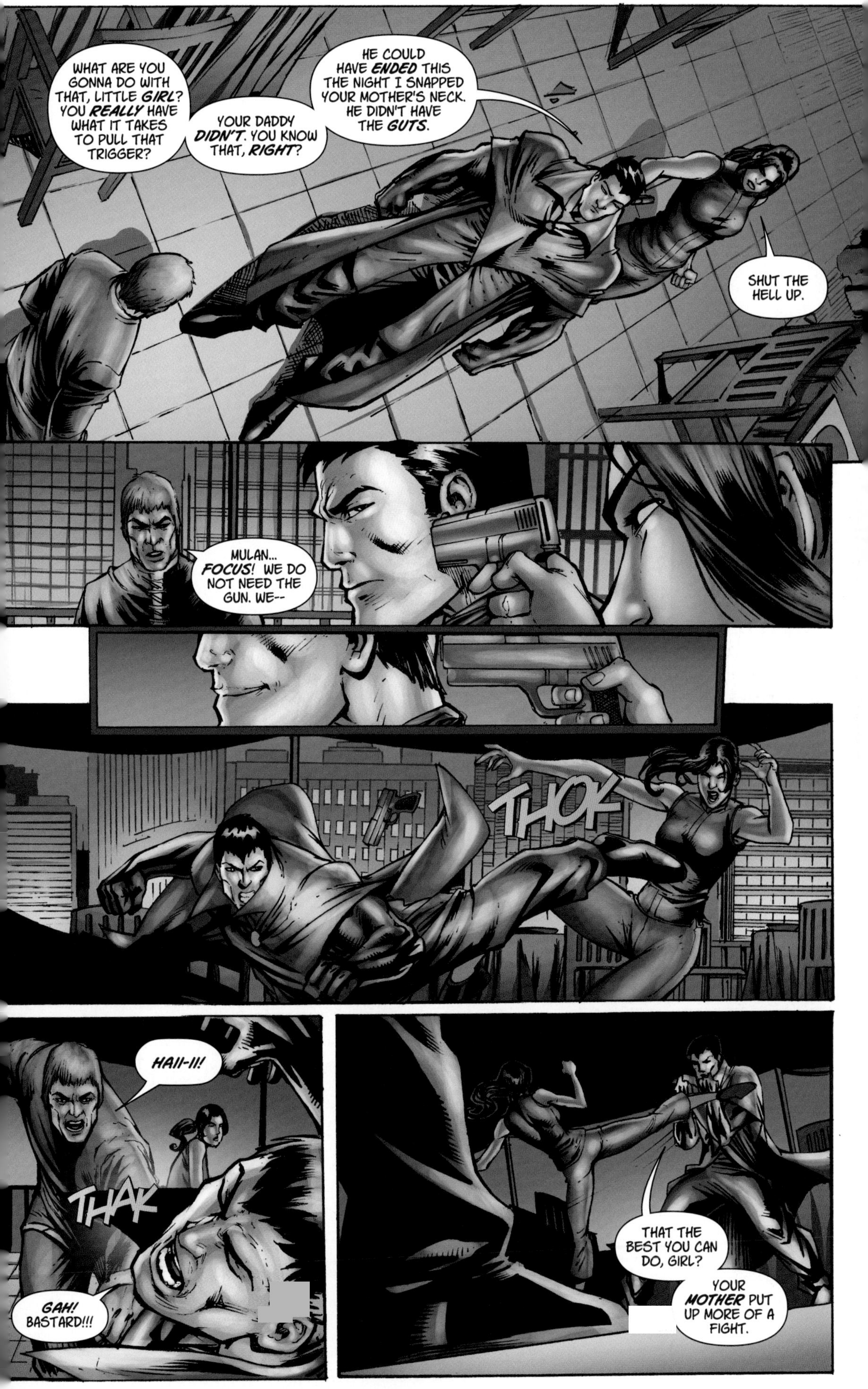
WHAT ARE YOU GONNA DO WITH THAT, LITTLE GIRL? YOU REALLY HAVE WHAT IT TAKES TO PULL THAT TRIGGER?
YOUR DADDY DIDN'T. YOU KNOW THAT, RIGHT?
HE COULD HAVE ENDED THIS THE NIGHT I SNAPPED YOUR MOTHER'S NECK. HE DIDN'T HAVE THE GUTS.
SHUT THE HELL UP.
MULAN... FOCUS! WE DO NOT NEED THE GUN. WE--
THOK
HAII-II!
THAK
GAH! BASTARD!!!
THAT THE BEST YOU CAN DO, GIRL?
YOUR MOTHER PUT UP MORE OF A FIGHT.

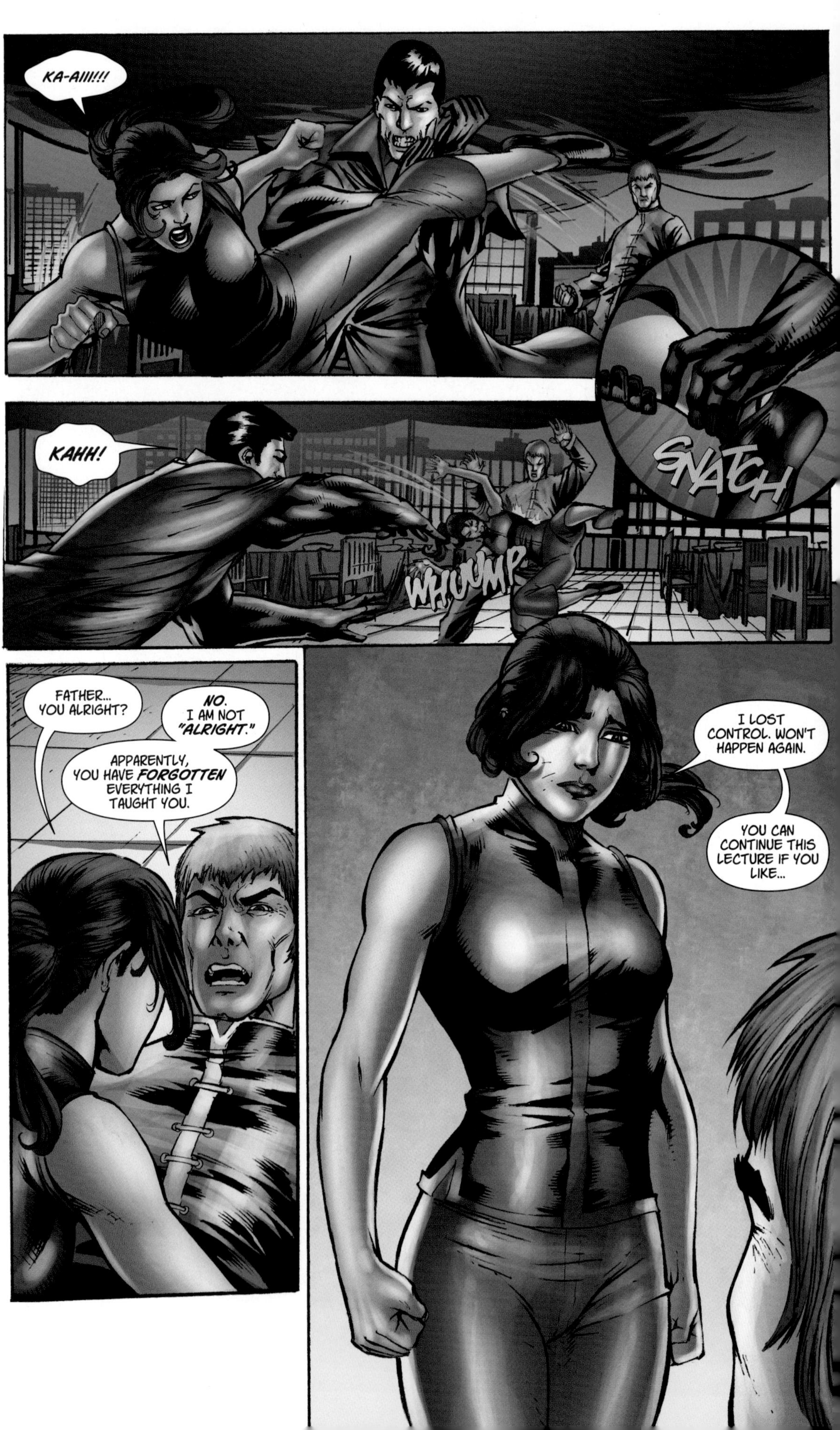
KA-AIII!!!
SNATCH
KAHH!
WHUUMP
FATHER... YOU ALRIGHT?
NO. I AM NOT "ALRIGHT."
APPARENTLY, YOU HAVE FORGOTTEN EVERYTHING I TAUGHT YOU.
I LOST CONTROL. WON'T HAPPEN AGAIN.
YOU CAN CONTINUE THIS LECTURE IF YOU LIKE...

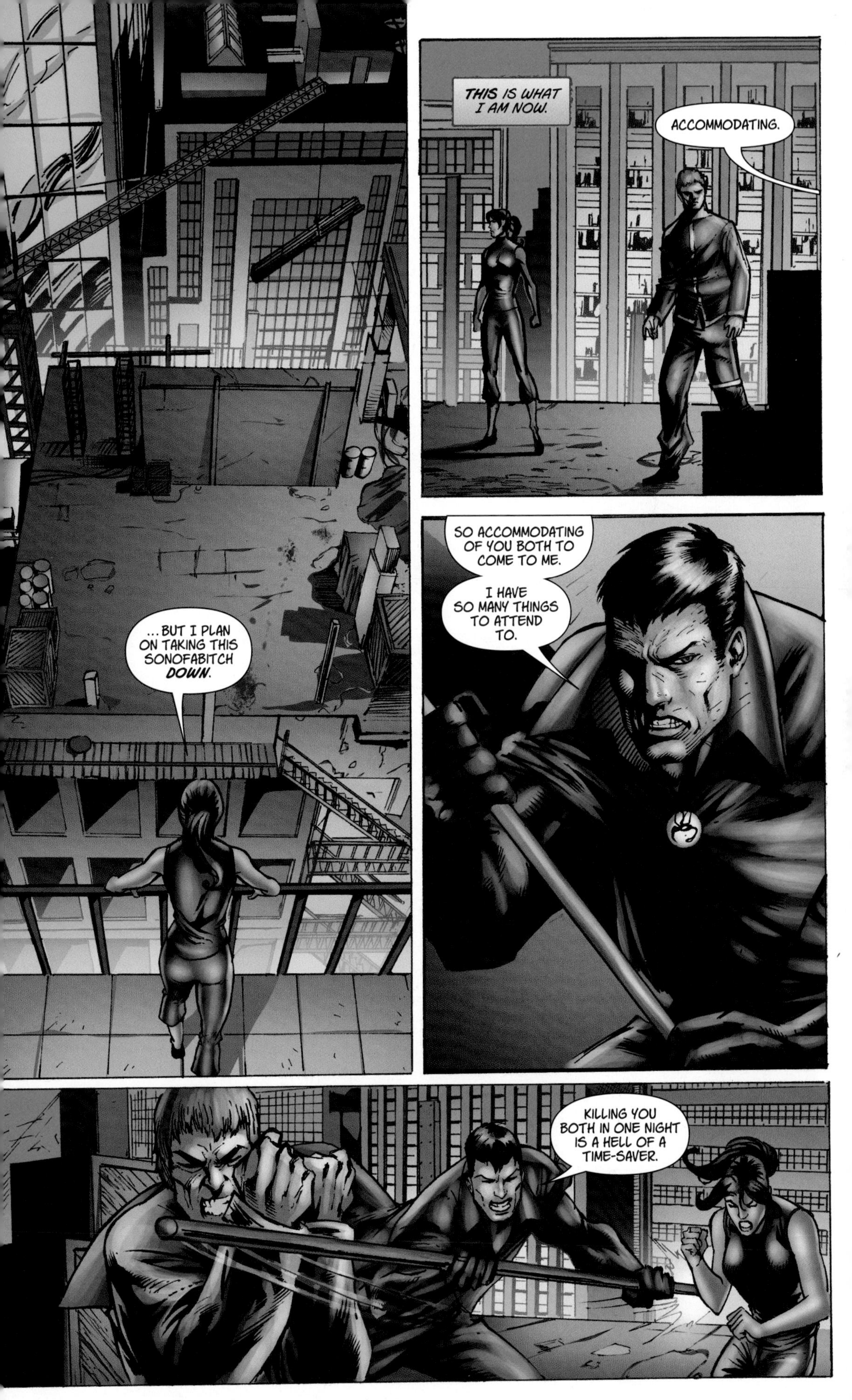
...BUT I PLAN ON TAKING THIS SONOFABITCH *DOWN*.
THIS IS WHAT I AM NOW.
ACCOMMODATING.
SO ACCOMMODATING OF YOU BOTH TO COME TO ME.
I HAVE SO MANY THINGS TO ATTEND TO.
KILLING YOU BOTH IN ONE NIGHT IS A HELL OF A TIME-SAVER.

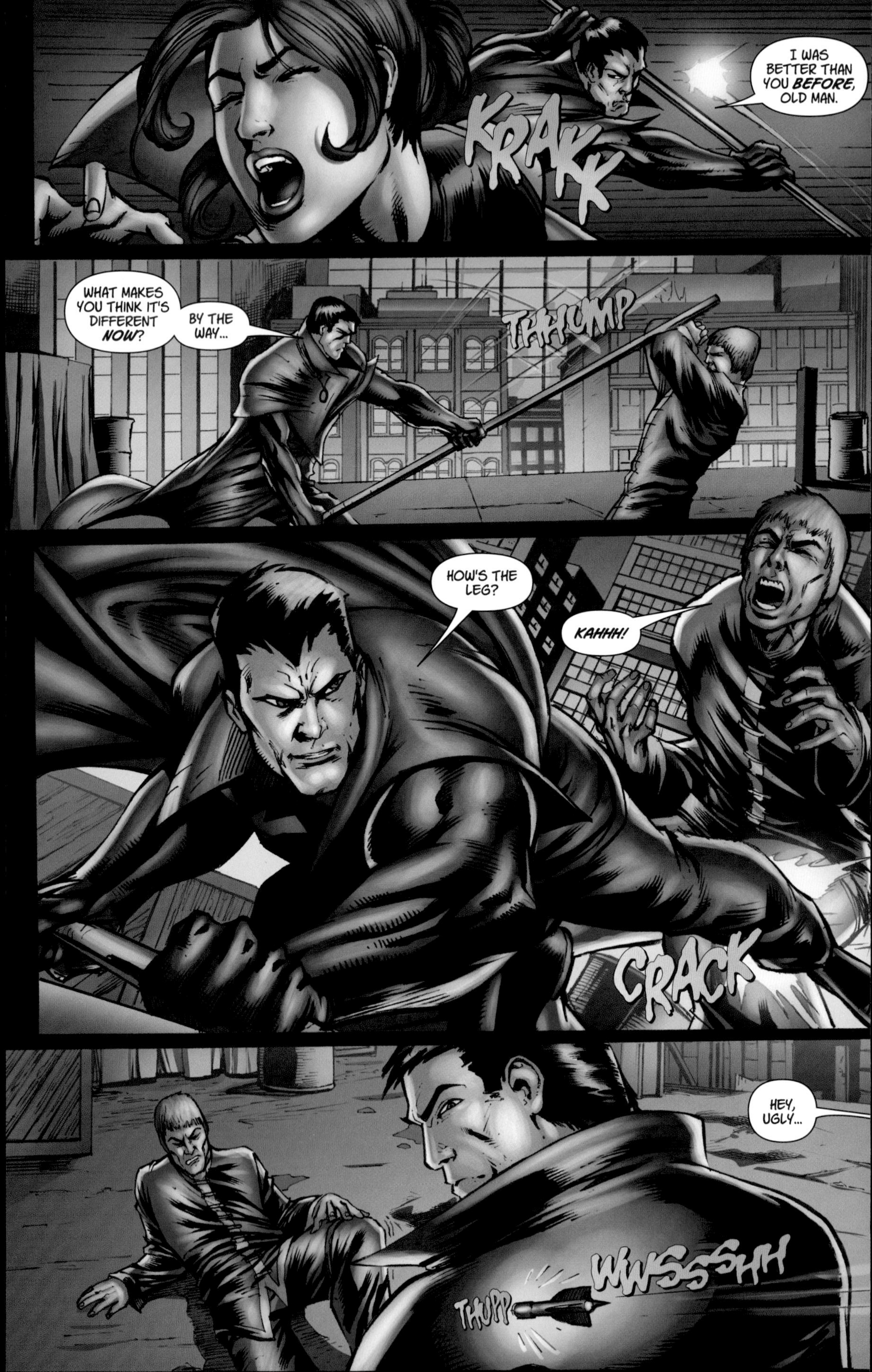
KRAKK
I WAS BETTER THAN YOU BEFORE, OLD MAN.
WHAT MAKES YOU THINK IT'S DIFFERENT NOW?
BY THE WAY...
THHUMP
HOW'S THE LEG?
KAHHH!
CRACK
HEY, UGLY...
WWSSSHH
THUPP

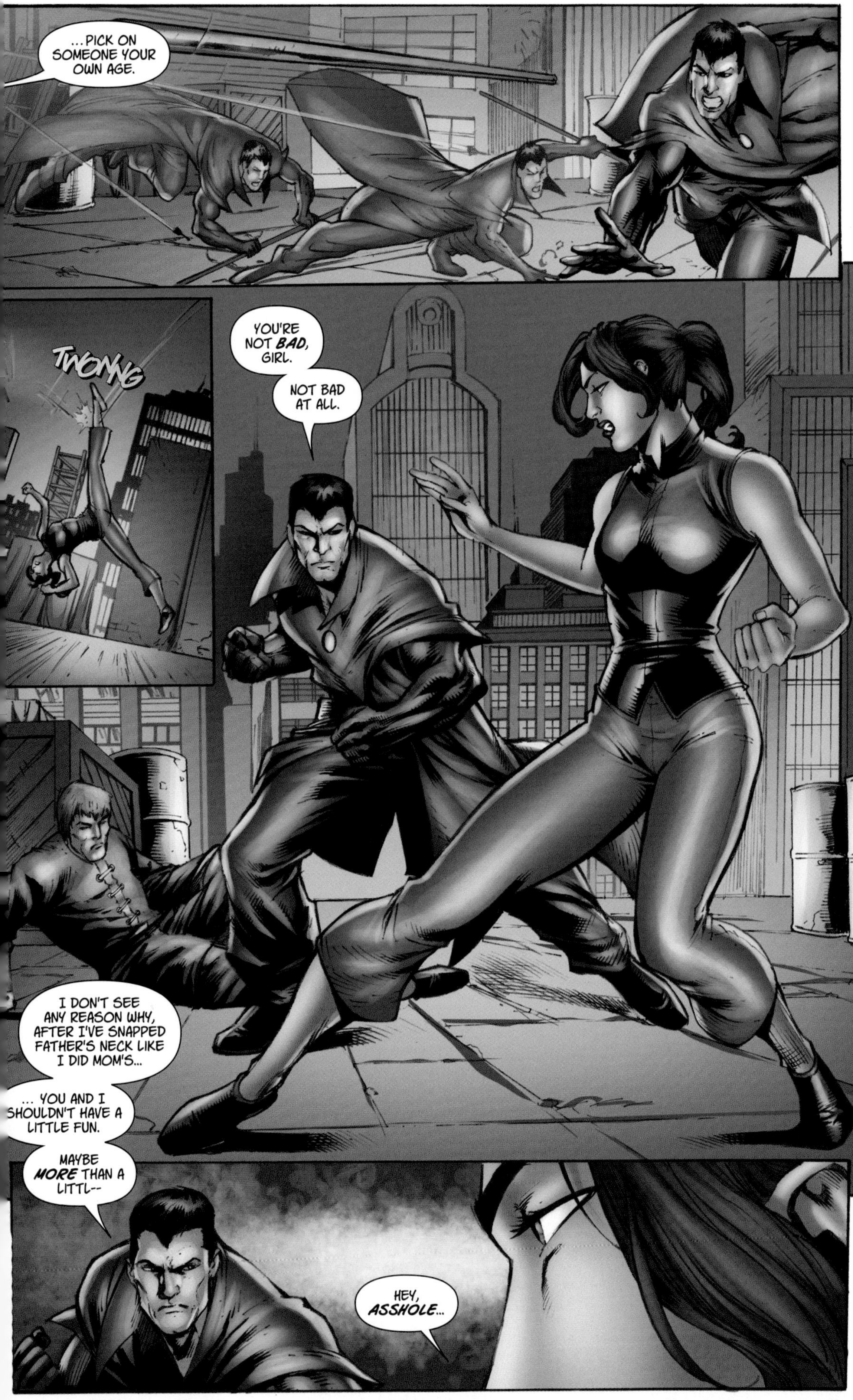
...PICK ON SOMEONE YOUR OWN AGE.
TWONNG
YOU'RE NOT *BAD*, GIRL.
NOT BAD AT ALL.
I DON'T SEE ANY REASON WHY, AFTER I'VE SNAPPED FATHER'S NECK LIKE I DID MOM'S...
... YOU AND I SHOULDN'T HAVE A LITTLE FUN.
MAYBE *MORE* THAN A LITTL--
HEY, *ASSHOLE*...

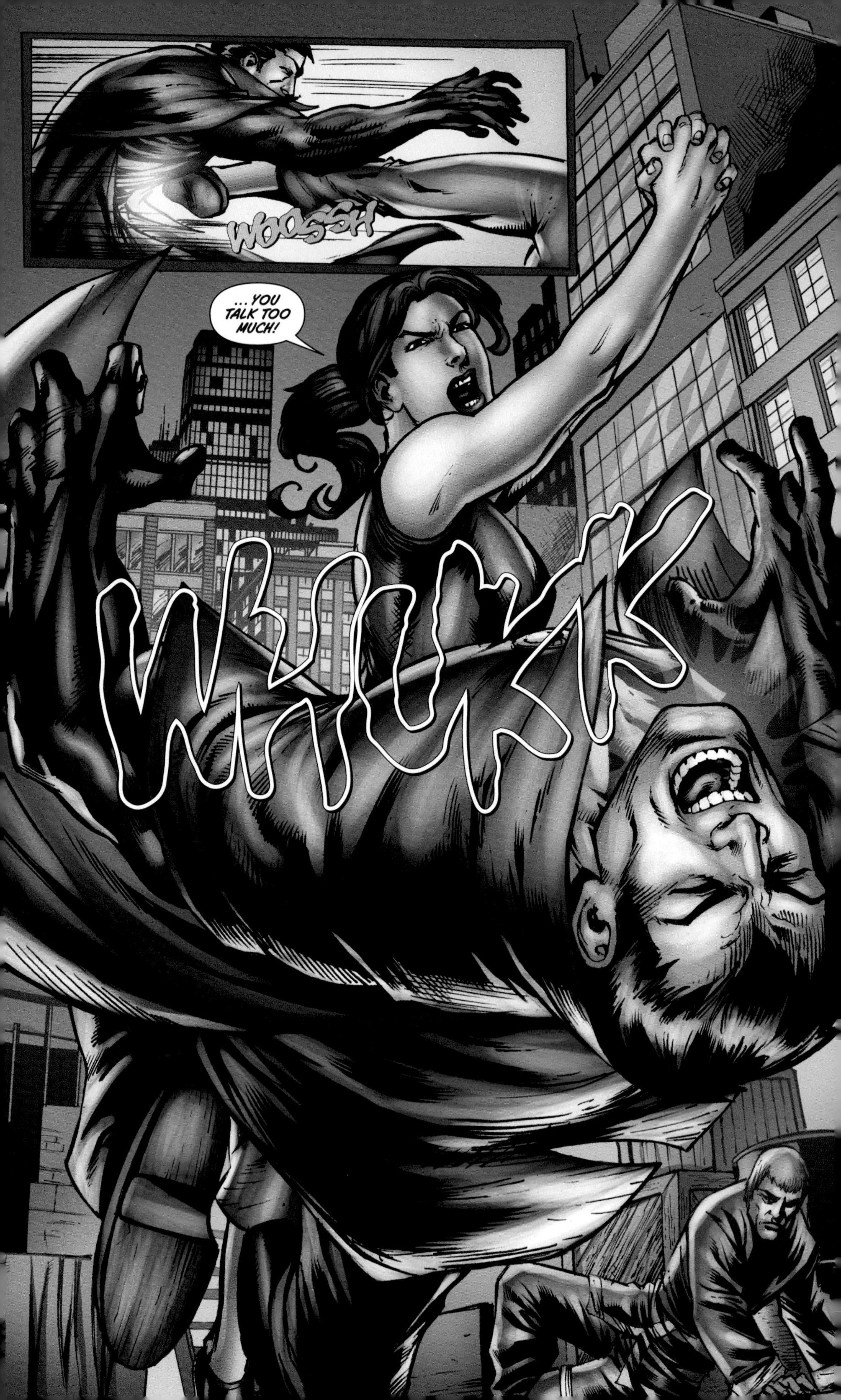
WOOSSH
...YOU TALK TOO MUCH!
WHUNK

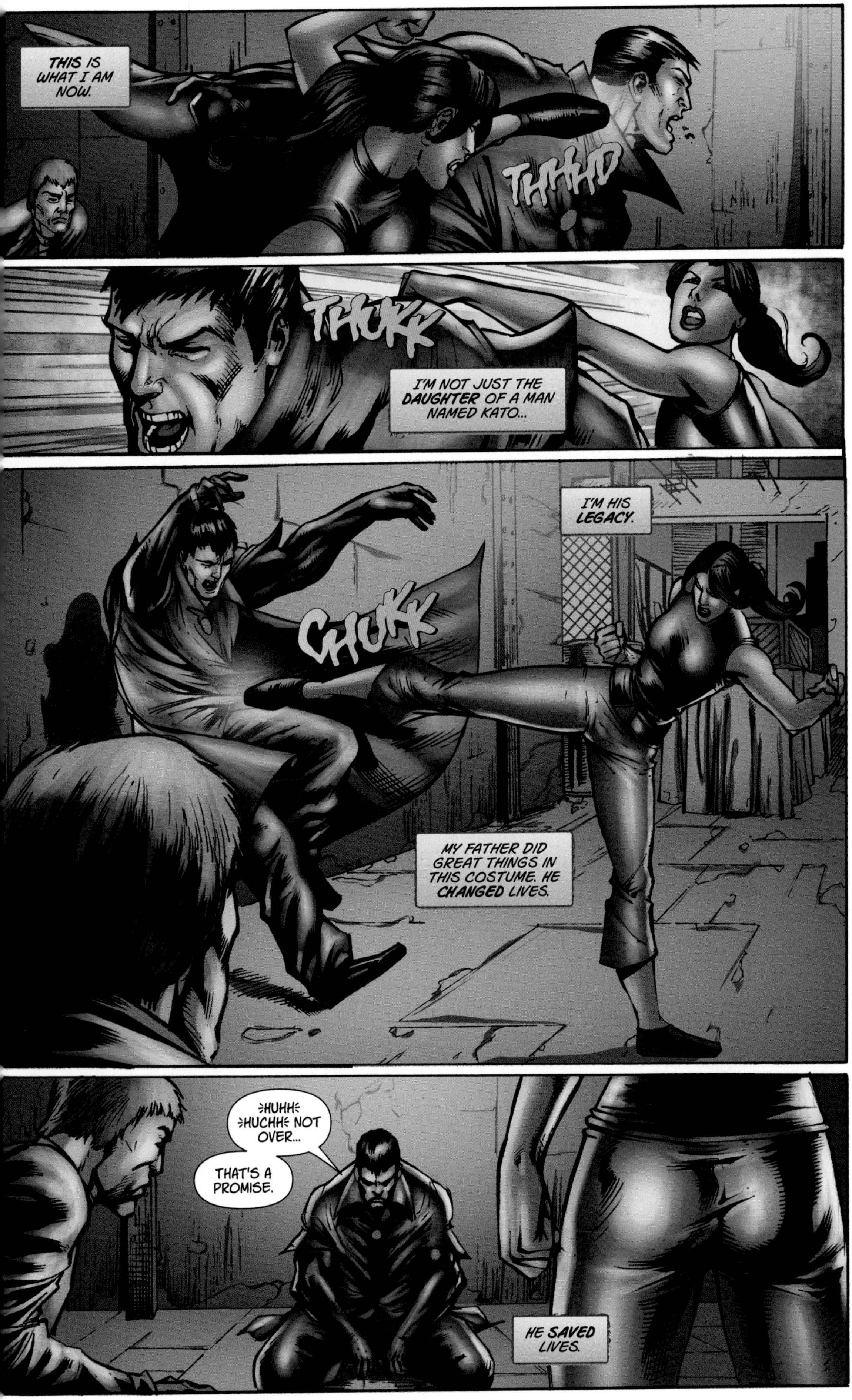
THIS IS WHAT I AM NOW.
THHUD
THUKK
I'M NOT JUST THE DAUGHTER OF A MAN NAMED KATO...
I'M HIS LEGACY.
CHUKK
MY FATHER DID GREAT THINGS IN THIS COSTUME. HE CHANGED LIVES.
HUHH HUCHH NOT OVER...
THAT'S A PROMISE.
HE SAVED LIVES.

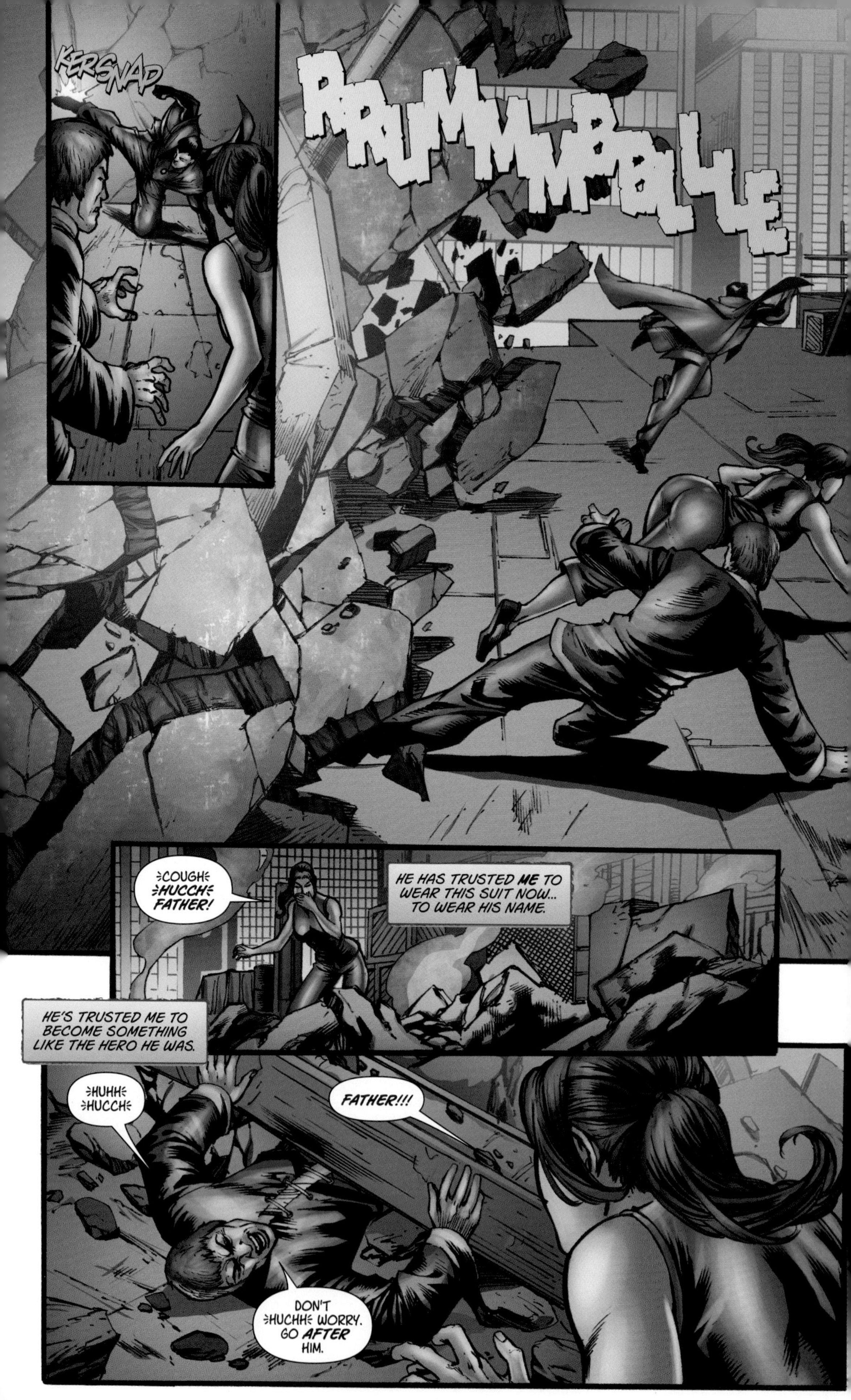
KERSNAP
RRUMMMBBLLLE
COUGH HUCCH FATHER!
HE HAS TRUSTED ME TO WEAR THIS SUIT NOW... TO WEAR HIS NAME.
HE'S TRUSTED ME TO BECOME SOMETHING LIKE THE HERO HE WAS.
HUHH HUCCH
FATHER!!!
DON'T HUCHH WORRY. GO AFTER HIM.

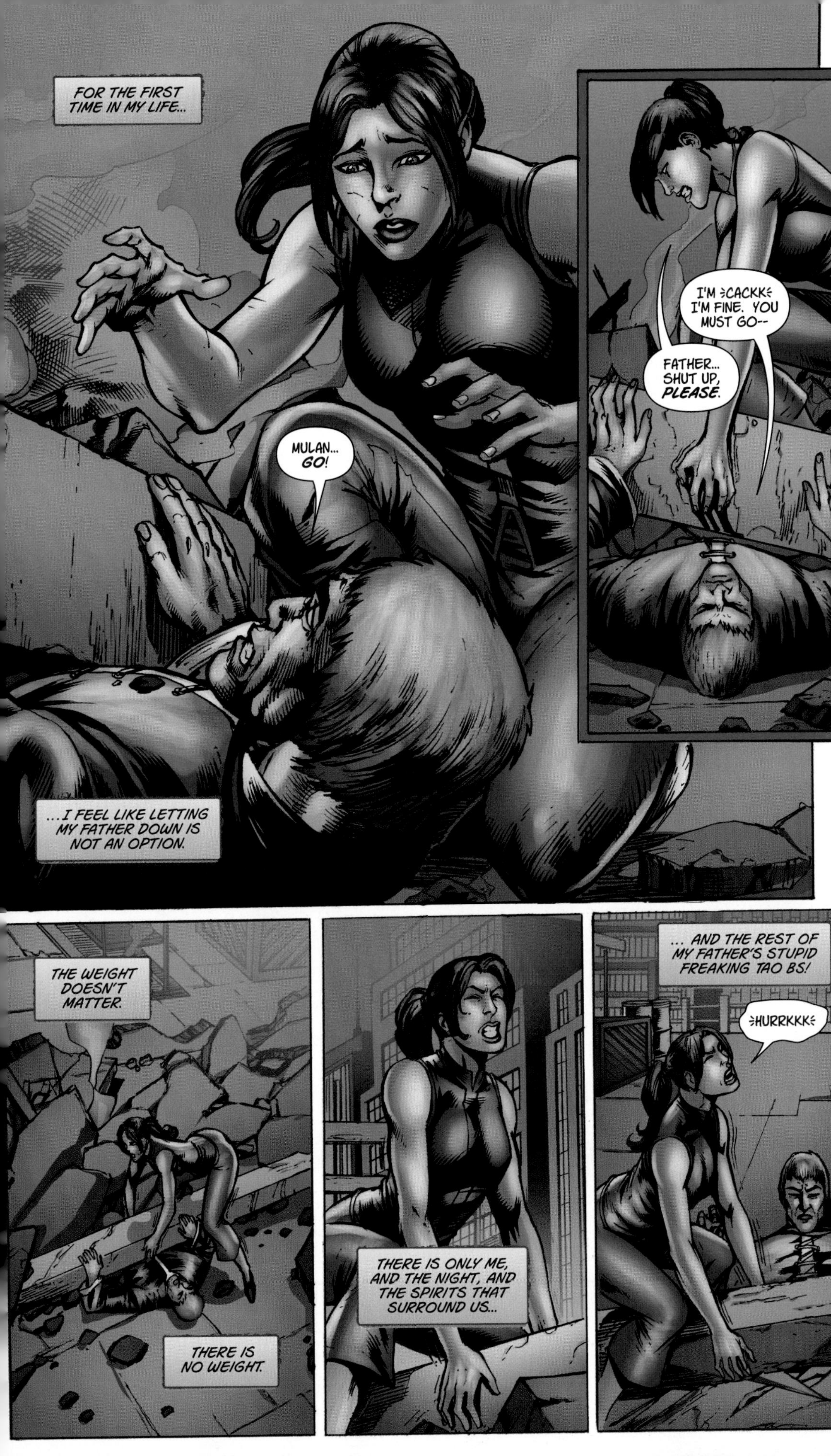
FOR THE FIRST TIME IN MY LIFE...
MULAN... GO!
...I FEEL LIKE LETTING MY FATHER DOWN IS NOT AN OPTION.
I'M ≡CACKK≡ I'M FINE. YOU MUST GO--
FATHER... SHUT UP, PLEASE.
THE WEIGHT DOESN'T MATTER.
THERE IS NO WEIGHT.
THERE IS ONLY ME, AND THE NIGHT, AND THE SPIRITS THAT SURROUND US...
... AND THE REST OF MY FATHER'S STUPID FREAKING TAO BS!
≡HURRKKK≡

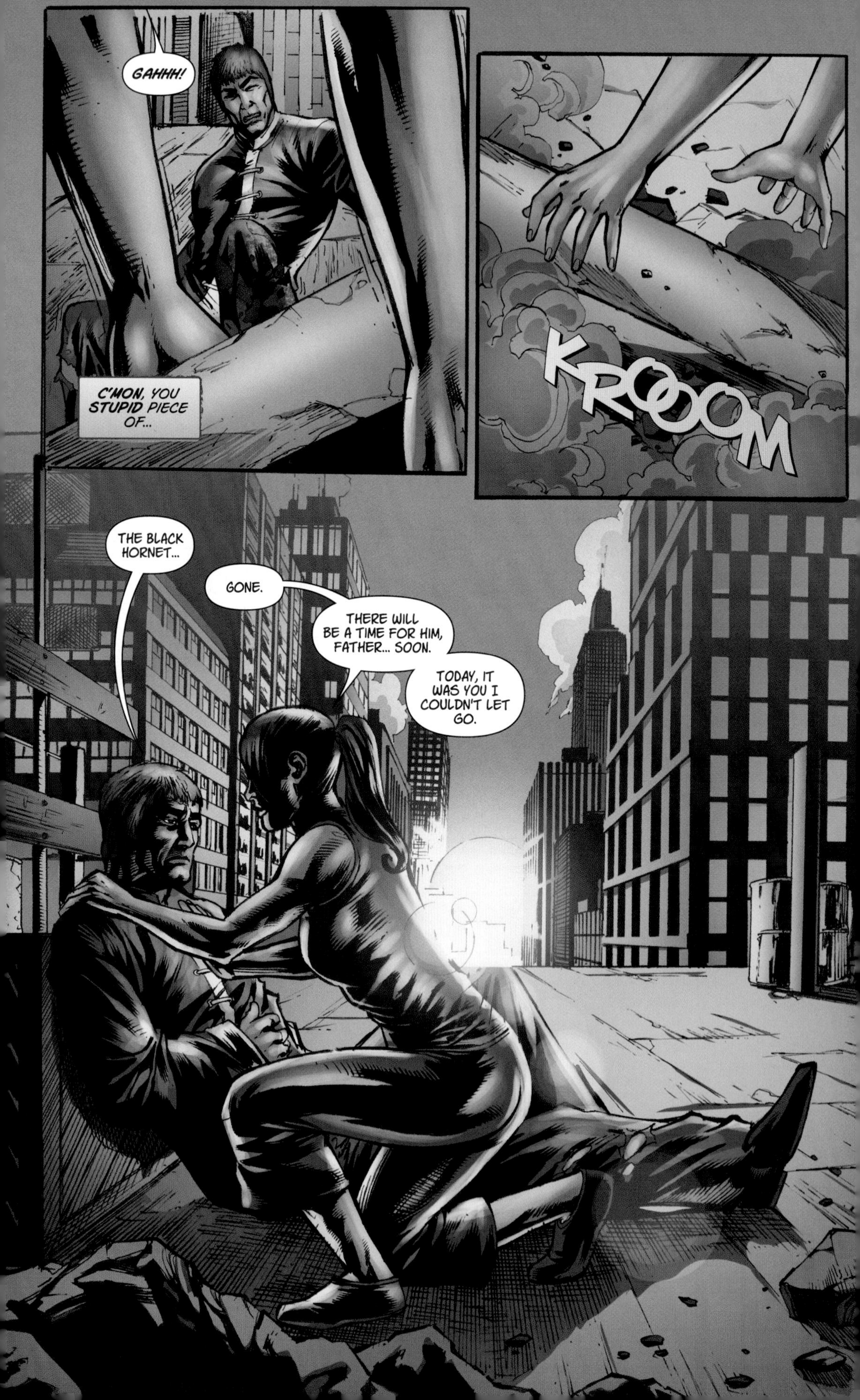
GAHHH!
C'MON, YOU STUPID PIECE OF...
KROOOM
THE BLACK HORNET...
GONE.
THERE WILL BE A TIME FOR HIM, FATHER... SOON.
TODAY, IT WAS YOU I COULDN'T LET GO.

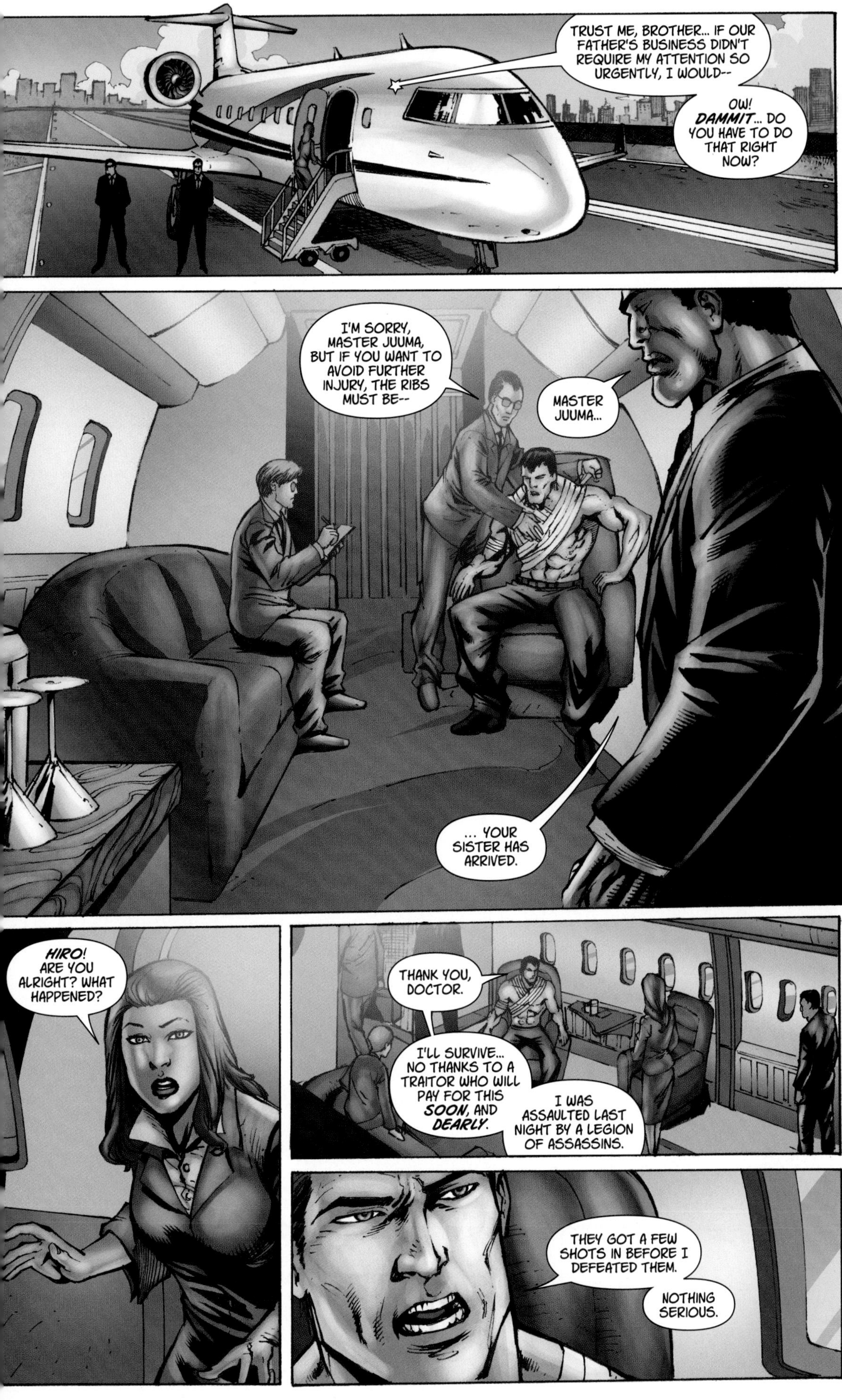
TRUST ME, BROTHER... IF OUR FATHER'S BUSINESS DIDN'T REQUIRE MY ATTENTION SO URGENTLY, I WOULD--
OW! DAMMIT... DO YOU HAVE TO DO THAT RIGHT NOW?
I'M SORRY, MASTER JUUMA, BUT IF YOU WANT TO AVOID FURTHER INJURY, THE RIBS MUST BE--
MASTER JUUMA...
... YOUR SISTER HAS ARRIVED.
HIRO! ARE YOU ALRIGHT? WHAT HAPPENED?
THANK YOU, DOCTOR.
I'LL SURVIVE... NO THANKS TO A TRAITOR WHO WILL PAY FOR THIS SOON, AND DEARLY.
I WAS ASSAULTED LAST NIGHT BY A LEGION OF ASSASSINS.
THEY GOT A FEW SHOTS IN BEFORE I DEFEATED THEM.
NOTHING SERIOUS.

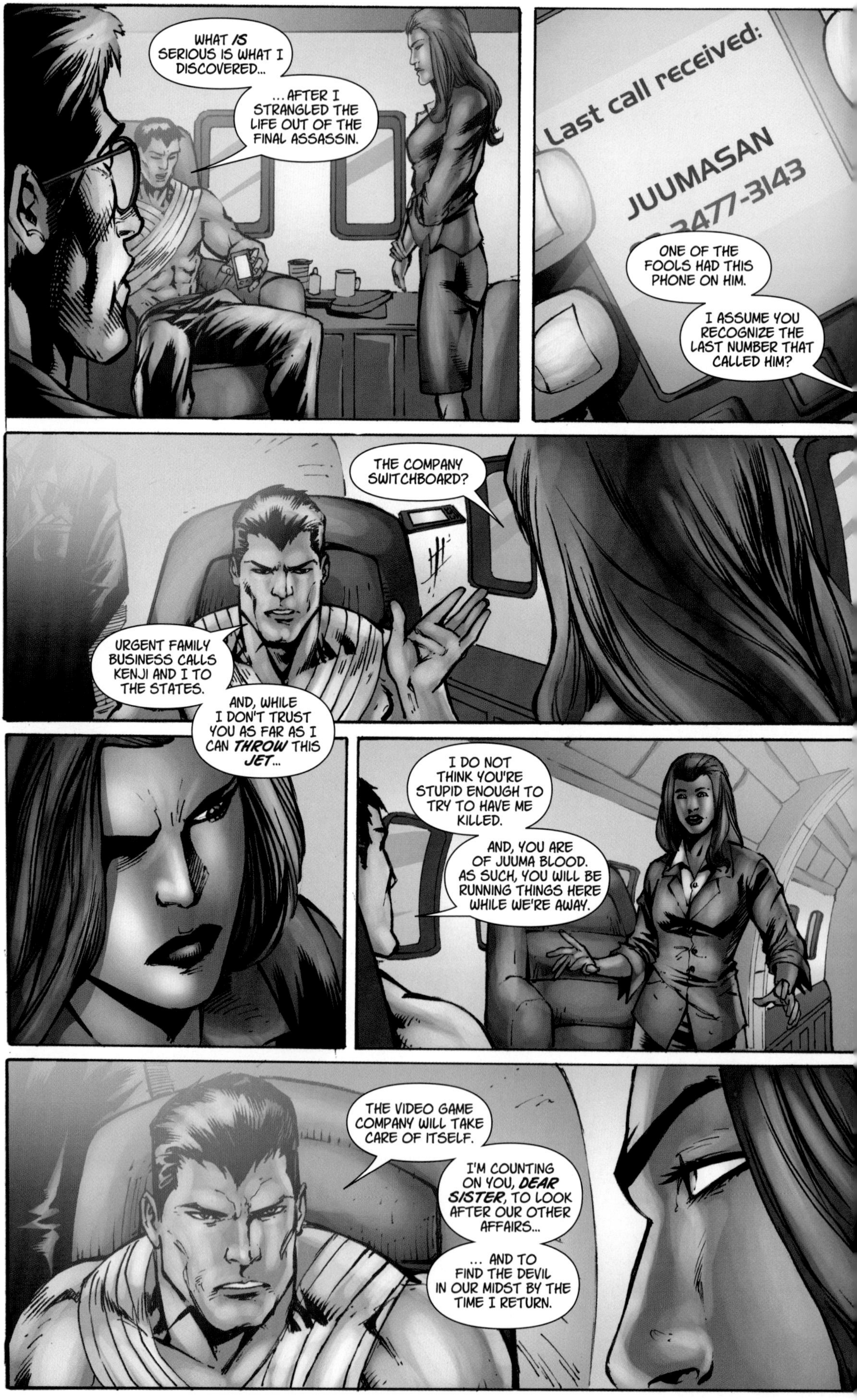
WHAT IS SERIOUS IS WHAT I DISCOVERED...
...AFTER I STRANGLED THE LIFE OUT OF THE FINAL ASSASSIN.
Last call received:
JUUMASAN
3477-3143
ONE OF THE FOOLS HAD THIS PHONE ON HIM.
I ASSUME YOU RECOGNIZE THE LAST NUMBER THAT CALLED HIM?
THE COMPANY SWITCHBOARD?
URGENT FAMILY BUSINESS CALLS KENJI AND I TO THE STATES.
AND, WHILE I DON'T TRUST YOU AS FAR AS I CAN THROW THIS JET...
I DO NOT THINK YOU'RE STUPID ENOUGH TO TRY TO HAVE ME KILLED.
AND, YOU ARE OF JUUMA BLOOD. AS SUCH, YOU WILL BE RUNNING THINGS HERE WHILE WE'RE AWAY.
THE VIDEO GAME COMPANY WILL TAKE CARE OF ITSELF.
I'M COUNTING ON YOU, DEAR SISTER, TO LOOK AFTER OUR OTHER AFFAIRS...
...AND TO FIND THE DEVIL IN OUR MIDST BY THE TIME I RETURN.

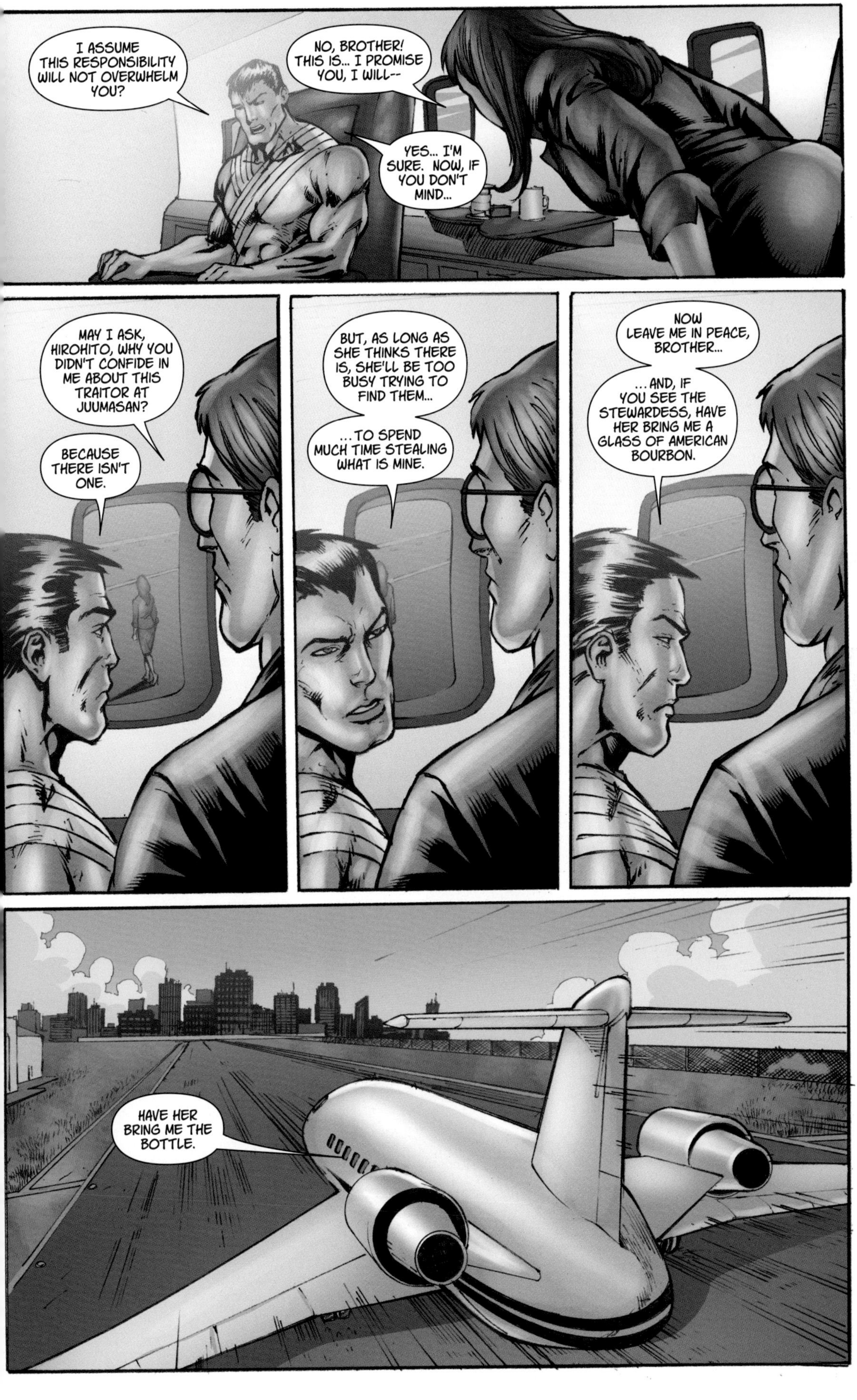

I ASSUME THIS RESPONSIBILITY WILL NOT OVERWHELM YOU?
NO, BROTHER! THIS IS... I PROMISE YOU, I WILL--
YES... I'M SURE. NOW, IF YOU DON'T MIND...
MAY I ASK, HIROHITO, WHY YOU DIDN'T CONFIDE IN ME ABOUT THIS TRAITOR AT JUUMASAN?
BECAUSE THERE ISN'T ONE.
BUT, AS LONG AS SHE THINKS THERE IS, SHE'LL BE TOO BUSY TRYING TO FIND THEM...
...TO SPEND MUCH TIME STEALING WHAT IS MINE.
NOW LEAVE ME IN PEACE, BROTHER...
...AND, IF YOU SEE THE STEWARDESS, HAVE HER BRING ME A GLASS OF AMERICAN BOURBON.
HAVE HER BRING ME THE BOTTLE.

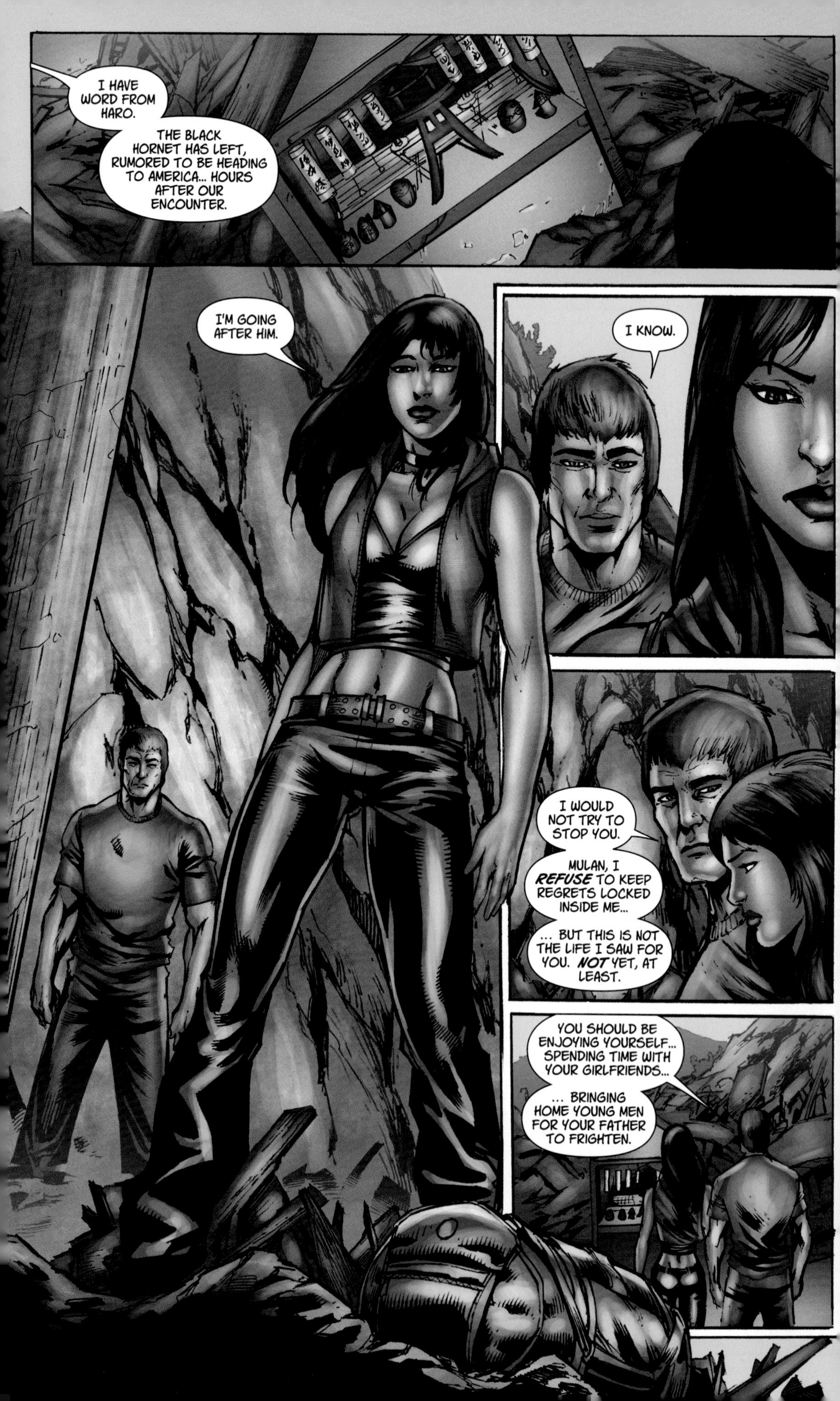

I HAVE WORD FROM HARO.
THE BLACK HORNET HAS LEFT, RUMORED TO BE HEADING TO AMERICA... HOURS AFTER OUR ENCOUNTER.
I'M GOING AFTER HIM.
I KNOW.
I WOULD NOT TRY TO STOP YOU.
MULAN, I *REFUSE* TO KEEP REGRETS LOCKED INSIDE ME...
... BUT THIS IS NOT THE LIFE I SAW FOR YOU. *NOT* YET, AT LEAST.
YOU SHOULD BE ENJOYING YOURSELF... SPENDING TIME WITH YOUR GIRLFRIENDS...
... BRINGING HOME YOUNG MEN FOR YOUR FATHER TO FRIGHTEN.

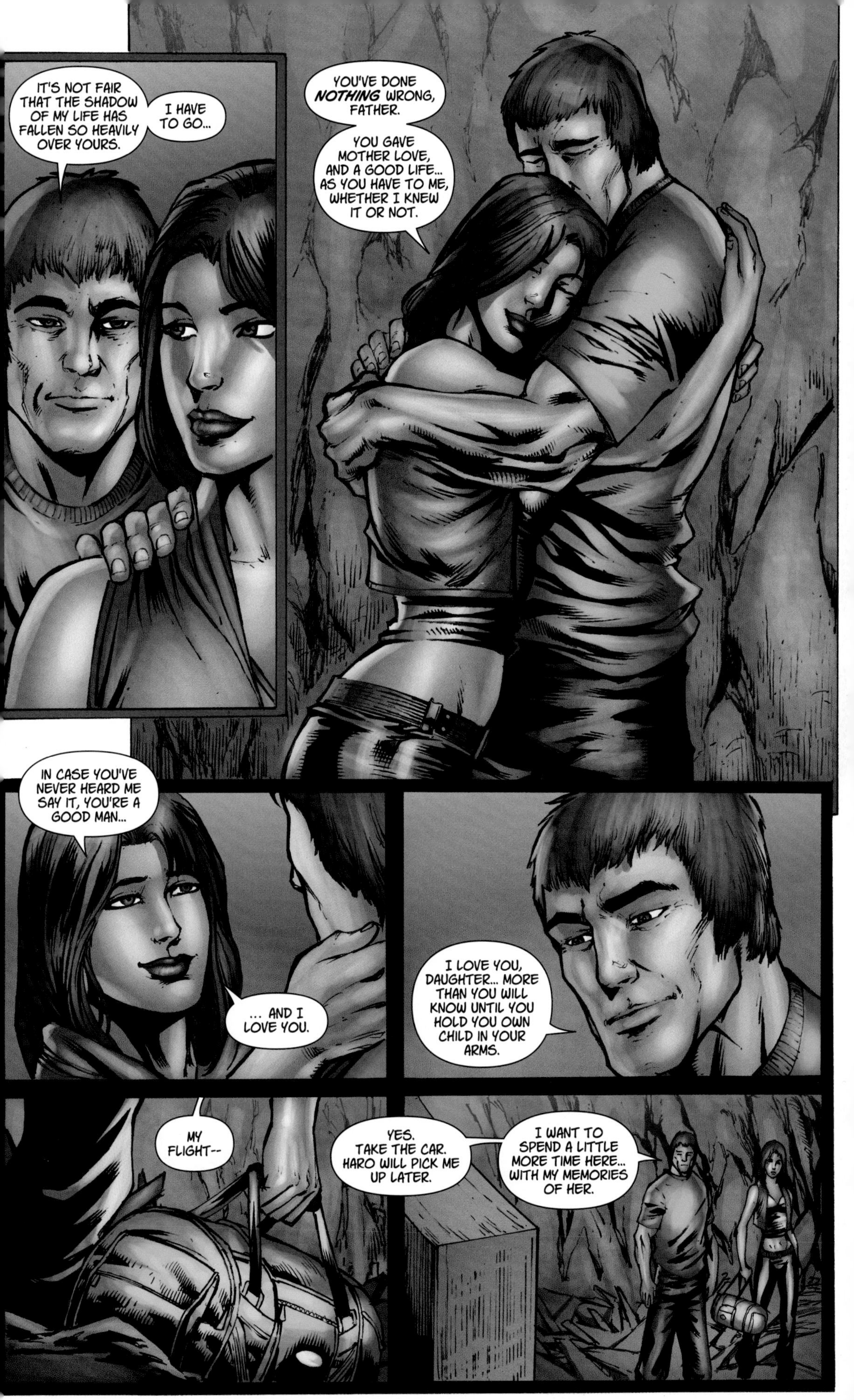
IT'S NOT FAIR THAT THE SHADOW OF MY LIFE HAS FALLEN SO HEAVILY OVER YOURS.
I HAVE TO GO...
YOU'VE DONE NOTHING WRONG, FATHER.
YOU GAVE MOTHER LOVE, AND A GOOD LIFE... AS YOU HAVE TO ME, WHETHER I KNEW IT OR NOT.
IN CASE YOU'VE NEVER HEARD ME SAY IT, YOU'RE A GOOD MAN...
... AND I LOVE YOU.
I LOVE YOU, DAUGHTER... MORE THAN YOU WILL KNOW UNTIL YOU HOLD YOU OWN CHILD IN YOUR ARMS.
MY FLIGHT--
YES. TAKE THE CAR. HARO WILL PICK ME UP LATER.
I WANT TO SPEND A LITTLE MORE TIME HERE... WITH MY MEMORIES OF HER.

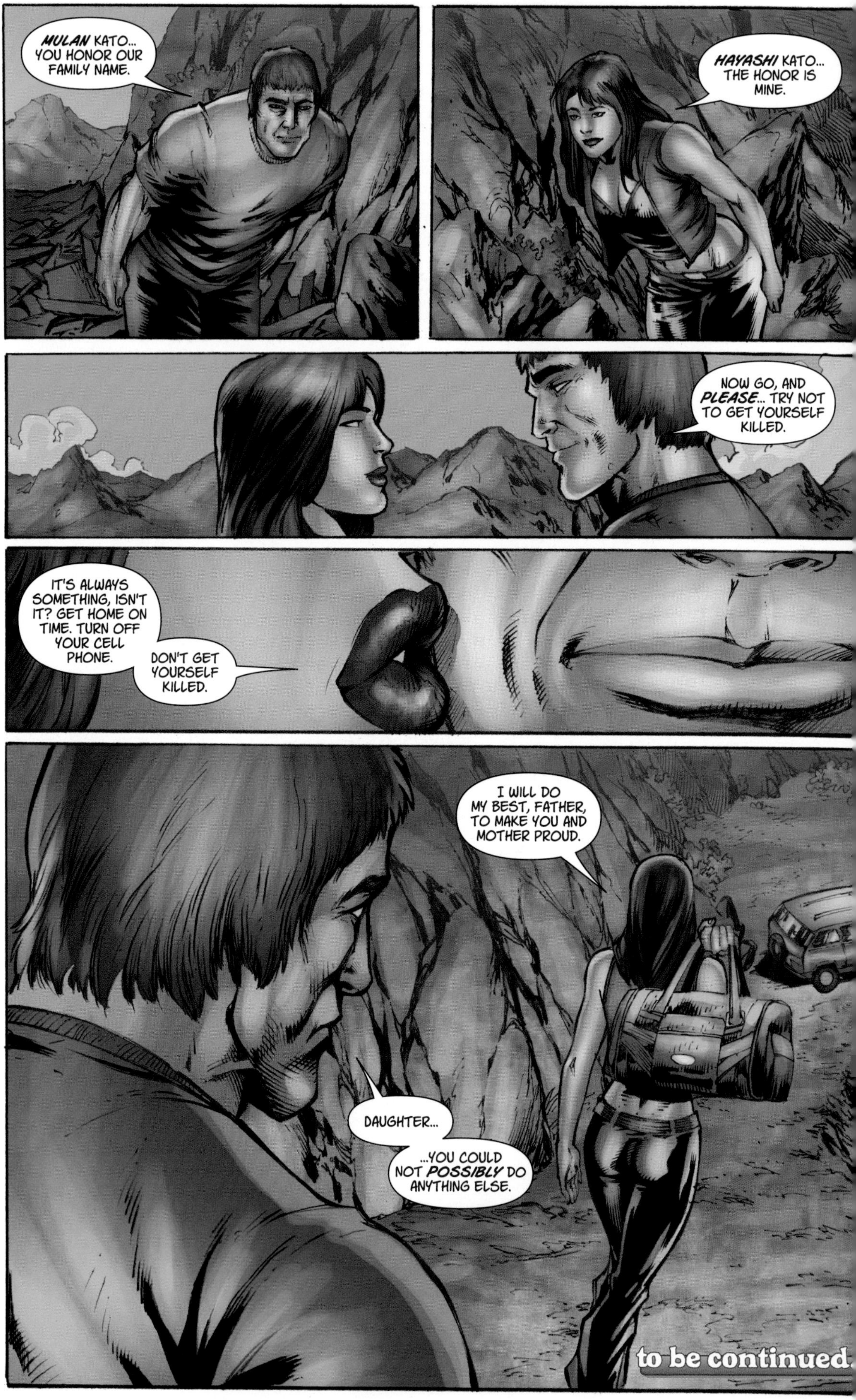
MULAN KATO... YOU HONOR OUR FAMILY NAME.
HAYASHI KATO... THE HONOR IS MINE.
NOW GO, AND PLEASE... TRY NOT TO GET YOURSELF KILLED.
IT'S ALWAYS SOMETHING, ISN'T IT? GET HOME ON TIME. TURN OFF YOUR CELL PHONE.
DON'T GET YOURSELF KILLED.
I WILL DO MY BEST, FATHER, TO MAKE YOU AND MOTHER PROUD.
DAUGHTER...
...YOU COULD NOT POSSIBLY DO ANYTHING ELSE.
to be continued.

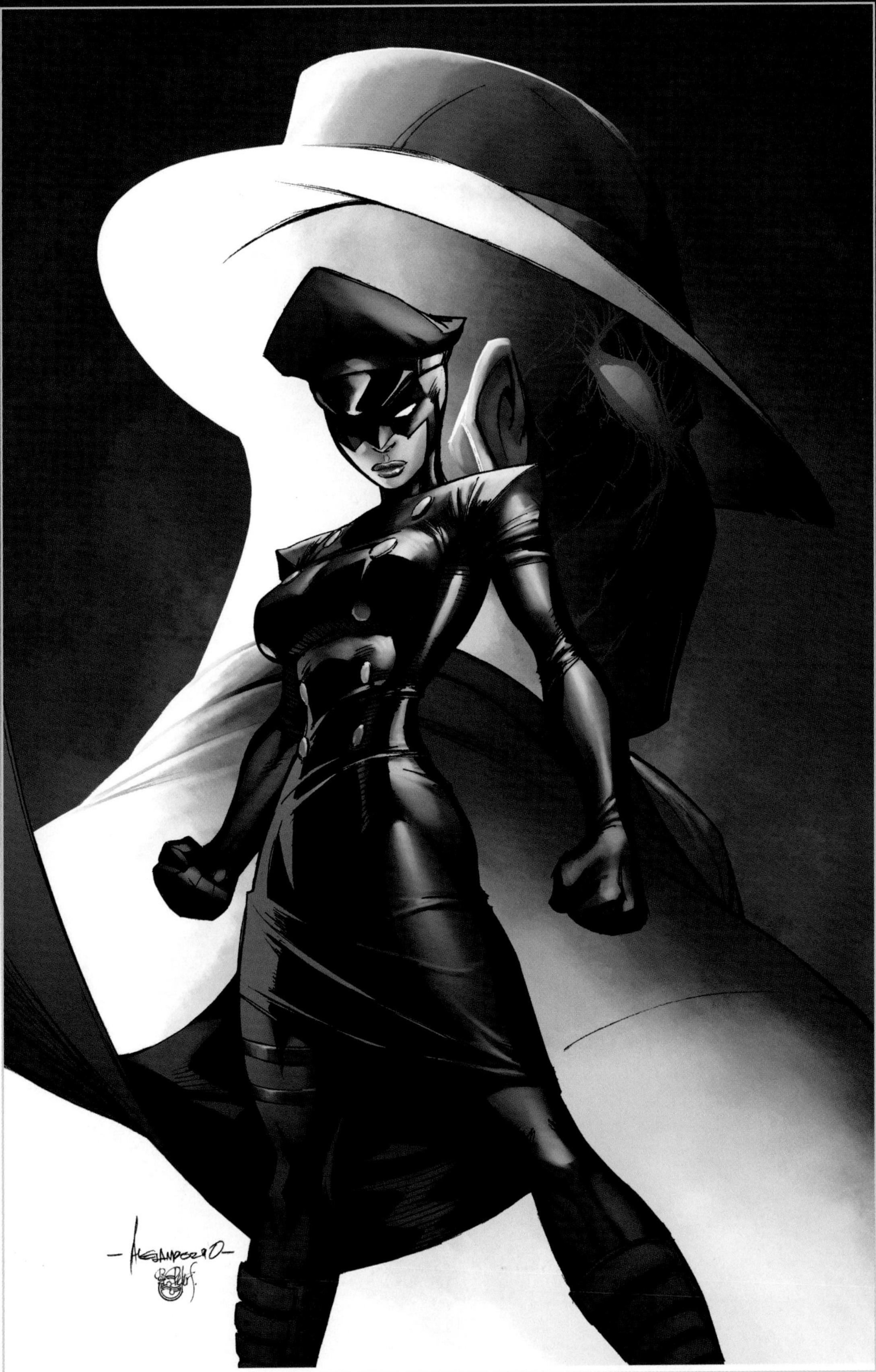

Issue one cover by **ALE GARZA**

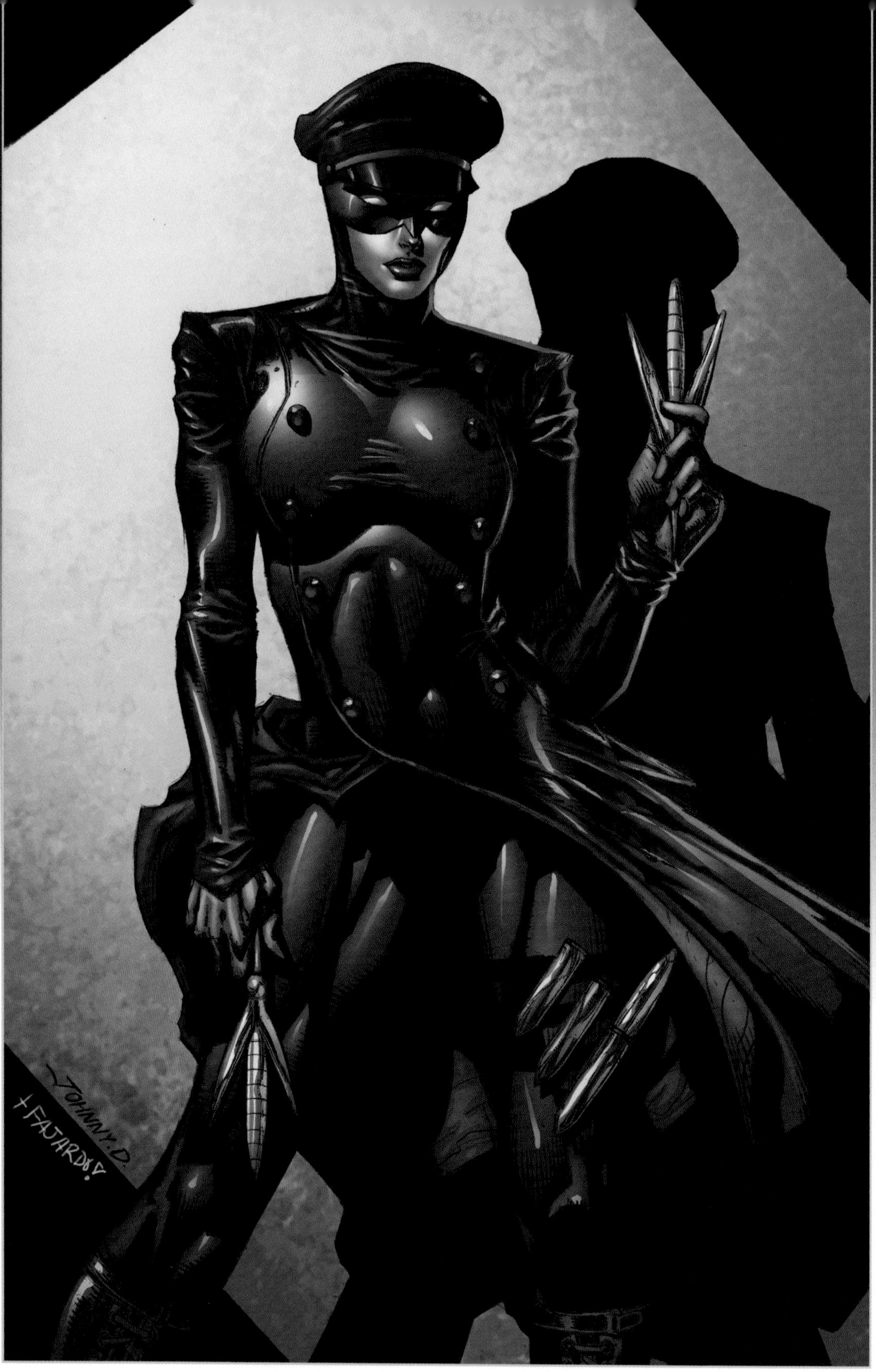
JOHNNY.D.
+ FAJARDO!

Issue one cover by **JOHNNY DESJARDINS**

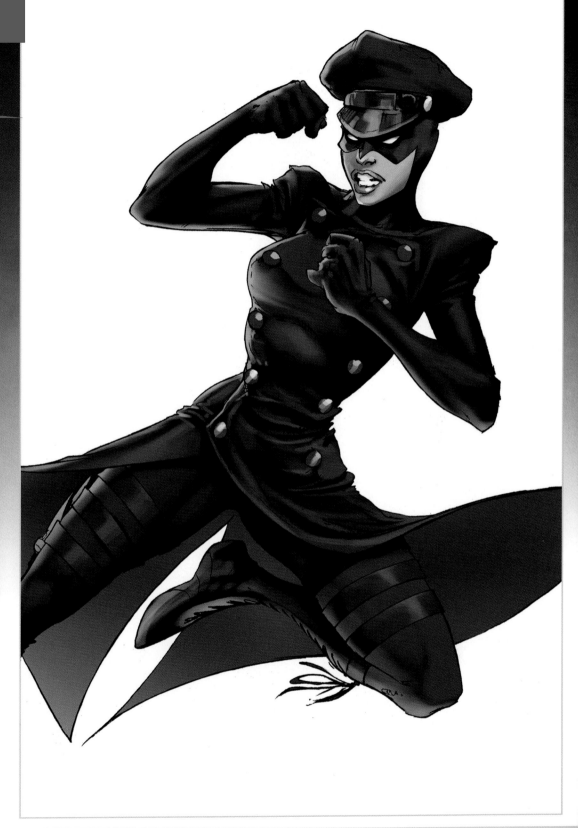

Issue one alternate cover by **JOE BENITEZ**

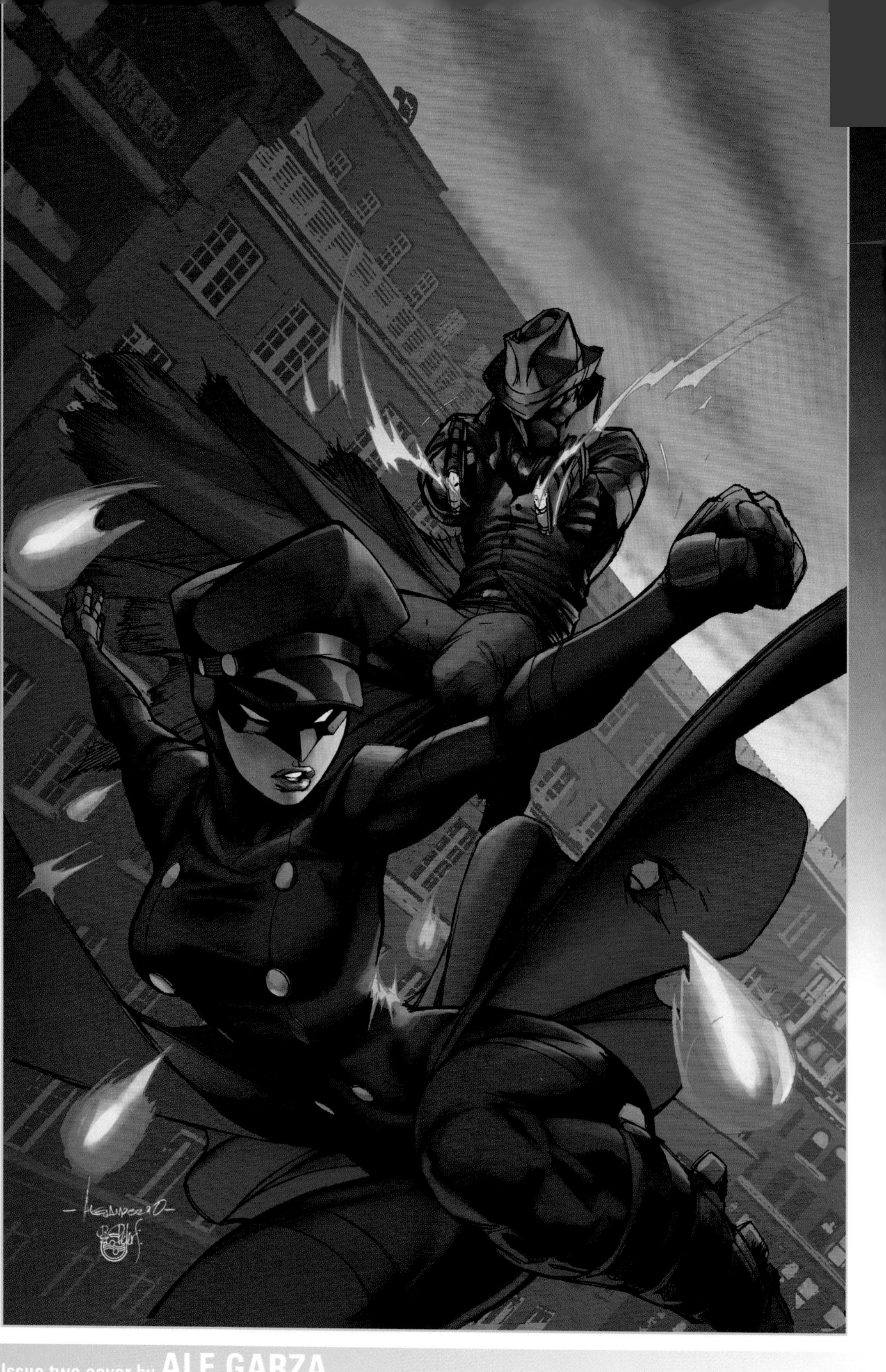

Issue two cover by **ALE GARZA**

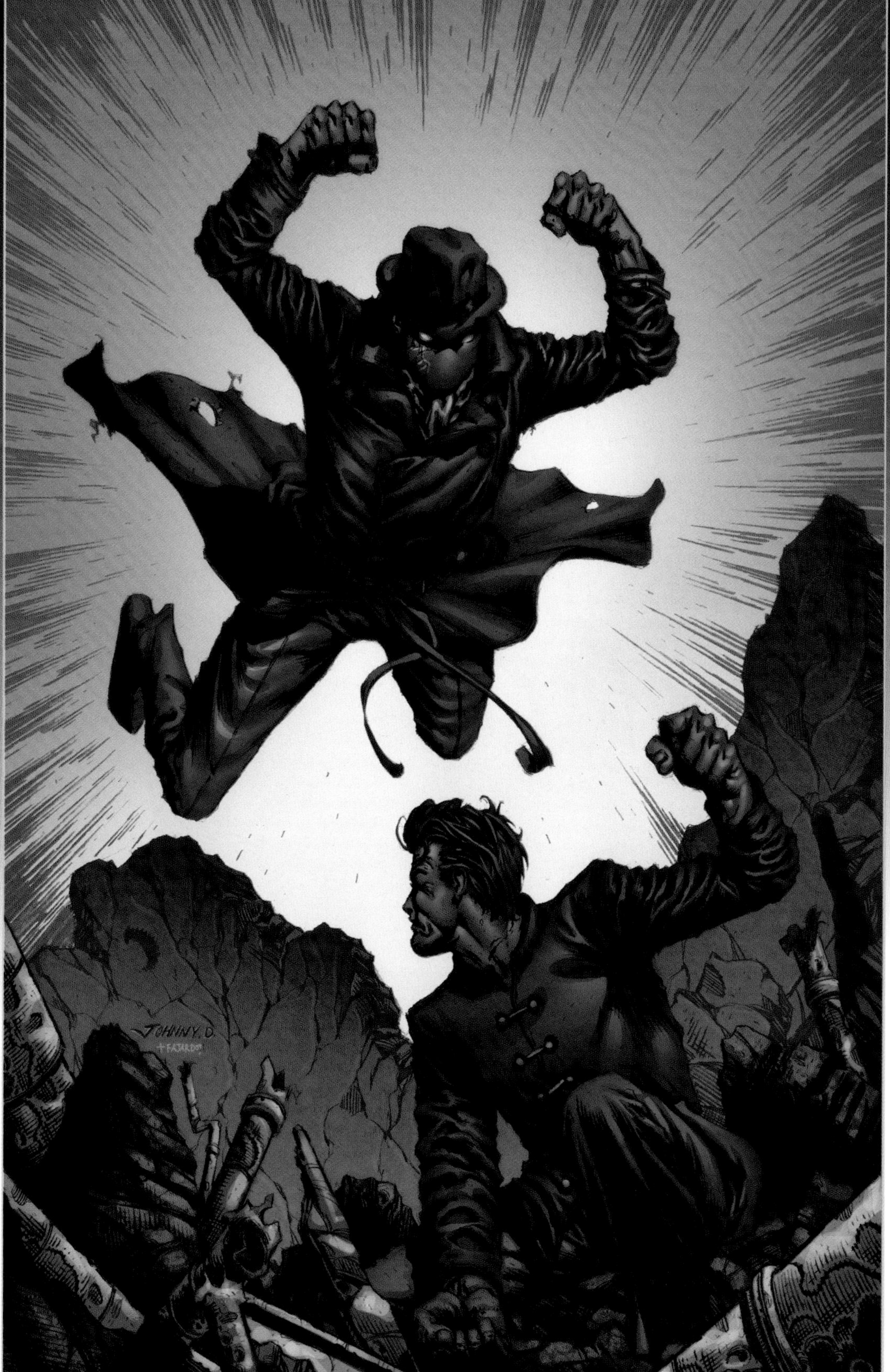
JOHNNY. D.

Issue two cover by **JOHNNY DESJARDINS**

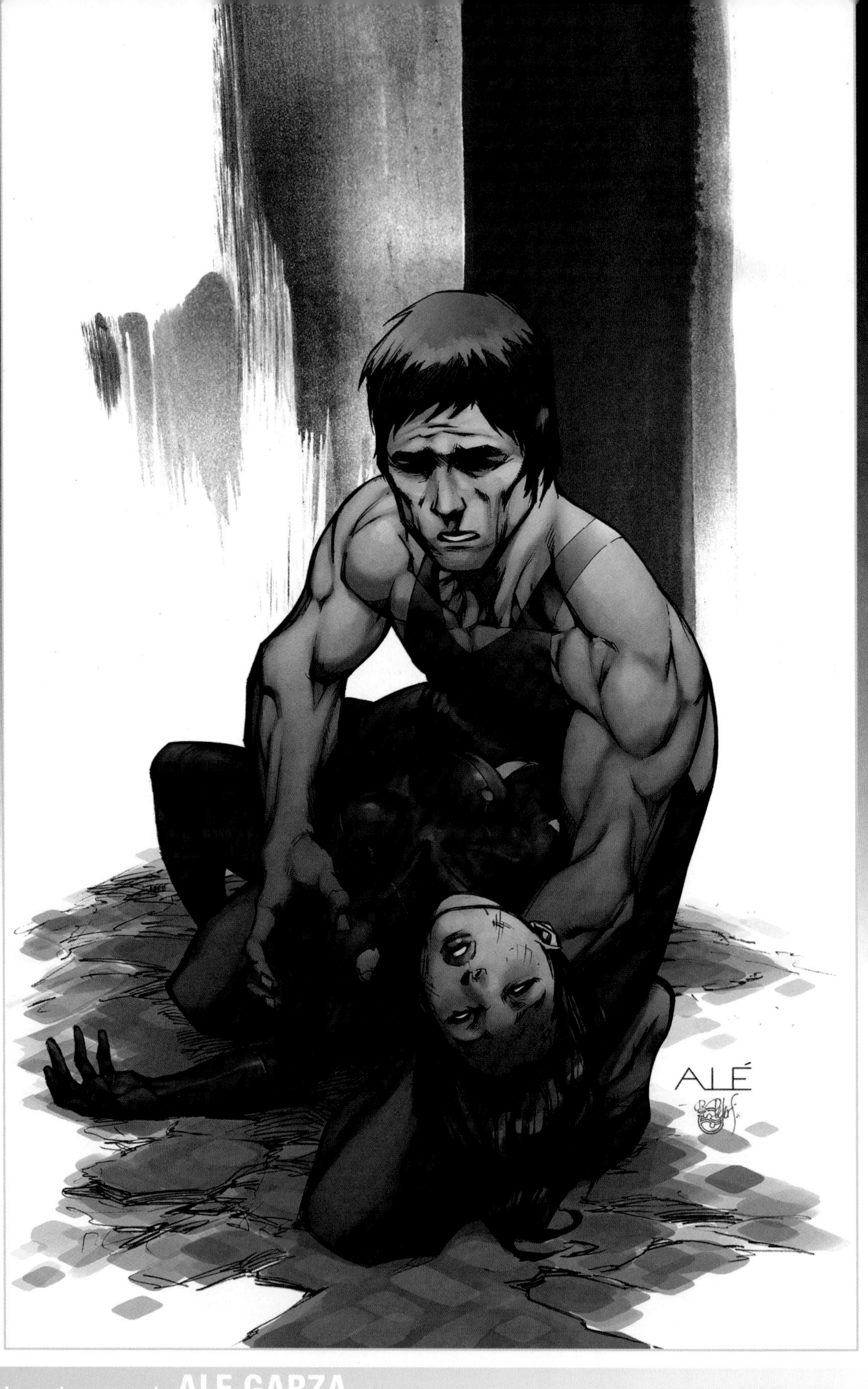
ALÉ

Issue three cover by **ALE GARZA**

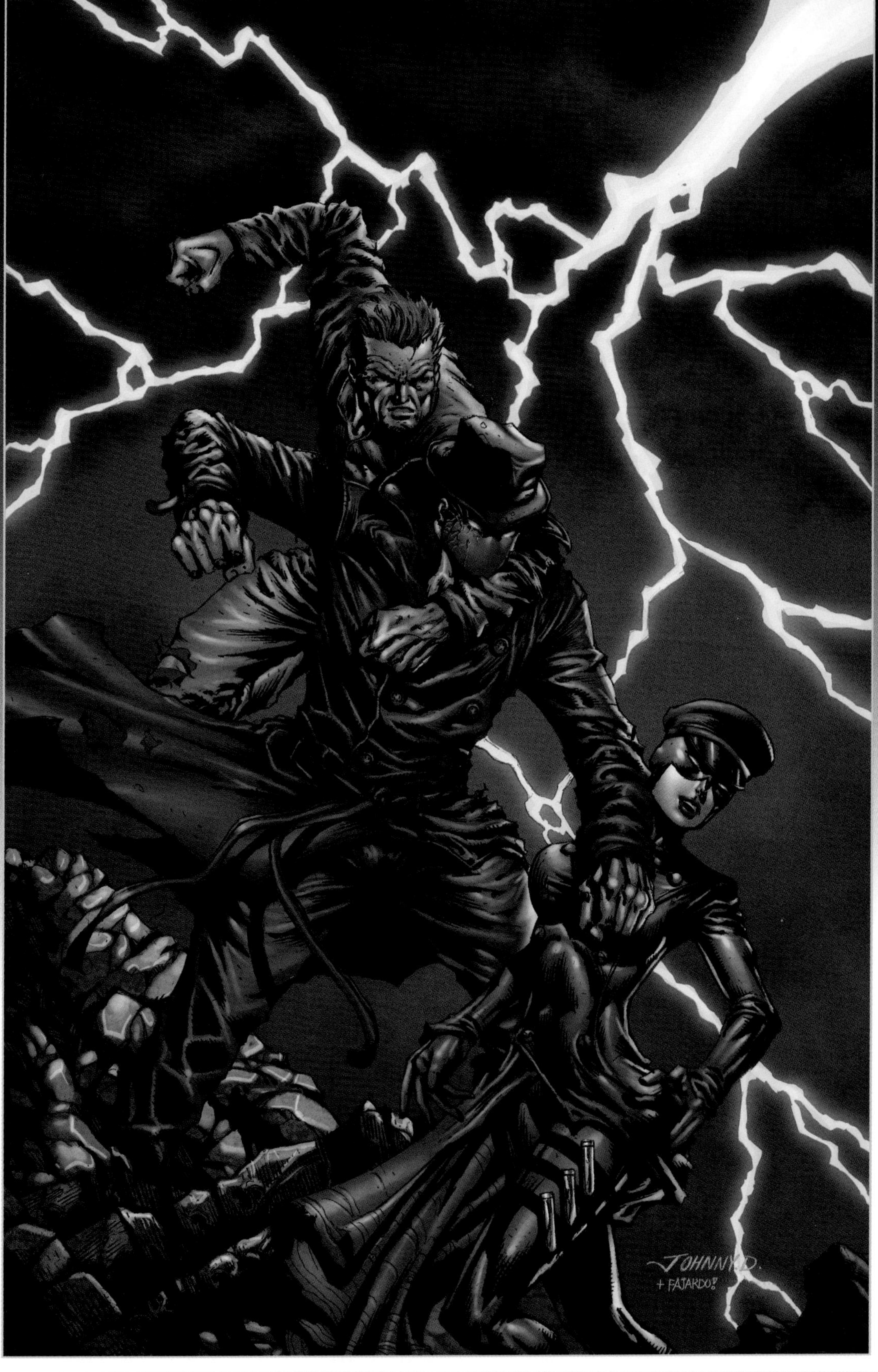
JOHNNY D.
+ FAJARDO!

Issue three cover by **JOHNNY DESJARDINS**

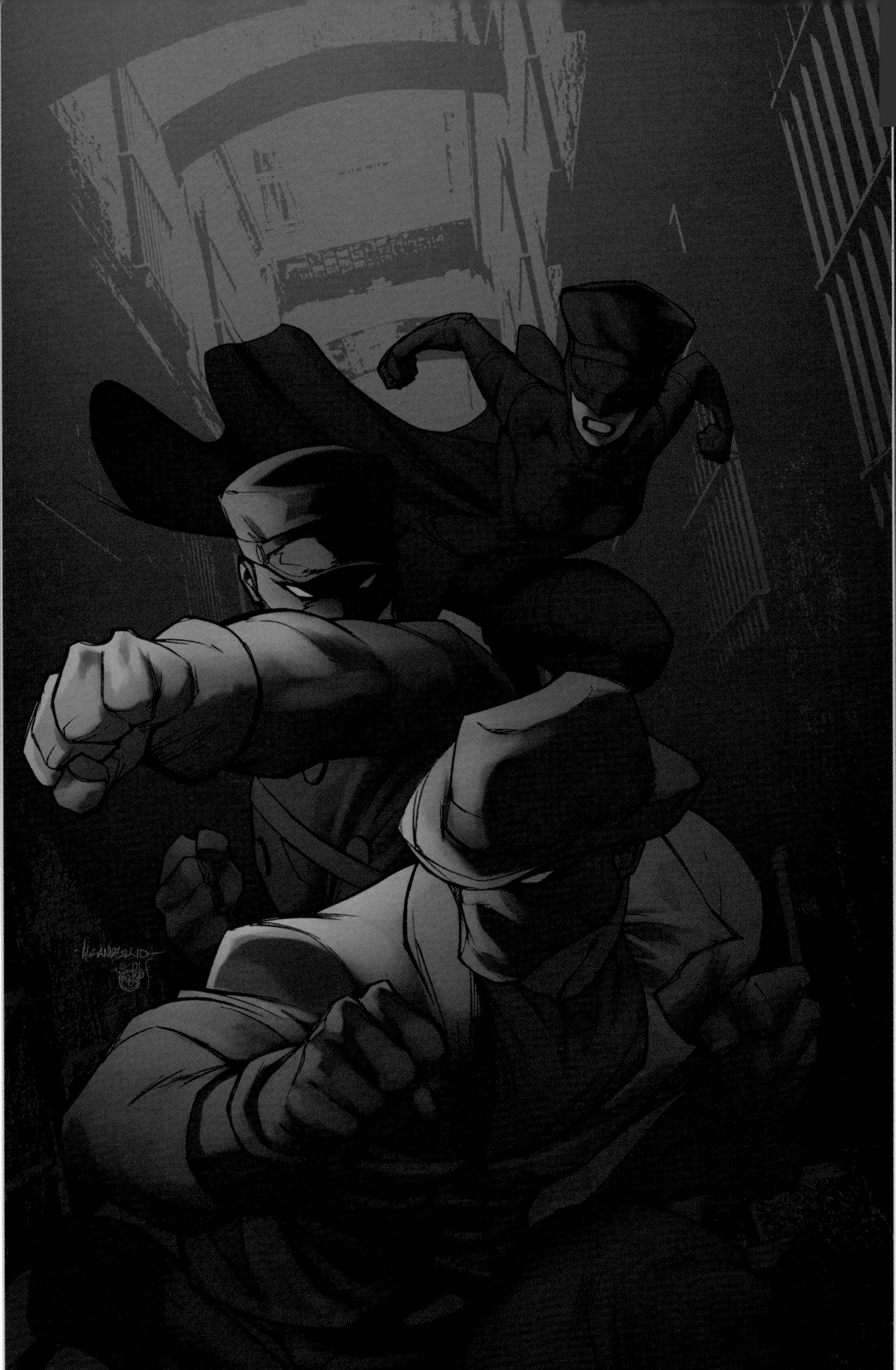

Issue four cover by **ALE GARZA**

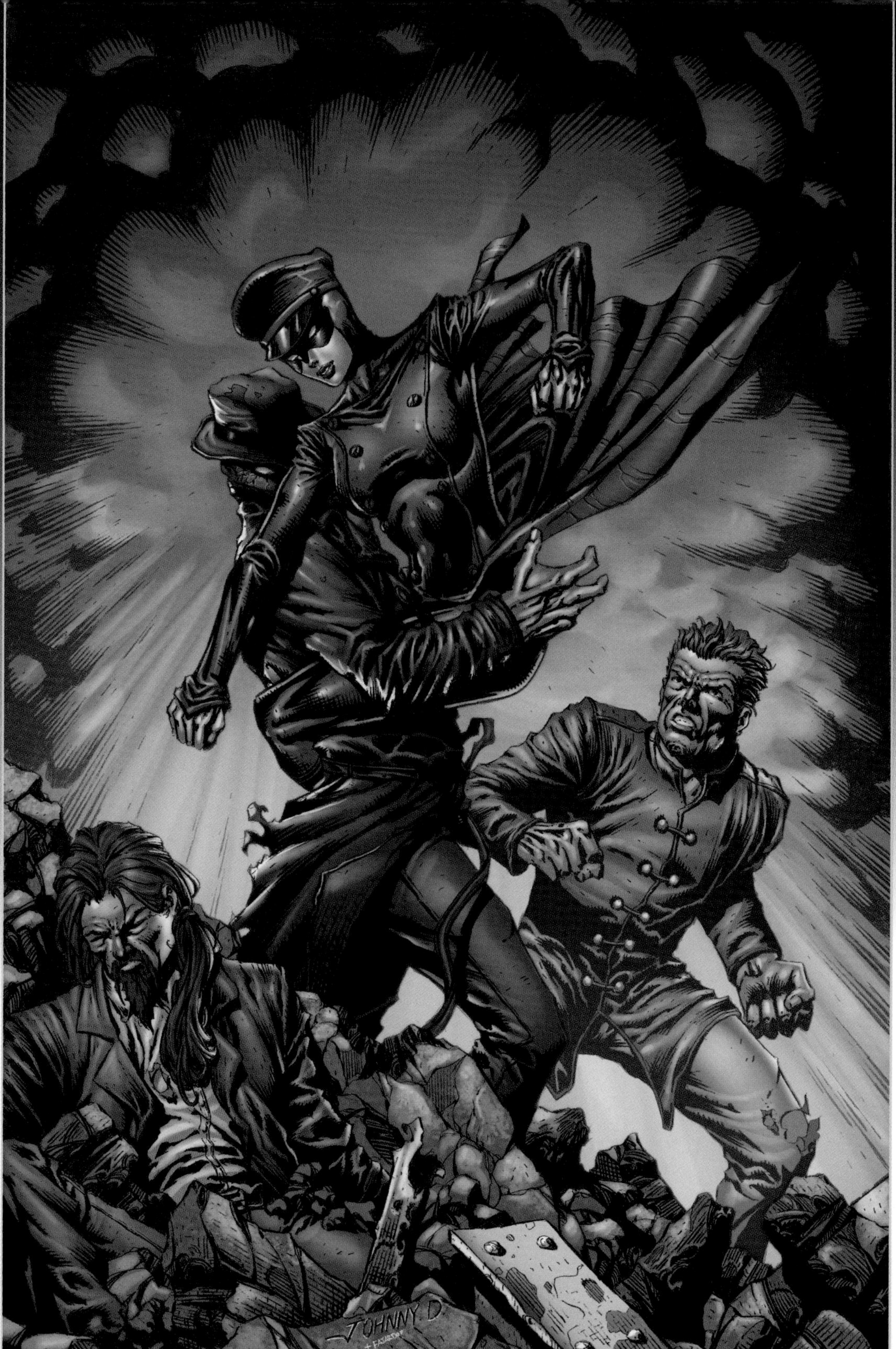
JOHNNY D

Issue four cover by **JOHNNY DESJARDINS**

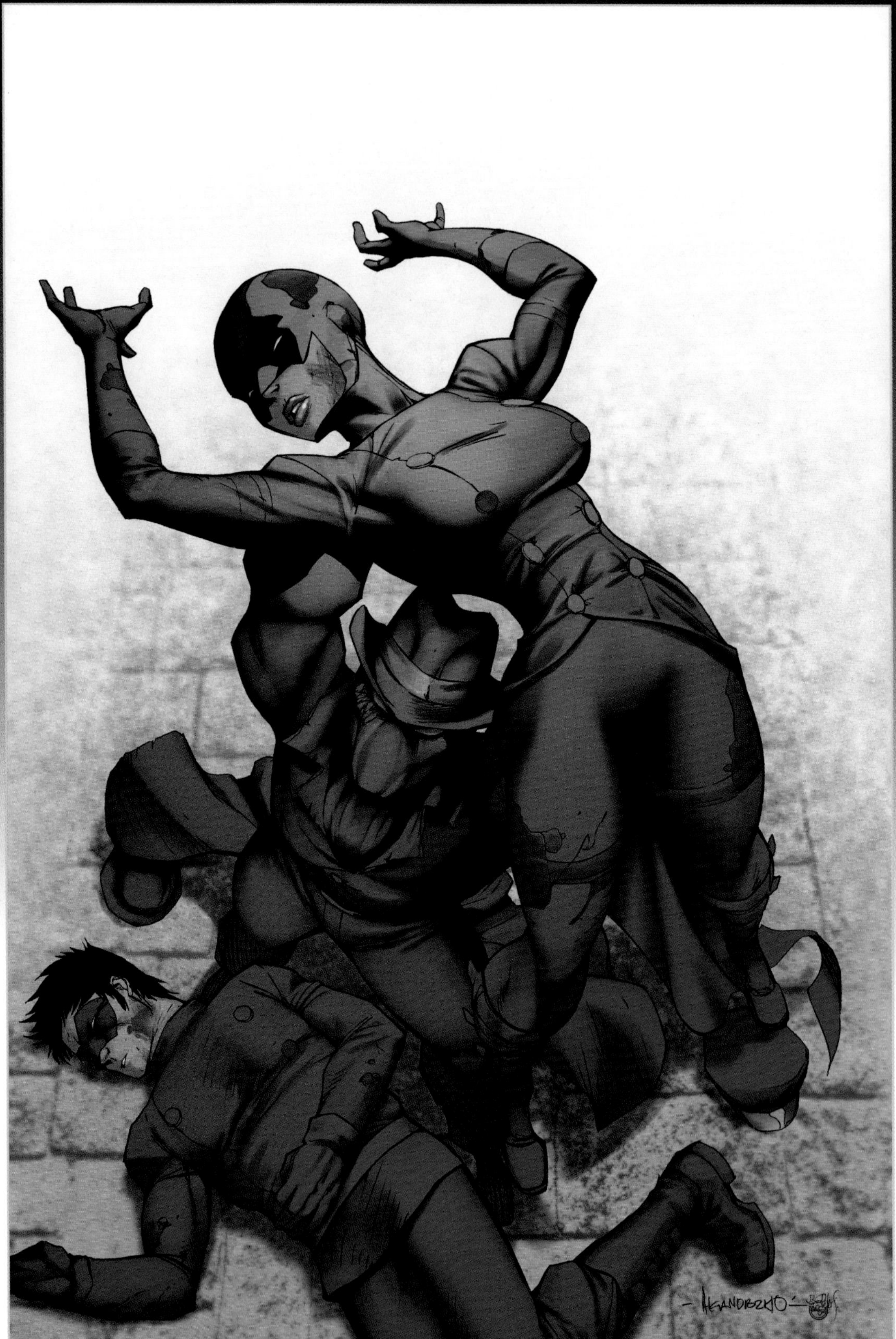

Issue five cover by **ALE GARZA**

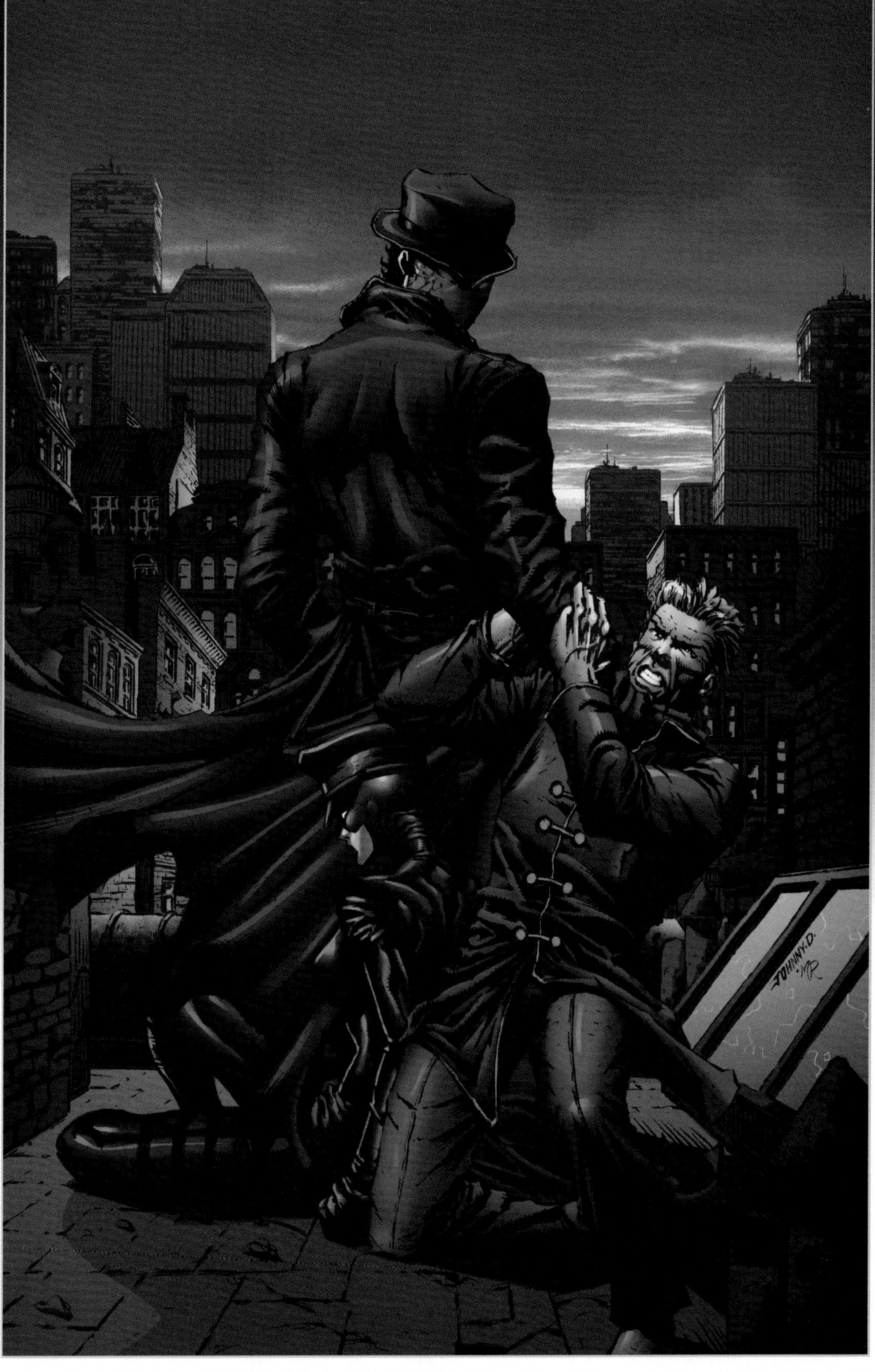
JOHNNY.D.

Issue five cover by **JOHNNY DESJARDINS**

KEVIN SMITH presents THE GREEN HORNET!

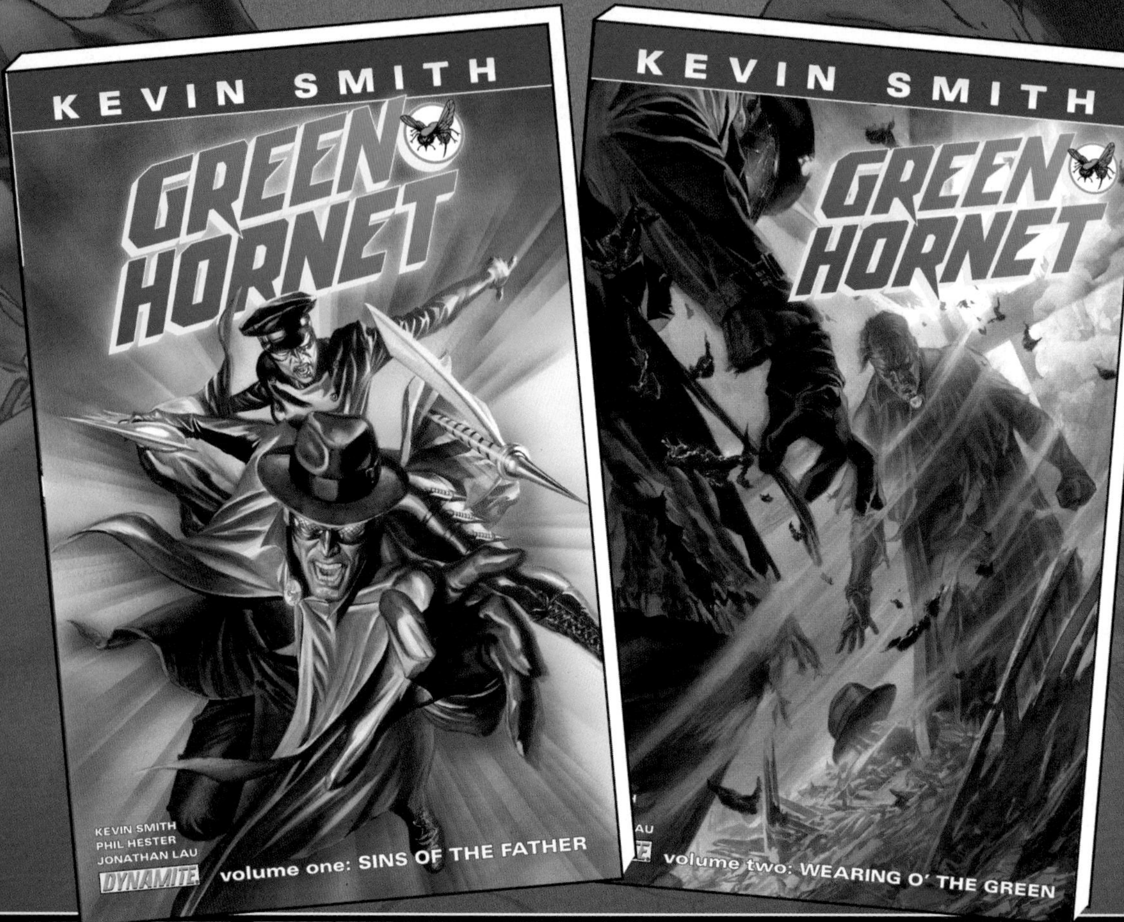
KEVIN SMITH
GREEN HORNET
KEVIN SMITH
PHIL HESTER
JONATHAN LAU
DYNAMITE
volume one: SINS OF THE FATHER
KEVIN SMITH
GREEN HORNET
volume two: WEARING O' THE GREEN

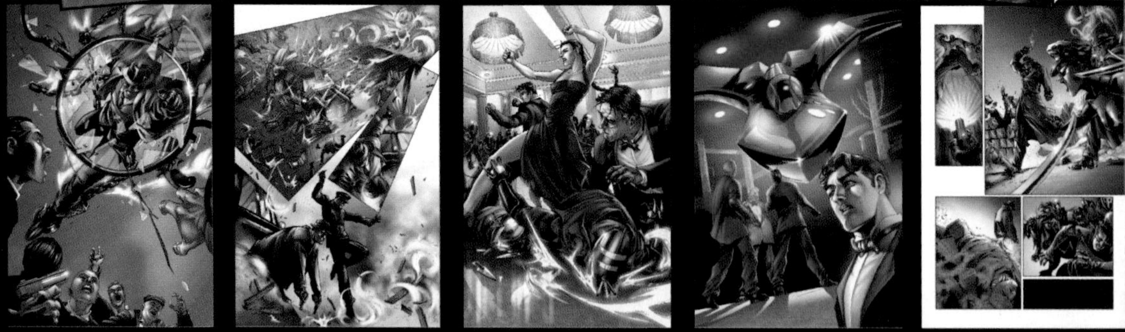

KEVIN SMITH'S GREEN HORNET

VOL. ONE: "SINS OF THE FATHER" & VOL. TWO "WEARING O' THE GREEN"

written by **KEVIN SMITH** art by **JONATHAN LAU** covers by **ALEX ROSS**

Playboy Britt Reid Jr. has lived a frivolous life of luxury. But when a mysterious figure from the past brutally and publicly murders his father, all of that changes. Now, driven by a thirst for vengeance and guided by two generations of Katos, this one time underachiever will find those responsible and take his father's place as Century City's greatest protector – The Green Hornet!

Volume 1 • In Stores Now! Volume 2 • Coming Soon!

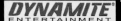

DYNAMITE ENTERTAINMENT WWW.DYNAMITEENTERTAINMENT.COM Newsletters • Contests • Downloads • Forums • Mor

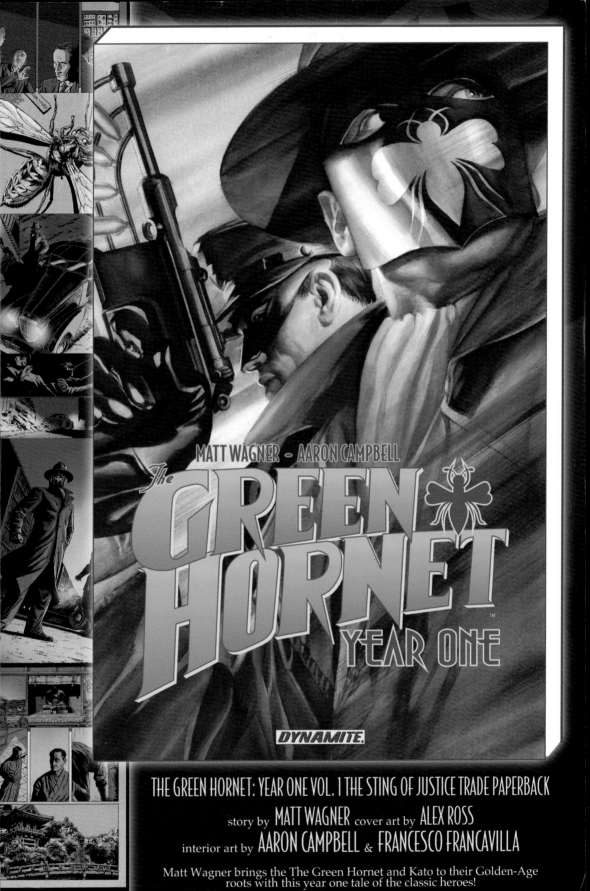

THE GREEN HORNET: YEAR ONE VOL. 1 THE STING OF JUSTICE TRADE PAPERBACK

story by **MATT WAGNER** cover art by **ALEX ROSS**

interior art by **AARON CAMPBELL** & **FRANCESCO FRANCAVILLA**

Matt Wagner brings the The Green Hornet and Kato to their Golden-Age roots with this year one tale of the classic heroes!

Reprinting issues #1-6, along with a complete cover gallery.